What Is Theology?

Foundational and Moral

Edmond J. Dunn

TWENTY-THIRD PUBLICATIONS
Mystic, CT 06355

DEDICATION

IN LOVING MEMORY OF MY SISTER,
RAMONA KOLAR
1934-1995

Twenty-Third Publications
185 Willow Street
P.O. Box 180
Mystic, CT 06355
(860) 536-2611
800-321-0411

ISBN 0-89622-742-1
Library of Congress Catalog Card Number 97-60965
Printed in the U.S.A.

CONTENTS

What Is Theology?

Introduction

My heart leaps up when I behold
  a rainbow in the sky:
So it was when my life began;
So is it now I am. . .

Wordsworth

You hold your new niece for the first time. Your team wins the game with a breathtaking shot. You find out your father's cancer treatment is working. Your high school classmate takes his own life. You see a comet in the early evening sky. A whole community mobilizes to build a sandbag dike; the mighty flood waters push it aside. Your boyfriend says he just wants to be friends. You flunk a test. Your girlfriend says she loves you. You get a call from home. And, you wonder . . . What does it all mean?

Wonder and meaning. We never know when uncertain reality is going to come up and stare us in the face. "What am I going to do?" "What am I going to *be*?" "*Who* am I going to be?" "What does it all mean?" We may or may not have been trained and taught well during the growing-up years in our families, churches, and schools, but as we enter adult life, or return to continue our education after having experienced a slice of life, new questions and challenges, new opportunities and avenues arise in many areas of our lives.

One of those areas encompasses wonder and meaning. Theology

as an academic discipline attempts to deal with the wonder experiences of our lives and what they may mean for living life to the fullest.

Theology is a critical approach to religious faith and practice. It is willing to "ask the hard questions" about what we believe and how we are to live because of our faith. That is what we will be doing in this book. The questions "Why?" "What does it really mean?" "What difference does it make for me? for us? for creation?" are all part of the game. Theology does not set out to destroy, threaten, or weaken faith, but it does bring faith and faith practices before the bar of critical reason. It attempts to make believing possible and meaningful for the person of faith entering the new millennium. As the old adage goes, "Faith builds on reason."

Theology does presuppose faith, however. It does not attempt to *prove* that God exists—an unlikely achievement in any discipline. The so-called proofs for God's existence, offered by people such as Anselm and Thomas Aquinas, came from individuals of deep faith living within faith communities. For those who have the gift of faith, the "proofs" can be helpful; for those who do not believe, they are not convincing. Theology, then, attempts to clarify, broaden, deepen, and enliven the *mysterious something* within us, within our communities, and within our relationships that keeps gnawing at us, "Why?" "What does this all mean?" "Where is it leading?" "Will I be happy?"

This particular text approaches these questions from a Christian perspective. For those who are not Christian, the book will provide a description of the basic questions and approaches that the followers of Jesus Christ encounter when they attempt to look critically at their own faith. There is no intention of criticizing other world religions. On the contrary a broad ecumenical perspective is employed. The other great world religions will be discussed briefly as Christianity relates to them, but the book is not a theology of world religions.

The particular faith community and tradition out of which I

come is Roman Catholic. The reader will find considerable material, questions, issues, and concerns that relate to this faith community. My theological education and interests, however, lie in the area of church unity and theological pluralism. I hope that people coming from the "mainline" Christian churches—Anglican, Lutheran, Methodist, Presbyterian, United Church of Christ, and Baptist, as well as others, will feel at home with the main thrust of the book. Again, there is no attempt or intention to "convert" anyone, although the hope of fanning the flame of faith in all believers is not absent.

Some expect a book of theology to be a book on the Bible. That is not the case here. Although holy Scripture is used throughout, the focus is on the role of Scripture in theology, the historical-critical approach to Scripture needed to make it useful for theology today, and the various theologies found in Scripture, especially within the New Testament.

Theology today must be in dialogue with other disciplines of learning. It has had a long relationship with philosophy, but today the human and physical sciences must also be brought to bear on theology. Theology in the future must be open to, and in dialogue with, the evolutionary processes of the new cosmology, as well with the minute findings of quantum physics—the vast worlds within and without. The present text, as an introduction to theology, can only give fleeting treatment to this rapidly developing area of study and dialogue. The notes to chapter five provide additional sources for the reader interested in pursuing this topic.

The book features frequent excursus that arise out of the main discussion. Such excursus may momentarily divert the reader's attention away from the main discussion either to deal with a related question or to give a more detailed account or example of the issue at hand. These excursus are indented and presented in smaller print.

The book is divided into two parts. The first, *Foundational Theology*, takes up the basic questions surrounding faith—of what we believe as Christians, and why. The second part, *Moral*

Theology, considers the way of life that seems fitting for one who claims to be a follower of Jesus Christ. An organizing principle in both parts of the book is the concept of relationship. We come to be who we are through sharing within our relationships, whether that relationship is with God through Jesus in the Spirit, with a spouse and children within married and family life, with the poor and marginalized as brothers and sisters in the Lord, or with the earth, of which we are a part and for which we share responsibility.

The mystery that invites and enables our various relationships is love, and love is the ultimate name for our God. "Live by love though the stars walk backward," e.e. cummings, tells us, and "trust your heart if the seas catch fire." To be touched by wonder and begin to ask the meaning of it all—that is what theology is all about. The reader is invited to enter into the process of "doing" theology as we proceed.

Part I
Foundational Theology

Chapter One

Theology: A Definition

> Blow on the coal of the heart,
> The candles in churches are out.
> The lights have gone out in the sky,
> Blow on the coal of the heart
> And we'll see by and by. . .
>
> Archibald MacLeish,
> from the verse play, *J.B.*

A death in the family, the loss of friendship, the discovery of new love, the birth of a child, the elation of reaching a long-sought-for goal, the awareness of the awesome beauty of a sunset or a symphony—there are times in all of our lives that cause us to ask, "why?" or "what does this all mean?" These questions lead us to the brink of theology. When Sarah returns to J.B. in MacLeish's modern setting of the book of Job, they have lost everything—their children, possessions, environment—everything except that mysterious ember in the depths of the heart. They must fan into flame that mysterious "something within," Sarah urges J.B., and thus find the strength to go on, to continue the search for the "meaning of it all."

The great twentieth-century Protestant theologian Paul Tillich has called that "mysterious something" that is found in our experience of the heights and the depths as well as the ordinary, the

7

ground of our being, the *cause of our ultimate concern*. In the Jewish-Christian tradition we name that mystery God. When we attempt to reflect upon this mystery in relation to our lives and our world, when we begin to tell stories about our experience of this mystery and begin to write them down, we are approaching that discipline called theology, a topic to which we now turn.

What Is Theology? *Word about God*

One way to begin to describe theology is to examine the word itself. The word theology is made up of two Greek words, *theos* and *logos*. The names of many areas of study—biology, psychology, anthropology, theology—end with the suffix *ology*, which is popularly defined as "the study of." Some define theology as the study of religion. We shall see that this definition is inaccurate.

The word *logos* itself means "word." A common English word, *logo*, refers to a sign or symbol used for identification. Our world makes extensive use of logos—from sports teams to manufactured products to causes. Each has its logo. We can see the close relationship between a word and a logo. In a sense words are logos, symbols standing for something else. When one writes the word *dog* we understand what it means but we also understand that the word *dog* is not apt to bark or enjoy being petted. The word *dog* is a logo, a sign or symbol for the animal we know by that name.

The word *theos* means "God." The name Theodore or Theodora signifies one who is a gift of God. The word God, of course, is also a symbol, a sign standing for the greatest of all mysteries. The word *theology*, then, means "word" about "God," making words about God, talking about God, or at least making an attempt to talk about God. In theological jargon, theology is "God talk."

In Greek philosophy *logos* also refers to the order or reason in the universe. Combining *word* and *order* or *reason*, we can see how the popular description of theology as the *study* of God came to be. When theology is defined as God talk, it is presumed that it involves order and reason. This definition of theology, derived from the word itself, is an etymological definition. Later we shall see that it is an accurate but not adequate definition of theology.

What Is the Problem in Theology?

The problem in theology is, simply, God. The subject that theology attempts to talk about is absolutely incomprehensible, as another great twentieth-century theologian, Karl Rahner, has said. It doesn't mean that we cannot know God somewhat, but it does mean that we cannot fully understand, encompass with our finite minds, the One who is Wholly Other, Absolute Transcendence, Pure Spirit, the Great Mystery. As the writer of the first letter of John says, "No one has ever seen God" (1 John 4:12).

In the Hebrew Scriptures, in the book of Exodus, Moses encounters God both up on the mountain and within the pillar of cloud that would descend upon the tent of meeting when Moses would enter. Once Moses prayed that God would reveal to him God's very goodness, God's glory. Moses wanted to be able to address by name the Mysterious One who had called him by name. God responded, "I will make all my goodness pass before you, and will proclaim before you the name, 'The Lord' [Yahweh]...." "But," God said, "you cannot see my face; for no one shall see me and live." And the Lord continued, "See, there is a place by me where you shall stand on the rock; and while my glory passes by I will put you in the cleft of the rock, and I will cover you with my hand until I have passed by; then I will take away my hand, and you shall see my back; but my face shall not be seen" (Exodus 33:18–23).

What are we to make of such talk? As we enter the third millennium in a world dominated by science and technology, is there any place or need for such stories concerning Moses? God doesn't have a hand or a face or a back. Is this foolishness? Has not science made such stories obsolete?

Something happened up on the mountain and within the tent of meeting. We are told that after these encounters the face of Moses shone so brightly that the people were afraid to come near him. He had to cover his face with a veil. He would only take it off when he went to speak before the Lord (Exodus 34:33–35).

We can say with John that no one has ever seen God, or with Moses that no one has seen the face of God. We could declare the task of theology impossible for our day and close this book. But...people, even people today, claim to have talked with God, heard God speak to them, encountered God, felt the presence of God. When Billy Sunday, a popular evangelist of years past, was asked how he could believe in God, he replied, "I was just talking with God." How does one handle that? One might ask, "Did God leave a number?" "Can I call God?" "Does God have an e-mail address or a home page?"

We bring together the various ways people claim to have come to know God in the phrase "to have *experienced* God." And having experienced God, people have to tell about it. If they never talked, no one would know God or know about God. And when people talk about God (to bring our discussion full circle here) what are they doing? Theology, of course. Theology is making words about God, talking about God, God talk. The experience on which theology is based is commonly called *religious experience*. We must now turn to examine the characteristics of religious experience.

What Are the Common Characteristics of Religious Experience?

Those who have studied the phenomenon of religious experience have identified certain characteristics common to those who claim to have encountered the Holy One, the Transcendent Other. Early in the twentieth century, philosopher William James, in *The Varieties of Religious Experience*,[1] and German Protestant theologian Rudolf Otto, in *The Idea of the Holy*,[2] were pioneers in the critical approach to the topic. On the other hand, Sigmund Freud, the founder of psychoanalysis, would say that the religious sense of "something more," of the "numinous," of God, is illusion. It is a product of wish fulfillment, a way of avoiding the responsibilities of adulthood. Karl Marx would say religion is a *delusion*, a kind of "opiate" that keeps the masses down by promising them rewards in an afterlife.

To examine the common characteristics of religious experience we shall draw on certain insights of Rudolf Otto and at the same time use as a model an incident from the New Testament. This episode, like the one involving Moses, takes place on a mountain. It is commonly called the transfiguration. It is found in the gospels of Matthew, Mark, and Luke. We shall use the account from chapter 17 of Matthew.

Jesus took Peter, James, and John up the mountain and was transfigured before them, ". . . his face shone like the sun, and his clothes became dazzling white." Then they saw Moses and Elijah talking with Jesus. When a cloud overshadowed them and they heard a voice from the cloud, they were overcome with fear and fell to the ground. Who, in the midst of such an experience, would not have done the same?

One of the characteristics common to those who claim to have encountered the Holy One is that of *fear*, mixed with *awe* and a feeling of *unworthiness*. When Moses, in Exodus 3:2–6, saw the burning bush and heard the voice tell him to remove his sandals because he was on holy ground, we are told that Moses hid his face, "for he was afraid to look at God." When the prophet Isaiah received his call and the temple shook and was filled with smoke, Isaiah cried out, "Woe is me! I am lost, for I am a man of unclean lips..." (Isaiah 6:5).

A second characteristic of a religious experience is the feeling of *well-being* or *wholeness*. In the transfiguration story even though the disciples experienced fear in the presence of the Holy One, they still experienced a fascination and deep peace. When Peter looked up and saw Moses and Elijah conversing with Jesus (Moses the great giver of the law and Elijah the great prophet), everything fit together—the law, the prophets, and Jesus. Peter's exclamation is one of the most memorable in Scripture, "How good it is for us to be here!"

One might ask if there is any difference between what we are describing as a religious experience and the experience of those who claim to have encountered the evil one, Satan or the devil. (We must leave aside at this time the question about the personification of evil as a corrupt but powerful being or beings, and the question

of possession. It would seem, however, that the insight of the ana-
lytical psychiatrist Carl Jung on the role and power of the "shadow
side" of the self—obsession rather than possession—deserves careful consideration.) Fear and awe can understandably be a part of
the experience of those who claim to have encountered evil per-
sonified. But the second characteristic is hardly apt. Rather than
well-being and wholeness, an encounter with evil brings turmoil
and disintegration. The legend of Faust is a classic literary account
of a human's attempt to enter into relationship with the evil one.

The third common characteristic of religious experience is a
desire for it not to end. This follows from the experience of well-
being, wholeness, and peace. When Peter makes the rather strange
statement, "Let us build three tents here, one for you, one for Moses,
and one for Elijah," he is expressing this characteristic. A tent is a
place in which to dwell, to stay. What Peter, James, and John were
experiencing on the mountain they wanted to go on forever.

Although the transfiguration story is a model of a religious experience, not every religious experience has these characteristics in
exactly the same way, in the same order, or to the same degree. But
the transfiguration does give us a chance to gain some understanding of the phenomenon of religious experience that is the basis of
theology.

How Common Is Religious Experience?

Andrew Greeley, a sociologist of religion, has found that a considerable percentage of young people admit to having had some type
of religious experience. He speaks of a *wonder experience* that causes one to ponder the deeper meaning of ordinary happenings—the
first view of the ocean or the mountains, a dazzling starry night, the
birth of a child, the budding of a rose, falling in love.[3] When one
falls in love is there not an element of fear and awe in the first
encounter, even a sense that one may not be worthy of the other?
And as the relationship grows is there not a feeling of wholeness
and well-being in the presence of the other? ("We just talk and talk
and talk!" "You bring out the best in me!" "I could have danced all

night!") If the relationship continues we may find ourselves saying, "We will be together forever; even death can't part us now." This is not to say falling in love is a religious experience, but the characteristics of a deep love relationship are not unlike the characteristics described by those who claim to have encountered the great Mystery, whom we identify as God.

Much has been written about those people who have experienced "clinical death" and then continued to live. The way these people describe their experience finds a definite parallel in the three characteristics we have been discussing. From the awe of the "out of body" experience and the movement through something like a tunnel toward light, to the well-being and peace in the presence of the Holy One, to the desire not to have to return to ordinary life (or to return with a wholly different perspective on life and death), we see here again those common characteristics of religious experience.

If death is defined as that from which you do not return, then these people were not really dead; but according to modern medicine the flat brain wave is the indication of "clinical death." Whether these people actually experienced death and afterlife is not the point here. Nor is it our intention to argue that these experiences prove from a scientific point of view that there is a life after death. Rather, what is described by those who have gone through a "near death" experience is similar to the basic characteristics of a religious experience. In the annals of the saints there are similar accounts, like the "mystical death" experience of St. Catherine of Siena, a great Italian mystic of the sixteenth century.

Is One Always Aware that One Is Having a Religious Experience?

Sometimes it is only by looking back that we realize the full import of a religious experience. Most assuredly one does not analyze the experience as it is happening—now I am experiencing fear and awe, now well-being, etc. Another story from the New Testament will serve as a model for "looking back" and realizing the full impact of a religious experience in hindsight.

We shall examine what happened to the disciples as they were leaving Jerusalem on the road to Emmaus (Luke 24:13–35). They were very downhearted because Jesus had been put to death and their hopes had been shattered. As they walked along, someone joined them and began talking with them, asking them why they appeared so dejected. "Are you the only stranger in Jerusalem who does not know the things that have taken place there in these days?" they replied. Then they told him how Jesus, a prophet from Nazareth powerful in deed and word, had been crucified even though he was innocent. The stranger then began discussing with them the law and the prophets and how the Messiah had to suffer and then enter into his glory. As it was getting late, they asked him to stop with them to eat. They went into a roadside inn and ordered some food. As they began to eat (breaking the bread), suddenly their eyes were opened and they recognized that the stranger was Jesus, the one who had been put to death. Then we are told, "he vanished from their sight."

At this point we shall leave the Emmaus story and our examination of hindsight in religious experience (we will return to them later) and pursue something that must have perplexed the disciples in this encounter with the risen Lord, as well as it perplexes us—the resurrected body of Jesus. As Christians we believe in the resurrection of the body. Immortality of the soul may help us understand the resurrected body, but the latter is what distinguishes us and our belief in eternal life.

Focus:
What can we
learn from
the disciples'
experience of the
resurrected body
of Christ?

What the disciples experienced of the bodily presence of the risen Christ gave them hope for their own resurrection, as it should give hope for ours. Can we make any sense out of this belief in the resurrection of the body in our scientific, technological world? One thing that can be said about the resurrected body in light of the disciples' Emmaus experience is that it is radically changed. They didn't recognize the stranger as the one they had been with just three days before. Nor do we hear the disciples asking, "Man, what's wrong with your hands?" or "Those feet look mighty sore." And yet in another encounter with the risen Lord, in the upper room, according to John's gospel, Jesus showed them his hands and his feet and asked doubting Thomas to put his hand into the wound in his side.

The resurrected body is radically changed. It is not limited by time or space. Time and space define the dimensions of our earthly life. To think outside of either time or space is difficult enough. But to think outside of both time and space is most difficult. When the disciples recognized the risen Christ in the inn on the road to Emmaus, we are told, he disappeared. That does not mean that he slipped into the rest room and then out the back door. The risen Christ did not have to spend the night somewhere. When he appeared in the upper room we are told that the doors were closed. Try appearing in the middle of a room when all the doors are closed. The resurrected body is not limited by time or space.

The risen body is not a resuscitated corpse. Jesus did not come out of the tomb with a body constituted in exactly the same way as he went in. When Jesus called Lazarus forth from the tomb, as recorded in chapter 11 of John's gospel, Lazarus was a resuscitated corpse. Lazarus took up his life where he left it off. Lazarus still had to die. The risen Christ would never die again. He had passed through death into new life. Following the Emmaus story in Luke's gospel, the risen Christ appears to the disciples and asks them for something to eat. "They gave him a piece of broiled fish, and he took it and ate it in their presence" (Luke 24:43). This is what in biblical studies is called crass realism. Luke uses such imagery to get across to his people that the risen Christ is truly the one the disciples had known before his death. If the risen Christ did eat the fish, it is unlikely that it added to his body weight or that he had to go to the bathroom afterwards. Bodily form, yes, but a radically transformed, glorified body.

It would be foolish to think that, at our resurrection, our own human bodies will be reconstituted of

Focus: What can we learn from the disciples' experience of the resurrected body of Christ?

Focus:
What can we
learn from
the disciples'
experience of the
resurrected body
of Christ?

the exact same material they possessed when they were placed in the grave. When one ponders the several millions of years of human existence, the innumerable bodies that have been buried and become a part of the earth again, it would be preposterous to think that each should find his or her own physical body. The seventeenth-century English poet John Donne captured the spectacle in one of his Holy Sonnets: "At the round earth's imagined corners, blow / Your trumpets, Angels, and arise, arise / From death, you numberless infinities / Of souls, and to your scattered bodies go."

The longest sustained discussion of the resurrected body in Scripture is found in chapter 15 of Paul's first letter to the Corinthians. There Paul teaches about the different kinds of bodies. As far as the human body and death and resurrection are concerned, "what is sown is perishable, what is raised is imperishable. It is sown in dishonor, it is raised in glory. It is sown in weakness, it is raised in power. It is sown a physical body, it is raised a spiritual body."

From the resurrection appearances of Christ, perhaps we can think of life beyond death as life "in another dimension." As our earthly body is returned to the earth we are clothed with a new, spiritual body. Bodily, because we are not who we are without our bodies. Karl Rahner speculates that in the resurrected life we are joined with matter in a more general way, still maintaining our unique individuality (unlike those who propose a series of reincarnations until we are finally absorbed into the One, the All).

The disciples' experience of the risen Christ was a religious experience. The risen Lord was available through the eyes of faith. He could not have been observed by a disinterested outsider. Our belief in the resurrection of our own bodies need not be understood within the parameters of a crass resuscitation of a corpse. As St. Paul assures us, in the "twinkling of an eye" we will all be changed—a new life, not limited by time or space.

We return now to the Emmaus experience. We left the scene just as Jesus was recognized by the disciples in the breaking of the bread and "he disappeared." The very next words in that passage reflect the principle that the full impact of a religious experience is often recognized only in retrospect. "They said to each other, 'Were not our hearts burning within us while he was talking to us on the road, while he was opening the Scriptures to us?'" "Our hearts burning within us...even back there...on the road...Did you experience it the way I did?" In the midst of a religious experience we may not be consciously aware that "I have a sense of fear and awe...now a sense of well-being...I don't want this to end." Often the full impact of a religious experience is realized in looking back.

What Is the Nature
of the Language of Religious Experience?

Theology is an attempt to talk about God—God talk. In the examples and models of religious experience discussed above, we used expressions such as seeing the "back but not the face of God" (Moses), seeing Jesus with his "face like the sun and clothes bright as snow" (Peter, James, and John), and "our hearts burning within us" (disciples looking back on the Emmaus experience). What are we to make of such language? Because in theology we are attempting to express the inexpressible, in a sense, *all theology is poetry*. Theology takes ordinary words and stretches their meaning. God is completely Other, and all we have are human words. The one who falls in love and then attempts to express that love in words becomes a poet—not necessarily a good poet!—and phrases come forth, "your eyes are like the oceans...your hair softer than silk." One cannot express it, and yet one has to try.

Poetry, poetic language, is used to express religious experience, which is at the root of theology. Also story is often used, as well as metaphor, symbol, and myth. The use of the term *myth* in theology is criticized at times, but that is usually because the word is misunderstood. When Paul Tillich was challenged in his identification of Christ as only a symbol, he replied, "Only a symbol? I never allow my students to say *only* a symbol."[4] In a similar way, a student of theology should never say, "*only* myth." Myth is our attempt to get at the deepest level of truth. For those who say there is no such thing as "deeper truth," that there is "nothing more" than meets the eye, then myth is legend, mere fantasy. They likewise would say that religious experience is fantasy. But for those attempting to express the "something more," myth becomes a story "on this side" about "the other side."

In his book *The Jesus Myth*,[5] Andrew Greeley identifies Jesus as myth. This is not to say that Jesus is legend or fantasy, but that Jesus is a story on this side about the other side. Jesus is a parable of God. Jesus is the key to that deeper truth. In Jesus we come to know what God is really like and what we are capable of becoming. What is God really like? In Jesus' life, teachings, actions, example, death, and resurrection, we come to know what God is really like. God is like the daffy old dad or mom who, when the wayward kid finally decides to come home, runs out with open arms of welcome and then throws a party (Luke 15:11–32). God is like the owner of a vineyard who hires workers throughout the day and then pays them all a full day's wage. When challenged by those who worked from early morning the owner replied, "Haven't I given you what I promised, or are you criticizing me for being generous?" (Matthew 20:1–16). That is God. God is like the one who would leave ninety-nine to go after one lost sheep (Matthew 18:12), who would make the sun to shine and the rain to fall on both the bad and the good (Matthew 5:45), who would gather the little ones under wing like the mother hen (Matthew 23:37).

According to John's gospel, Jesus said that the one who sees him sees the One who sent him. God is like the one who eats with sinners, tax collectors, and prostitutes (the outcasts); who heals the lame, the blind, the deaf, the speech-impaired; who shows a "preferential option for the poor," as it is described today; who, though innocent, endured crucifixion for love of all sinners and then, from the cross, forgave those who put him there. That is what God is like. In Jesus we come to know what God is really like. Jesus is one with God, God's very Word who remains with us now through the power of the Holy Spirit.

In Jesus we come to know what we are capable of being. Jesus is one with us, our brother. He is bone of our bone, flesh of our flesh, and blood of our blood. He ate and drank with people like us. He rejoiced and suffered; he died and rose again. In him we see that it is possible for us to be loving, forgiving, reconciling, merciful, peaceful, and just. In him we come to realize that we can become at home with ourselves, at home with others, and thus be at home with the Lord—saved. In Jesus, through the power of the Spirit, we come to know that we need not be afraid to love him, our brother, another human being, with the absolute love of God, to face death confident that we will fall helplessly into the arms of a loving God, and to face the future knowing that the victory has been won, that in the end good shall prevail, justice and peace shall reign.

In Jesus it all comes together. In him we come to know the deepest level of truth. Jesus is the story "on this side about the other side." Jesus is myth. What is more, this same process of mythical interpretation could be applied to the Supper of the Lord, the Eucharist. In that ritual reenactment we remember what God has done for us in Jesus, we celebrate his risen presence through the power of the Spirit in the bread and wine we share, and we look forward to his coming in glory to usher in the fullness of the reign of God. In the Lord's Supper, the deepest meaning of God's offer and our response is symbolized.

Is Faith Necessary for Doing Theology?

A classic definition of theology comes to us from the eleventh-century monk, theologian, and later archbishop of Canterbury, Saint Anselm. Theology for Anselm is faith seeking understanding. Although faith and revelation will be explored more fully in the following chapter, let us relate Anselm's definition to the earlier definition that comes from the word itself, namely, theology as God talk. Anselm's definition presupposes faith. Yet one can talk about God without believing, without having faith. One can say, "There is

no God." That is God talk, but is it theology? One way of expressing this dilemma is to say that all theology is God talk, but not all
God talk is theology.

All theology is God talk. That is the meaning derived from the
word itself. Therefore the definition is accurate. And yet, following
Anselm, not all God talk is theology because not everyone who
talks about God has faith in God. Following Anselm, theology is
done from within the community of faith. One cannot do theology
without faith. Theology as *God talk*, therefore, is *accurate* but not
adequate. It does not make the necessary distinction between talking about God and talking about God from the faith perspective.
The faith perspective and the community of faith will be discussed
in the next chapter. The faith community will be seen in a broad
sense as *that group of people who admit there is "something more"
inviting them, and attempt to respond to it.*

What About Those
Who Talk About God but Do Not Believe?

It is evident that one can talk about God without believing in God.
Those who study communities of faith or religious groups from the
"outside" are engaged in legitimate inquiry. The object of their study
is religion. At the beginning of this chapter it was suggested that to
define theology as the study of religion was inadequate because, as we
can now see, that definition does not take into consideration the faith
dimension required for doing theology. Religion can be described simply as a group of people organized to some extent around a belief system (*a creed*), a way of worship (*a cult*), and a way of life (*a code*).
Those who research and write about the way these groups have lived
through a period of years are involved with the *history of religion*.
Those who inquire about how these groups organize themselves and
interact with other groups are involved in the *sociology of religion*.
Those who study the inner workings of the mind and emotions of
those who make a commitment to such groups are involved in the
psychology of religion, and those who ponder the possibility of believing from the point of view of reason are involved in the *philosophy of*

religion. All of these are legitimate areas of study. One can be involved with them and also have a faith commitment, but faith is not required. Indeed the social sciences attempt to remain above commitment, to adopt a value-free approach. In theology, on the other hand, there is a faith commitment. Admittedly, one may pass a course in theology with honors and still be an unbeliever. It is a matter of definition. According to Anselm the course for that person would not be theology, however, but a study *about* a faith community.

Can One Have Faith without Theology?

To turn the question around is to ask whether one can have faith without talking about it, without attempting to understand it. One's first response might be, "Of course. I know many who have faith but never talk about it." But in a broader context, if *no one* ever talked about faith, or about God or religious experience, how would we know, and how would we know if we know? We touch here on the question of human knowledge and how it is acquired. Some may choose to follow the philosopher Plato and insist that humans have innate ideas. Knowledge from this perspective is *remembering* from the prior realm of the spirit before we were imprisoned in these earthly bodies. Most accept, following Aristotle, that our knowledge comes from *the outside* through our senses by some type of communication. We come to be who we are through dialogue and sharing. The dialogue begins at birth between parent and child—expressions, words, phrases, sentences, stories—and it lasts a lifetime. Sharing or communion is the other basic element in our coming to be who we are. It too begins in childhood, from the "everything is mine" of early childhood to the complete self-giving and mutual sharing of friendship and married and family life.

What is true of our everyday human condition must also be true of our life in the Spirit, our life in relationship to God, our life of faith. We are compelled to talk about it, to theologize about it, to share it in order to understand it. As we are reminded in 1 Peter 3:15–16, "Always be ready to give reason for this hope of yours, but do it with gentleness and respect." According to our human condi-

tion we couldn't have faith without expressing it; we couldn't have faith without theology.

What Are the Ways, Approaches, or Methods in Doing Theology?

Although there are many approaches to theology, three basic ways of doing theology will be identified and discussed here. We are speaking of methods in theology. The three can be designated as the biblicist method, the doctrinalist method, and the correlative method.

The Biblicist Method

The biblicist method or the biblicist approach to theology insists that all theology is biblical theology. Karl Barth, perhaps the greatest Protestant theologian of our time, held this opinion. In other words, the role of theology is to explain, defend, and disseminate that which is contained in holy Scripture. There is no way that we humans can approach God except as God is revealed to us through the Word of God, Jesus Christ, as found in the New Testament.[6]

Barth was reacting to a late nineteenth- and early twentieth-century movement in Protestant theology known as Liberal Protestantism. "Liberal" in this context refers to theologians who identified revelation with a universal human experience and downplayed its divine origin. Jesus was looked upon as a great ethical teacher and not much more. Barth saw Liberal Protestantism as watering down the powerful teachings of the sixteenth-century reformers Luther and Calvin. Because of this "return to the roots" of Protestant thought, Barth's theology is often called "neo-orthodox." God's action in Christ alone saves us. Humans can do nothing but accept in faith the saving message.

To claim that God could be found by reasoning based on human experience, as the great nineteenth-century theologian Friedrich Schleiermacher held, could only lead to a human construct that Barth identified with *religion*. True Christianity found its roots, its "raw material," only in *revelation* as it comes to us through Christ in the New Testament.

From this perspective Barth built his magnificent theological system in the multivolume *Church Dogmatics*.[7] Barth entered into a critique of philosophy, the human sciences, the humanities, and other world religions in discussing the various aspects of Christian theology. (In systematic theology, there is a place for everything and everything has its place.) But all of the critique is done in light of the revelation that comes to us through Christ in Scripture.

Indeed there is a biblical theology. In fact, in the Bible there are many theologies. Barth, however, harking back to the Reformation principle of *Scripture alone*, insisted that all theology must be biblically based. There is no "general revelation" apart from Christ, according to Barth. Even if God were available in the world and in everyday experience through some "natural revelation," still God could only be rightly recognized and understood there through the revelation in Christ. God's revelation to the Hebrews through the law and the prophets was preparatory for the coming of Christ. The Old Testament itself, Barth claims, can only be rightfully understood through God's revelation in Christ as found in the New Testament.

In our time many evangelical preachers and theologians have pushed the position of Barth to an extreme that is known as *biblical fundamentalism*. From this perspective the Bible is not only the sole legitimate source for theology, it must be interpreted literally. Biblical inerrancy is insisted upon. Yet Barth was no fundamentalist. He would not be able to identify with the contemporary biblical literalists.

The Doctrinalist Method

A second approach to doing theology employs the doctrinalist method. The task of theology from this perspective is to interpret, defend, and disseminate that which is contained in the official teachings or doctrines of the church. Its roots are in the late New Testament writings addressed to Timothy and Titus, the so-called Pastoral Epistles. Here the Good News flowing from the Christ event is reduced to preserving sound doctrine and authoritative teaching.

Faced with those who were spreading what was regarded as false teachings and unacceptable practices, the role of Timothy and Titus was to guard what had been entrusted to them. Job descriptions and qualifications for those seeking to be bishops and deacons are found here, and the earlier openness to both men and women in ministry, stemming from Jesus' own practice, is strongly opposed. "I permit no woman to teach or have authority over a man; she is to keep silent," we find in 1 Timothy. It was the woman, Eve, who was deceived, not Adam. "She became a transgressor. Yet she will be saved through childbearing..." (1 Timothy 2:11–15).

The post-apostolic and post-New Testament periods found theology being developed by a group of teachers known as apologists. They defended the faith in the face of persecutions from without and dissension from within. Bishops began to meet in regional synods to combat heresy. In the fourth century came the first great ecumenical council, a meeting representing the "whole wide world," which met at the urging of the Emperor Constantine in Nicea in 325. The fourth and fifth centuries were dominated by the dogmatic teachings of the councils held at Constantinople (381), Ephesus (431), and Chalcedon (451). All of these councils met in the East. During this same period, and extending into the seventh and eighth centuries, writers we identify as church fathers (and mothers) had a major influence on the doctrinal development of the church. Among them St. Augustine stands out for his lasting influence on the church.

The medieval period contributed in many ways to the further development of the doctrinalist approach to theology. Among these contributions were the election of a number of powerful reform-minded popes, and ecumenical councils meeting in the West. The codification of canon law, with its effects on moral theology and the sacraments, eventually brought about a juridical vision of the church. The laity, religious, and lower clergy were to obey the directives of the church's duly constituted authority. Power would gradually become centralized in the offices of the pope and the curia, the administrative and governing bureaucracy of the church. The oath of obedience that the pope required the bishops to make resembled the feudal oaths that bound vassals to the lord.

At the beginning of the thirteenth century universities began to be formed, and a theological revival ensued, culminating in the work of the great Dominican theologian, Thomas Aquinas. Opening to the thought of the pre-Christian Greek philosopher Aristotle, Aquinas fashioned his masterful *Summa Theologicae* (Overview of Theology). The *Summa*, like the work by Barth discussed above, was a work of systematic theology. The overarching means of interrelating the various aspects of theology was not Scripture, as in the case of Barth, but primarily Aristotelian thought.

The theological views of Aquinas dominated the theology of the Roman Catholic church up until the contemporary period, but it became less Aquinas's own thought than the thought of those who interpreted him in what became known as scholasticism—that work coming out of the schools (the universities) produced by the schoolmen (scholars). Theology gradually became rigid, arid in its distance from Scripture, and authoritarian.

In the aftermath of the Reformation, the Council of Trent (1545–1563) consolidated Catholic teaching in answering the challenges of the reformers. In the eighteenth century both the French Revolution and the emergence of the philosophical movement known as the Enlightenment challenged the "old order." Revolution and enlightenment challenged all authority while exalting intellectual freedom and moral autonomy. The Roman Catholic church found itself more and more in a posture of defensiveness and isolation from the world.

During his long reign in the third quarter of the nineteenth century, Pope Pius IX condemned Liberalism in the *Syllabus of Errors* (1864). Liberalism in this context meant an acceptance of the emerging understanding of the rights of the individual, the freedom of religion, of speech, and of the press. All of these ideas challenged traditional authority. Pius IX also presided over the First Vatican Council (1870) in which papal infallibility was defined as a dogma of the church. With the loss of the Papal States and the position of the pope as a secular ruler, Pius IX became, as he described himself, "a prisoner in the Vatican" within the newly united Kingdom of Italy. Theology became the defensive weapon of true doctrine in the face of a hostile world.

Under the leadership of Pope Leo XIII there was a brief period of being more open to the world. His encyclical *On the Condition of Workers* (1891) was the beginning of the modern social teaching of the popes. Leo XIII's encyclical encouraging the study of Thomas Aquinas gave a boost to the return to Aquinas's own thought.

This period of openness was followed by the pontificate of Pius X, in which the movement called *Modernism* was condemned as heresy (1907). (Modernism had certain parallels with Liberal Protestantism discussed above.) Every bishop, priest, seminary rector, and theology professor was required to take an oath against Modernism. Theological progress on the Catholic scene basically came to a halt. A defensive, neo-Scholastic/Roman theology dominated the Catholic theological climate from the early part of the twentieth century until the Second Vatican Council (1962–65).

It is out of this basic historical overview that the doctrinalist method in theology must be understood. The theologian was supposed to explain, defend, and make known what was contained in the official teaching of the church. *Denzinger*[8] (a compendium of all creedal, papal, and conciliar teaching), canon law, papal and curial decrees and letters, and Scripture (as a church document to be interpreted officially) became the raw material of theology. Some persons today, still following this method, would hold that theologians today now need do nothing more than explain and defend the recent universal *Catechism of the Catholic Church*[9] and make its contents known.

There most assuredly is a doctrinal theology. Indeed the doctrine and teaching of the church reflect many theologies. Pushed to the extreme, a doctrinal theology can result in what is known as *doctrinal fundamentalism*. All teaching of those in authority in the church must be taken in a literal, inerrant sense. This is true especially of the teachings of the pope. This position, which Rome itself does not accept, ignores the historical and cultural contexts in which teachings arise, the primary questions the teachings are attempting to address, and the level of solemnity with which the teachings are promulgated.

What are the weaknesses of the biblicist and doctrinalist methods of doing theology?

The primary weakness in both the biblicist and doctrinalist approaches to theology is that they presume that the "raw material" of theology, the subject of theology (which is ultimately God), is available in some tangible source. These approaches eliminate the "problematic" nature of theology. Even though we are dealing with God, who is totally Other or Pure Spirit, there is no problem in theology from the biblicist's or doctrinalist's perspective, for there are tangible sources for theology—the Bible or the doctrine of the church. The questions these approaches leave unanswered are, how did these sources come to be? Did the Bible drop from heaven in completed form? Does the doctrine come from some mysterious treasury of tradition available only to church leaders?

Because these two approaches presuppose that the "raw material" of theology is "deposited" in some tangible source, the biblicist and doctrinalist approaches to theology have been labeled *positivistic*. This term is borrowed from a contemporary philosophy of the same name, *logical positivism*, in which the only "real" is held to be the tangible, that which is available to the senses. If it cannot be seen, touched, or tasted, it doesn't exist. The "something more," or as it is called in traditional philosophy, *metaphysics*, is unreal. "God" is a meaningless term, and to say that "God is good" is a double fallacy. Karl Barth has been accused of having a positivistic view of revelation (God's Word deposited in the New Testament). The uncritical objectification of God's Word coming only through hierarchical teaching or doctrine is likewise positivistic. For both the doctrinalists and the biblicists the material of theology is completely deposited in the past; God's availability in ordinary human experience, in religious experience, can have no effect on the theological enterprise.

The Correlative Method

A third approach to theology, one that attempts to take seriously both the "message" and the "situation," is called the correlative method. Borrowed from Paul Tillich's call for the correlation between faith and culture,[10] this method incorporates the best of the biblicist and doctrinalist methods and interrelates them with the "signs of the times," the "big questions" that people are asking today. Most mainline theology today comes out of some variation of this method of correlation. (David Tracy, an outstanding contemporary Catholic theologian, suggests *critical* be added to the description—thus, critical correlation.[11])

Before we can understand the process of correlation, the terms *message* and *situation* both need to be examined in the context in which they are used here. *Message* refers to God's Word. Once again we encounter the Word. We have already examined the Greek word for *word*—*logos*. *Word* in Greek is the name for something. It is an identifying tag, like a logo.

In Hebrew the word for *word* is *dabar*. In Hebrew, word denotes not only name but also situation or action. Hebrew understands *word* as "doing what it says." For example, in the beginning of the Hebrew Scripture, in the book of Genesis, God says, "Let there be light," and..."there was light." God did not have to think, "Now let's see. If I had a couple of dried sticks, or two flints... I could use my Zippo Lighter...." Rather God spoke, and it came to be. Likewise Adam and Eve got to "name" the animals and also had control over them. Anyone teaching a group of kindergarten students understands the power of being able to "name" the children for the sake of good order. Moses on the mountain wanted to know the name of the Lord. Knowing the name, being able to pronounce the name, Yahweh, implied a relationship. Indeed when Adam "knew" Eve (in the biblical sense implying a relationship), she had a baby! When the angel told Mary she was to have a son and name him Jesus (which means "he will save"), she questioned, "How can this be since I do not *know* man?"

The prophet Isaiah says on the Lord's behalf, "As the rain and snow come down from heaven and do not return until they have watered the earth..., so shall my word be that goes out from my mouth; it shall not return to me empty, but it shall accomplish that which I propose, and succeed in the thing for which I sent it" (55:10–11). In the New Testament St. Paul reminds us that the word of God comes to us in power. That is why Luke, writing about Paul's encounter with the Greek philosophers on the Areopagus (Acts 17:16–34), misses the mark when he relates that they tell Paul they must discuss these matters—his preaching—again sometime. For Paul, preaching was not raising questions for discussion. The power of the word should have picked them up and turned them around! Luke is reflecting more the Greek than the Hebrew understanding of preaching the word.

John begins his gospel, "In the beginning was the Word [the Logos], and the Word was with God and the Word was God.... And the Word became flesh and dwelt among us." Although writing in Greek, John must also have had in mind the Hebrew understanding of *word*. God spoke and the Word, the very self-expression of God, became one of us—bone of our bone, flesh of our flesh. We were so created that, when God wished to become one with us, humanity fit God like a glove. It was not, as the theologian John Shea says, "like trying to put eighteen clowns into a Volkswagen." Jesus, therefore, is the Word of God, the ultimate self-disclosure of God. And the message, from the Christian point of view, is Jesus. Not just what Jesus said or taught, but his whole life and his death and resurrection. The message is the Christ event. That message comes to us through the New Testament as well as through the teaching, doctrine, and tradition of the community of his followers, the church. This message, the Christ event, is correlated with the situation that the followers of Jesus find themselves in at every age—the here and now.

The situation consists of the "big questions" that people ask; the things we think about when we are not thinking of anything else; the background music of our lives. Who am I? What am I to do, to be? Will I be happy? In light of the joys and sorrows, the successes and failure, the wins and losses, in my life and the lives of others, what does it all mean? Is there any meaning at all? As it once was expressed in a popular song in a movie, "What's it all about, Alfie?"[12] Does it mean anything?

If you were asked to write a statement of your belief (a creed) or an instruction for others about faith (a catechism), or if you were asked to put together in an ordered way all of the aspects of faith (a systematic theology), where would you begin? Isn't it likely that you would begin, "I believe in God," or "We believe in God"? Or would you begin with, "In the beginning God created the heavens and the earth," or "In the beginning was the Word, and the Word with God"? Both ways have been used in theology. They represent two ways of beginning to theologize. The first is called the anthropological approach. It begins with the human, with the questions, the yearning, hopes, and fears that people have. As St. Augustine put it, "My soul is restless until it rests in Thee." The other is the cosmological approach—starting with the way things are "out there," not within me or us. Theology from this perspective begins from above, with God: "Who is God?" Both approaches are necessary. Both must be interrelated. But the approach of most contemporary theology is to start from below, with the questions people are asking.

The correlative method in theology starts from those big questions people ask in their lives and then relates those questions to the message, to Jesus Christ and what he offers for those who are searching for meaning. The questions are clarified and reformulated; the message is better understood and reinterpreted; and the correlation continues back and forth. Faith seeking understanding; understanding deepened by faith. As Karl Barth has said, "One must go through life with the Bible in one hand and the newspaper in the other." This is true, but not *just* with the Bible, or *just* with the newspaper, unless the Bible represents the *message* in the broad sense in which we have discussed it, and the newspaper represents our *human situation* and the big questions we ask.

How Can the Correlative Method
Be Expressed in a Working Definition of Theology?

We will use the method of correlation in this book. We are now ready to formulate a working definition of theology from this perspective, taking into account the issues discussed above. These issues are summarized as the definition takes form.

Theology is our attempt to express

[*our*—theology is done from within the community of faith; faith is necessary to do theology.

attempt to express—God is completely Other, we have only human language, we attempt to express the inexpressible.]

in clear and concise language

[the poetic language of religious experience is analyzed, systematized, the various aspects compared, interrelated according to some system. Theology to this extent—following Aquinas in the opening of his *Summa*—is a science, not in the physical, positivistic sense, but similar to the human sciences.]

what we presume to be the self-disclosure of God

[*we*—again, within the faith community.

presume to be—the problematical aspect of theology is recognized: we could be wrong; theology could be self-projection (Feuerbach), illusion (Freud), delusion (Marx).

self-disclosure of God—what is revealed is God's very self, not just information about God.]

in persons, nature, history, everyday human experience

[*in persons*—people claim God has been disclosed to them within themselves in dreams and visions, through others—prophets, holy ones, the saints.

in nature—"the heavens proclaim the glory of God," the

mountains, the ocean, the budding of a rose, the birth of a child.

in history—our Jewish-Christian-Muslim traditions claim that God has been disclosed in the mighty deeds of history; God identifies God's self to the chosen people—"I led you out of the land of Egypt, I fed you manna in the desert, I gave you the promised land"—and from the Christian perspective: "I send my only Son." The record of God acting is found in the Bible, the Qur'an.

in everyday human experience—people still claim that God is disclosed to them in a variety of ways here and now.]

and, for Christians, in an ultimate way in Jesus of Nazareth.

[to make the definition one of Christian theology, the final, full, unique disclosure of God in Jesus must be taken into account.]

The centrality of Jesus in Christian theology needs further amplification. It has been said that if one were taking a course in Christian theology and the professor asked a question to which you did not know the answer, raise your hand and say, "Jesus Christ," and you'll probably be right! Christians see all of theology (God talk) in and through the self-disclosure of God that comes to us through Jesus Christ in the power of the Holy Spirit. As the beginning of the letter to the Hebrews states, "Long ago God spoke to our ancestors in many and various ways by the prophets, but in these last days he has spoken to us by a Son, whom he appointed heir of all things.... He is the reflection of God's glory and the exact imprint of God's very being, and he sustains all things by his powerful word."

Vatican II has described Jesus as the "center, the focal point, the meaning of all history." This Christian claim for Jesus is called the scandal of particularity. Of all the billions of persons to have lived in the world, this one from Galilee is unique.

In the popular film *Oh God!,* when God finally spoke and

answered the question of whether Jesus was truly his son, God said, "Jesus is my son, Moses is my son, Muhammed is my son...." Christians would have to raise an objection to this. No, Jesus does not just take his place as a great prophet among others. Jesus is unique, the ultimate, final, full self-disclosure of God. In light of the various ways in which God has spoken, and continues to speak, and in light of our growing need for dialogue among all the world's great religions, we can say that Jesus is *unique,* but not *exclusive.*

The name Jesus of Nazareth, rather than Jesus Christ, was used in the definition of theology we have just constructed. It is about the human being from Nazareth that we make such claims. Christ—the Greek translation of Messiah, the Anointed One—is a title, a profession of faith in Jesus. Christ is not Jesus' second or last name. It is Jesus *the* Christ whom we profess as Lord, the Word of God, the Wisdom of God.

Questions for Reflection and Discussion

1. Was the understanding of theology that you had before you read this chapter both *accurate* and *adequate?* How has it changed?

2. What are some of the *wonder experiences* you have had in your life? Can you relate them in any way to what people describe as a *religious experience?*

3. Does the description of the resurrection appearances of Christ to the disciples in the New Testament help you understand your own hope for resurrection? If so, how?

4. How would you explain to someone how poetry, myth, and symbol enter into our attempt to *talk about God?*

5. Have you experienced in your life any of the *big questions* that have been at least partially resolved by correlating them with the *Message* we identify as Jesus Christ?

Suggestions for Further Reading

Edwards, Denis. *Human Experience of God.* New York: Paulist Press, 1983. See chapter 1, "Why Speak of 'Experience of God'," pp. 1–15, and chapter 2, "The Mysterious Dimension of Our Lives," pp. 16–26.

Greeley, Andrew M. *The Great Mysteries: An Essential Catechism.* New York: HarperCollins, 1985. See "Introduction," pp. xi–xxii, and chapter 1, "The Mystery of God," pp. 1–11.

Johnson, Elizabeth A. *She Who Is: The Mystery of God in Feminist Theological Discourse.* New York: Crossroad, 1994. See chapter 3, "Basic Linguistic Options: God, Women, Equivalence," pp. 42–57.

Lane, Dermot A. *The Experience of God: An Invitation to Do Theology.* New York: Paulist Press, 1981. See chapter 1, "Experience, God and Theology," pp. 1–31.

Sloyan, Gerard S. *Jesus in Focus: A Life in its Setting.* Mystic, CT: Twenty-Third Publications, 1994. See chapter 20, "The Man Raised from the Dead," pp. 157–165.

Chapter Two

Revelation and Faith

In Carlo Menotti's opera *The Medium*, there is a moving scene between a lovely young woman and a young man her mother has brought into the home as a servant. The young man is a deaf-mute. He can neither hear nor speak. The two fall in love, and in this particular scene the young woman sings a beautiful duet—but, of course, she has to sing both parts. She sings and acts out in a lovely dance what she knows the young man wants to say in expressing his love for her. Then, in turn, she sings her loving response to him, and they celebrate their love in a dance of joyous ecstasy.

As people of faith we believe that our God has communicated with us. We see traces of God in the beauty of nature and the wonders of the universe. As humans we believe that God has invited us into a love relationship that cannot be expressed in human words, and yet we are anxious to try. Our response to God's invitation to a loving friendship is perhaps something like the young couple's dance of joy. It is this mysterious invitation on God's part, and our attempted response, that will be the main topic of this chapter.

What Is the Meaning of Revelation?

Theology is our attempt to express in clear and concise language what we presume to be the self-disclosure of God in persons, nature, history, everyday human experience, and, in an ultimate way, in Jesus of Nazareth.

In this working definition of theology, formulated at the end of the first chapter, we should be able to find a definition or description of *revelation*. To reveal is to disclose or to uncover. In the theological sense, revelation is *the self-disclosure of God*. To be more modest, taking into account the problematical character of theology—as well as revelation—we can define revelation as *what we presume to be the self-disclosure of God*. We should remember here the cautions mentioned in the previous chapter about how we could be mistaken, and how social scientists such as Feuerbach, Freud, and Marx have challenged the reality of there being a God who reveals.

It should be noted as well that the definition speaks about the *self*-disclosure of God, not just information about God. One of the most serious misunderstandings about revelation comes from those who want to narrow it to information, especially information about the future. Although revelation has its content, its intellectualist and conceptualist aspects, it is not primarily *information* but *invitation*. God comes to us inviting us into a relationship, to be friends. And that offer goes forth to everyone, as we shall discuss later.

Are Revelation and the Book of Revelation the Same?

There is much interest and discussion these days about the book of Revelation, the last book of the New Testament. As we pass from the second millennium into the third, there are those who are convinced the world will come to an end. For many, revelation is identified with the prediction and graphic description of the end of the world and the judgment as it is depicted by the visionary John, who wrote from the island of Patmos toward the end of the first century. It will be worthwhile for us to take a diversion from our general topic of revelation and faith and examine briefly the type and purpose of the theological language in this work, which is known also as *The Apocalypse of John.* (Apocalypse is the Greek word for revelation.)

Two types or genre of writing can be identified in the book of Revelation. One is *apocalyptic*, the other is *prophetic*. Each has its particular style and purpose. Both are found elsewhere in the Bible as well. Apocalyptic writing comes into existence at times of great persecution. Its primary purpose is to encourage people to remain faithful, even in the face of suffering and possible martyrdom. In the end God will reward the righteous and destroy the wicked. Persecution and suffering (or probable persecution and suffering) are so threatening that human striving is no longer thought possible. God will have to intervene, and God will intervene very soon in a cosmic, cataclysmic way. There are signs to be read and there are visionaries who are to read them and to urge the people to remain faithful.

Focus: The book of Revelation— apocalyptic and prophetic writings

Apocalyptic writing is God talk that has lost its "cool." It makes use of exaggerated imagery and puzzling symbols and has a fascination for numbers. It is a type of underground communication, unintelligible to the outsiders, the persecutors, but understandable to the faithful. It is not possible here to get into the content of the book of Revelation, which has its fascination for poets and artists, as well as for fundamentalists. But we will consider a few examples of its use of language.

Exaggerated imagery is found in chapter twelve of the book of Revelation. A woman, clothed with the sun, with the moon under her feet and wearing a crown of twelve stars, is about to give birth when a great red dragon with seven heads and ten horns and seven diadems on his horns sweeps a third of the stars out of the sky with his tail and hurls them down to earth. The woman is the heavenly representative of God's people, Israel. This is the primary symbolic meaning of the woman. It is from the people of Israel that Jesus was born, the child caught up to the heavens.

The second symbolic meaning of the woman is the Christian faithful, the church, whom the dragon (Satan) is persecuting. A few verses later there is a battle in heaven, and Michael and his good angels overcome the dragon or serpent and his followers and throw them out.

A puzzling symbol, also involving numbers, is the sign 666 written on the forehead of the beast who had "two horns like a lamb" and "spoke like a dragon" and made the people worship the first beast whose "mortal wound had been healed." Greek and Hebrew letters have numerical equivalents, and one likely combination of letters equaling 666 is the letters spelling Nero. Not that Nero was the source of persecution in the book of Revelation; rather the Roman Emperor Domitian, who reigned from 81–96, was looked upon by the Christians as Nero come back to life. The "mortal wound...healed" may refer to the legend that Nero, who apparently committed suicide by slitting his throat, was supposed to come back to life. It is similar to references to Saddam Hussein during the Gulf War as "Hitler alive again." The hype about 666 being a fearful sign of Satan needs to be balanced by remembering that it is a metaphor for a Roman emperor, Domitian, who persecuted the Christians at the end of the first century and was compared to Nero, who persecuted the Christians earlier.

The fascination with numbers in the book of Revelation is evident in numerical equivalents such as the example above, or in the interpretations of the symbolic value of certain numbers. There are seven lamp stands and seven scrolls, seven trumpets and seven bowls. Seven, the perfect number, represents God's way finally being achieved. The twenty-four elders before the throne of God represent the twelve tribes of Israel and the twelve apostles. The twelve thousand from each of the twelve tribes who are to be saved, equaling one-hundred and forty-four thousand, the total number of saved, also refers to the squaring of twelve.

The overall message (revelation) of the book of Revelation is not the actual prediction of the time and manner of the end—when it was written they believed the end had to come soon—but a condemnation of the evil ones. (The absolute mercilessness with which the evil ones will be judged—thrown alive into burning seas of sulfur, birds gorging on their flesh—caused Martin Luther to question if the work were even Christian. As we shall see later, the book of Revelation did have a difficult time getting into the New Testament canon.) The message is one of courage for those undergoing persecution. The book ends with a glorious vision of the final reign of God where the martyrs with white robes washed in the blood of the lamb rejoice in the new heaven and the new earth. There every tear will be wiped away, there will be no more mourning, crying, or pain. All things will be made new. The final cry of the book of Revelation is, "Come, Lord Jesus!"

Revelation in the apocalyptic sense is the message that God is with us through everything, and in the end accepting his invitation will bring us total fulfillment. Revelation is not so much information about the end: Jesus told us the time is not for us to know. Neither is it primarily about how the end will come, nor about how many will be saved. Rather it is the assurance that God's invitation is valid even in the face of great persecution and suffering.

Prophetic writing, in contrast to apocalyptic writing, is down to earth, practical, often political in nature. "Thus says the Lord...," the common prophetic introduction, warns, cajoles, urges, begs the people to act kindly toward the poor and the weak, to act justly in matters of the world, to refrain from alliances with outsiders that may compromise the covenant and turn the nation against their God. In other words, you *can* act justly, live uprightly, remain faithful—and you'd better!

Focus:
The book of
Revelation—
apocalyptic
and prophetic
writings

Focus:
The book of
Revelation—
apocalyptic
and prophetic
writings

The great prophets warn of what will happen if the people stray from faithfulness, but it is a call for correction in the present more than a prediction of the future. Prophetic utterances remain in the Bible even if the results don't come to pass.

An example of prophetic writing is Amos proclaiming on behalf of God:

> Hear this, you that trample on the needy, and bring to ruin the poor of the land..., buying the poor for silver and the needy for a pair of sandals and selling the sweepings of the wheat....The Lord has sworn by the pride of Jacob: surely I will never forget any of their deeds....The time is surely coming...when I will send a famine on the land; not a famine of bread, or a thirst for water, but of hearing the words of the Lord....They shall run to and fro, seeking the word of the Lord, but they shall not find it. (Amos 8:4–12)

Though the book of Revelation is primarily an apocalyptic work, it also contains prophetic writing. In the seven letters addressed to the seven churches there are some down-to-earth warnings and calls to action—mixed with apocalyptic threats as well. In the fourth letter, addressed to the church in Thyatira, a commercial center whose trade guilds were known to sponsor idolatrous feasts, God speaks through the prophet John:

> But I have this against you: you tolerate that woman Jezebel, who calls herself a prophet and is teaching and beguiling my servants to practice fornication and to eat food sacrificed to idols. I gave her time to repent, but she refuses to repent of her fornication. Beware I am throwing her on a bed, and those who commit adultery with her I am throwing into great distress, unless they repent of her doings....

(In the Old Testament idolatry is often referred to as adultery.)

The book of Revelation, as well as other apocalyp-

tic writing found in the Bible, is indeed a part of the
revelation of God. But it is not all that revelation is.
Further, the message of apocalyptic writing is not so
much prediction about the end of the world; it is God's
word addressed to those in great distress urging them
to remain faithful in spite of suffering and persecution.

Focus:
The book of
Revelation—
apocalyptic
and prophetic
writings

How Can the Correlative Method
Be Expressed in a Working Definition of Revelation?

We can return now to our general discussion of revelation and faith
and formulate a working definition of revelation.

Revelation is God's gracious self-disclosure

[*self-disclosure*—it is ultimately God's self that is disclosed, not information about God.

gracious—revelation is wholly free on God's part, it is
not something that belongs to us humans by right; it is
sheer grace.]

reaching out to humans as an invitation (as well as promise) to
participate in God's own life of unfathomable love

[*invitation to participate*—God's self-disclosure is primarily an invitation to enter into a relationship, a friendship—
but it is not commanded, it can be refused.

promise—revelation is promise in the sense of God's
faithfulness to the covenants made with humans and the
final assurance of the reign of God.

life of unfathomable love—we are graced with the capacity to go beyond ourselves and enter the mystery of God's
very self, whose essence is love.]

mediated to us through persons, nature, history, everyday experi-
ence, and ultimately in and through God's very Word, Jesus
Christ.

[*mediated*—God, being pure spirit, and we being embodied spirits, there can be no such thing as "pure" revelation; it must be mediated; all creation can mediate God's revelation but in Jesus the medium embodies the very message.]

The mysterious self-disclosure or revelation of God reaching out to us in the form of an unspoken invitation—God's very presence, uncreated Grace—is taken a step further in holy Scripture and in the Tradition and doctrines of the church, where it is interpreted, articulated, and reflected upon in conceptual form. Here revelation gets its intellectual content in written and spoken form—the theology of revelation.

What Is Faith?

We have defined revelation as

> *God's gracious self-disclosure reaching out to humans as an invitation (as well as promise) to participate in God's own life of unfathomable love, mediated to us through persons, nature, history, everyday experience, and, in an ultimate way, in and through God's very Word, Jesus Christ.*

If revelation is described as God's gracious *invitation* to friendship, then faith is our *response to* and *acceptance of* the invitation. Revelation and faith are like two sides of a single coin. God discloses God's self as invitation; we respond in faith. That we can respond and thus enter into a relationship with God is also God's gift. Although we are free to accept or refuse, our acceptance is God's gift, God's grace. Coming to know God in faith, especially through his Word, Jesus Christ, means *knowing* in that deep sense that involves one's whole self. The outcome or result of this loving relationship from our perspective is *discipleship*—a way of living and loving that touches every aspect of our lives including worship and moral behavior.

Faith at its root is *preconceptual*. It is mysteriously present to us before we attempt to put it into words, before we conceptualize it.

It is something like the person who walks into a room and is "zapped" by the particular presence of another. As a song from *South Pacific* put it, "Some enchanted evening you may see a stranger across a crowded room. And you know even then...."

When we attempt to conceptualize our response to this mysterious invitation, when we attempt to put it into words, we are, of course, doing theology. It may not be good theology, it may not be sophisticated, but it is theology nonetheless. Again, with Anselm, it is faith seeking understanding. The conceptualization of faith, which results in the content of faith, to which we give intellectual assent, takes various forms. A summary of our faith in words is called a *creed*. A proclamation of the faith is called preaching or testimony. An organized presentation used to pass on the faith to others is called a *catechism*. Poetry, hymns, and stories are other ways of putting faith into words. More formal theologizing results in doctrines and dogmas.

A brief aside on the distinction between doctrine and dogma will be helpful here. I hope it will open paths to ecumenical dialogue.

Focus: What is the difference between doctrine and dogma?

Both doctrine and dogma are teachings. They are human formulations of the truth of God's revelation that has come to us in its fullness in Jesus Christ. *A dogma is a doctrine that has been officially declared a norm.* Every organization has its dogmas, although they are not usually given the name. For example, if you want to be a member of the swim team you will: (i) have a swimsuit, (ii) have a physical, (iii) not miss more than three practices without an excuse, (iv) not miss any meets. If you do not follow these norms you are not a member of the swim team.

The bottom-line dogma in Christianity is that Jesus is Lord, the Messiah, the Savior, God's very Word. That dogma has been the cornerstone of the Christian community from the beginning. If you do not accept it, you are not Christian. In a general sense, the whole saving truth of revelation that comes to us through Christ and is reflected upon in the

Focus: What is the difference between doctrine and dogma?

Scripture and Tradition of the church is dogma. More particularly, dogmas are specific definitions directly related to matters of the faith and the way of life of those who profess to be disciples of Christ. They are proposed by the legitimate leaders of the church and are binding on its members.

Some churches put more emphasis on dogma, understood in this more specific sense, than do others. The Reformation churches and the Orthodox churches generally accept the dogmatic character of the saving truth found in holy Scripture and the early councils of the church. The Roman Catholic church, following the principle of *the development of doctrine,* insists that further binding definitions concerning Scripture and Tradition are possible and necessary.

Two fairly recent dogmas of the Roman Catholic church are especially difficult for Protestants to accept. One has to do with the teaching authority of the pope, the bishop of Rome. The other relates to Mary, the Mother of Jesus. We will comment briefly on each of these dogmas—the infallibility of the pope and the assumption of the Blessed Virgin Mary into heaven.

In 1870 the First Vatican Council, meeting in Rome, and with the approval of Pope Pius IX, declared as a dogma that the pope could teach infallibly, that is, without error, in matters of faith and morals. This dogma, much misunderstood both within and outside of the Catholic church, should be examined within the context of the signs of the times of the second half of the nineteenth century. The long-reigning Pius IX saw the church as being battered on every side by the challenges of science, popular democracy, and freedom of press, speech, and religion (liberalism). Further he saw his own authority waning with what appeared to be the inevitable loss of the Papal States to the forces that were struggling for the unification of Italy. With this dogma at least he would reign supreme in the spiritual realm.

The actual teaching on infallibility is a very restrictive one. First of all papal infallibility is more of a negative or protective concept than a positive one. It protects the pope from leading the church astray on matters of faith and morals—what church members are to believe and how they are to live. It is not a source of special knowledge; it is not a "hot-line" to heaven. The pope must research, study, and consult like anyone else. The charism or gift of infallibility is only there if it is used. Popes who don't employ it, don't have it. It is not a personal possession of the individual pope.

The dogma states that the infallibility of the pope is the same infallibility that Christ gave the whole church. The promise, "I will be with you all days," at the end of Matthew's gospel, may be exercised by the universal pastor, the pope, under certain conditions for the good of the whole church.

Further restrictions in the teaching include the following three:

(i) *The matter being defined must pertain to faith and morals; it must be directly related to the saving truth reflected in Scripture and the Tradition of the church.* The pope cannot teach infallibly about science, art, or even sports.

(ii) *The pope must be exercising his role as universal pastor, as the one who cares for the unity of the flock of Christ's disciples.* The pope cannot teach infallibly about some local dispute or private concern.

(iii) *The pope must intend to be teaching infallibly, of defining a facet of faith binding for the whole church.* The pope cannot let something "slip out" and then be bound by infallibility.

Finally, the Second Vatican Council's teaching on *collegiality* has opened the path for dialogue on the teaching of papal infallibility with Protestants and the Orthodox. Collegiality means that the bishops share with the pope in ultimate authority in the church, and that the most solemn form of teaching is the ecumenical council with the pope.

The dogma of infallibility has been employed only

Focus:

What is the difference between doctrine and dogma?

Focus:
What is the
difference
between
doctrine and
dogma?

once since 1870, and that was in 1950 when Pope Pius XII defined the dogma of the assumption of Mary into heaven body and soul.

The first question that Protestants propose concerning the dogma of the assumption is, where is this found in holy Scripture? Of course, it isn't. The Catholic (and Orthodox) response is that it is part of the Tradition of the church. (The relationship between Scripture and Tradition will be taken up in the following chapter, so it will not be dealt with here.) The scriptural material on Mary is sparse, but the teaching on the assumption could be said to derive from Scripture in the following way. Mary was asked to be the Mother of the Savior, and she consented. Because of this she was hailed as "full of grace" and "blessed among women." Mary was the faithful one, open to God's offer of friendship from the beginning of her life. She is the model of the redeemed one, and therefore she is with God and her Son, where one day we also hope to be.

One must not get caught up in literalism as far as the body being *assumed* is concerned. Mary's assumed body must be a resurrected body, one not limited by time or space. If her physical body were "taken up" to some "place" called heaven, it is not hard to imagine what would have happened to such a body at a certain altitude. When the Russians first put a person into space, the cosmonaut radioed back that no God was found up there; this should remind us that the language we use in a dogma such as the assumption is real, but still metaphorical.

The positive thrust of the dogma of the assumption is that it gives us hope for our own absolute future; it reminds us of our belief in bodily resurrection and that therefore the body, not just the soul or spirit, is good; that matter itself, of which the universe is made, is good and to be respected; and that the human body and all matter is destined to be transformed and saved.

However, neither of these dogmas is at the center

of our Christian faith according to Vatican II's hierarchy of truths. They should not be insoluble roadblocks to the movement toward Christian unity. Catholics take them seriously in their understanding and exercise of the faith and can hope that, with further development, they can be understood in a favorable way by other Christians. As Karl Rahner has reminded us, dogmas "point to" the truth that is incomprehensible. They are accurate but not adequate.

Focus:
What is the
difference
between
doctrine and
dogma?

We return now to the main discussion of revelation and faith. Because faith at its root is preconceptual, we can say that in a sense *there is only one faith*—that earnest desire to respond to God's gracious invitation—*but many beliefs.* It is when we begin to conceptualize our faith, talk about it, theologize, that we disagree. With this broad basic understanding of faith as a graced response to, and acceptance of, God's invitation to friendship, we come to realize the deep respect with which we should encounter anyone who shares that journey whether he or she be Christian, Jew, Muslim, Buddhist, Hindu, or part of any other faith community. Even Marxists or Humanists can be included (they may not wish to be) if they leave some space for openness to mystery. All should be engaged in a spirit of dialogue. Because God is available in human experience, we can be confident that somehow God is already with them in their search.

What Are the Dangers
of a Rationalistic Approach to Faith?

Two attitudes to be avoided in the revelation/faith question are a rationalist perspective and a fideist perspective. The rationalist approach insists that if you use your head you will arrive at faith. Those who do not believe are either hardheaded or hard-hearted.

A caricature of the rationalist approach would be the following: "Do you mean you don't believe? You have no faith? Take a look out there. Do you see the vastness of the universe, the order, the grandeur? Do you think that could just happen? God created all there is, and on the top of creation he put man and woman. They had it made but for some reason—the woman weakened first—they turned against God and so injured God that nothing could make up for it except the divine itself. So God sent his Son. He taught us things about God we would not know otherwise, he told us how we are supposed to live, and he proved he was God by his miracles, especially the miracle of his own rising from the dead. He stayed around for a while before he returned to heaven, but before he left…

[you can take one of two routes here—the Protestant or the Catholic; here is the Protestant]…he called together some of his friends and said, 'Get a pencil and paper and write this down because I'm leaving but you'll have this inspired book. As long as people read it and preach it and follow it, they'll be saved.' We still have that book today. It is the all-time best-seller in the world and if you would just read it with an open mind you can't help but find faith!"

[or, the second, Catholic, route would be]…he called together the twelve apostles and told them he was leaving but he wanted them to continue his work. So he made Peter the pope and told him to go to Rome and establish a church on a rock, and he made the other apostles bishops, and they were to help Peter. We still have the church and a pope who has succeeded in an unbroken line down from Peter, the longest lasting institution in the whole world, and if you would just start going to church you would find faith and save your soul!"

The main weakness with the rationalist approach is that it exaggerates the ability of reason to find God; it removes the gift-like character of faith. Such an attitude is reflected in the popular bumper sticker of a few years ago, "I Found It!" As a Lutheran pastor commented, "Near heresy if not absolute heresy. You don't find it. It finds you."

What Are the Dangers of a Fideistic Approach to Faith?

The other extreme to avoid is fideism—"faith-ism" to coin a word—or blind faith. This approach insists that there is no reason for belief. It is a blind leap. The more unreasonable or irrational faith is, the better! It shows one's complete surrender, including one's mind, to whatever God demands. As Danish philosopher and religious thinker Søren Kierkeggard said, "I believe because it is absurd!" One of the great examples of fideism in the Bible is Abraham's readiness to sacrifice his son, Isaac, upon God's command. It was through Isaac that God had promised offspring to Abraham. Still, Abraham took his son to the spot where he was to sacrifice him to the Lord and had the knife lifted ready to kill him. An angel of the Lord called from heaven and stopped him. Still, he had proved his loyalty to God.

If we are to take this story literally, we can say at best that the Lord God let Abraham, our father in the faith, know that God does not want human sacrifice. The Hebrew people abided by this prohibition even though they were surrounded with peoples who practiced human sacrifice. At worst, one could wonder about the wounded psyche of the son, to say nothing of the charge of child abuse to which Abraham would be liable.

A delightful interpretation of this story by comedian Woody Allen uncovers the weakness of the fideistic approach:

And Abraham awoke in the middle of the night and said to his only son Isaac, "I have had a dream where the voice of the Lord saith that I must sacrifice my only son, so put your pants on."

And Isaac trembled and said, "So what did you say? I mean when he brought this whole thing up?"

"What am I going to say?" Abraham asked. "I'm standing there at 2 a.m. in my underwear with the Creator of the Universe. Should I argue?"

"Well, did he say why he wants me sacrificed?" Isaac asked his father.

But Abraham said, "The faithful do not question. Now let's go because I have a heavy day tomorrow."

And Sarah, who heard Abraham's plan, grew vexed and said, "How doth thou know it was the Lord and not, say, thy friend who loveth practical jokes?"

And Abraham answered, "Because I know it was the Lord. It was a deep, resonant voice, well-modulated, and nobody in the desert can get a rumble in it like that."

And so he took Isaac to a certain place and prepared to sacrifice him, but at the last minute the Lord stayed Abraham's hand and said, "How could thou doest such a thing?"

And Abraham said, "But thou said—"

"Never mind what I said," the Lord spake. "Doth thou listen to every crazy idea that comes thy way?"

And Abraham grew ashamed. "See, I never know when you're kidding."

And the Lord thundered, "No sense of humor. I can't believe it!"

Abraham asked, "But doth this not prove I love thee, that I was willing to donate mine only son on thy whim?"

And the Lord said, "It proves that some people will follow any order, as long as it comes from a resonant, well-modulated voice."

And with that, the Lord bid Abraham get some rest and check in with him tomorrow.[1]

The fideistic perspective on faith leads parents to respond to their teenage or college-age children who are questioning their faith with something like, "It was good enough for your father and me, and it's good enough for you! Just go to church. It doesn't matter if it doesn't *mean* anything to you." The fideistic perspective might also lead other teenagers or college-age students to follow someone who said they had been told—in a vision or by an angel—that in order to be saved they would have to stand on their head for ten minutes every day. "Well if that is what is required, who am I to question?" Such blind following leads to situations like the poisoned kool-aid of the Jonestown tragedy or the Branch Davidian disaster in Waco, Texas. In both instances a community of men, women, and children were led to their deaths by fanatical, charismatic leaders who were being accused of coercion, mind control, and child abuse by family members outside the groups and by law-enforcement officials.

In contrast to the rationalistic and the irrational approaches to the question of revelation/faith, the mainline Christian tradition has been this: *Faith is neither rationalistic nor irrational, but reasonable.* That is, faith builds on reason or, as the First Vatican Council taught, faith must always be "consonant with reason." Christians may not be able to convince others to believe by argument from reason, but they should be able to give good reason for their own believing. We are back again at the saying from the first letter of Peter: "Always be ready to give reason for this hope of yours...."

How Can the Correlative Method Be Expressed in a Working Definition of Faith?

We are now ready to formulate a working definition of faith:

Faith is our freely given, graced response to God's invitation to a loving relationship

[*our*—although faith has its effects in each individual, faith is only found (mediated) in and through a faith community—for Christians, the Body of Christ or the church.

freely given—like the parent who invites his or her adult child to return the love given in a free, mature friendship, but cannot demand it, God, "who has first loved us," invites us to freely respond to the offer of sharing in the divine life, and although God could demand it, God respects the freedom in which we each of us were created.

graced response—this is a way of saying that even our acceptance of God's offer, the *potential* we have for faith, is God's gift, is sheer grace.

a loving relationship—God, who is *Love,* offers us a share in the very life of God, unfathomable Love.]

that begins in preconceptual form

[we are mysteriously *touched* by God in our innermost being before we attempt to conceptualize it, therefore anyone who *turns toward* Absolute Mystery is a sister or brother in faith.]

but takes its cognitive form in creeds, preaching, prayers, doc-trines, and dogmas of the faith community

[*cognitive form*—faith does have intellectual content and calls for an intellectual assent (recall the discussion in chapter one about whether one can have faith without the-ology.)

creeds, preaching, prayers, doctrines, and dogmas—these forms are an aspect, an expression of faith, but are not to be identified as faith itself—as one writer expressed it, "faith is a verb."]

and calls us to a discipleship of worship, personal transforma-tion, and action on behalf of justice.

[*a discipleship of worship*—faith not only involves the intellect—seeking understanding through theology, but it also seeks ritual expression (not unlike the young couple's love in Menotti's opera, *The Medium*). Many Christians experience this ritual expression through the sacramental life. An ancient saying, "the law of praying is the law of believing" (*lex orandi/lex credendi*) captures the idea that we seek to know the truth so we might praise God as we ought; or, in the expression of Karl Rahner, in the end all theology must turn into prayer.

personal transformation—accepting the invitation to par-ticipate in the very life of God through grace, calls us to conversion and repentance. Just as in a religious experi-ence, being in the presence of the Holy arouses in us a sense of fear, awe, and unworthiness, so entering into the life of God through the power of the Holy Spirit calls us to a change of mind and heart. We attempt to live the moral life in our personal and communal relationships.

and action on behalf of justice—clearly as disciples of Jesus Christ the life of faith must lead us to praxis on behalf of justice; "Not everyone who says, 'Lord, Lord,' will enter the Kingdom, but the one who does the will of the Father."

In the final judgment scene in Matthew's gospel, the will of the Father is clearly depicted in feeding the hungry, clothing the naked, caring for the sick, etc. From the Old Testament prophets through Jesus' preaching and example to the social teaching of the church, justice is an integral part of the Word of God we are invited to accept; a preferential option for the poor is clearly an essential aspect of the definition of faith.]

This, then, is our working definition of faith:

Faith is our freely given, graced response to God's invitation to a loving relationship that begins in preconceptual form but takes its cognitive form in creeds, preaching, prayers, doctrines, and dogmas of the faith community, and calls us to a discipleship of worship, personal transformation, and action on behalf of justice.

Up to this point we have been referring to God's Word coming to us in an ultimate way in Jesus Christ, himself the Message, yet reflected upon in the Scripture and Tradition of the church. We must now turn to that topic and examine the relationship between Scripture and Tradition and their respective roles in doing theology.

Questions for Reflection and Discussion

1. How would you explain the statement, "Revelation and faith are two sides of a single coin"?

2. How can limiting the understanding of revelation to *information*, and especially information about the precise time and manner of the end of the world, inhibit our understanding and appreciation of God's gracious invitation to all humans and all creation to enter into relationship?

3. How would you explain to someone the difference between doctrine and dogma? Would the phrase from *Animal Farm*, "All

animals on the farm are equal, but some are more equal than others," be of any aid in explaining what Vatican II calls a "hierarchy of truths," and the World Council of Churches calls a "sense of proportion"? Use as examples the basic Christian dogma, Jesus is Lord, and the Catholic church dogmas on the assumption of Mary or papal infallibility.

4. Why does faith always involve risk? What dangers can result when churches or groups attempt to remove the "risk factor" from theology? How does this relate to fundamentalism in Scripture or doctrine?

Suggestions for Further Reading

Brown, Raymond E. *Responses to 101 Questions on the Bible*. New York: Paulist Press, 1990. See questions 30–33 on the book of Revelation and fundamentalism, pp. 41–48.

Dulles, Avery. "Faith and Revelation," in *Systematic Theology: Roman Catholic Perspectives*, Vol. I., ed. Francis Schüssler Fiorenza and John P. Galvin. Minneapolis: Fortress Press, 1991, pp. 92–128.

Lane, Dermot A. *The Experience of God: An Invitation to Do Theology*. New York: Paulist Press, 1981. See chapter 2, "The Nature of Revelation," pp. 32–61, and chapter 3, "The Activity of Faith," pp. 62–89.

McBrien, Richard P. *Catholicism: New Edition*. New York: HarperCollins, 1994. See chapter 2, "Faith and its Outcomes: Theology, Doctrine, Discipleship," pp. 19–71.

Schillebeeckx, Edward. *Church: The Human Story of God*. New York: Crossroad, 1990. See chapter 1, "World History and Salvation History, History of Revelation and History of Suffering," pp. 1–45.

Schneiders, Sandra M. *The Revelatory Text: Interpreting the New Testament as Sacred Scripture*. New York: HarperCollins, 1991.

Chapter Three

Scripture and Tradition

The story is told of an old Jewish rabbi who, when misfortune was threatening his people, would go to a certain part of the forest to pray. He would light a fire there, say a particular prayer and miraculously the misfortune would be averted. Later, a disciple of the old rabbi would likewise go to the same place in the forest to intercede on behalf of his people. There he would say, "Master of the Universe, listen! I do not know how to light the fire, but I am still able to say the prayer." The disaster would be averted.

Still later, to save his people another rabbi would go to the forest and say, "I do not know how to light the fire, I do not know the prayer, but I know the place and this must be sufficient." The miracle was accomplished. Finally it fell to another rabbi to intercede for his people. Sitting in his armchair with his head in his hands, he spoke to God: "I cannot even find the place in the forest. All I can do is to tell the story, and this must be sufficient." And it was.

Elie Wiesel
The Gates of the Forest (paraphrased)

God created us because God loves stories. The Bible is the story of God's invitation and humanity's faltering response down through the ages. In the Jewish-Christian tradition a pivotal chapter is the encounter between God and Moses on the mountain—the place, the fire, the prayer, the covenant. In the Christian story it is the star, the stable, the angels' song, the miracle of Emmanuel, God with us. We continue to tell stories and live by the shared experience from one generation to the next. That is what Scripture and Tradition are all about, as I hope we will see in what follows.

Why Has the Relationship
between Scripture and Tradition
Been a Stumbling Block in the Christian Community?

The source of this question takes us back to the Reformation in the sixteenth century. The reforms called for by Martin Luther and John Calvin were based primarily on a return to Scripture. It was a biblical renewal. Luther claimed that the only way to reform the church was to use Scripture as the final arbiter. His "Scripture alone" (*sola scriptura*), along with "faith alone" and "grace alone," became the criteria for the reform. The Roman Catholic church responded to the challenge by insisting that not only Scripture but Tradition is a source of God's Word, God's revelation. Furthermore, because the reformers were challenging the teaching authority of the pope and the bishops, Tradition for the Catholic church became almost synonymous with doctrine. In the heated polemics of the time the stage was set for what was discussed earlier as the biblicist and doctrinalist approaches to theology.

Although "Scripture alone" became a criterion for reform, it was never followed strictly either by Luther or Calvin. The early church councils' teachings on the Trinity, the humanity and divinity of Christ, and the like were maintained. Luther also continued to accept the episcopal polity of the church (ruled by bishops as we shall see in the next chapter) as well as devotion to Mary the Mother of Jesus. But the reformers did believe they were following Scripture more strictly when they reduced the number of liturgical rituals known as sacraments from seven to two—baptism and the Lord's Supper.

A general rule of the mainline reformers was to allow or accept a practice or custom unless it was directly forbidden by Scripture. Moreover, particular questions should be considered in light of all of Scripture, not just a single passage. The radical reformers (further discussed in the following chapter) insisted on a much more literal interpretation of Scripture—what the Scripture allowed or disallowed should be strictly followed. Women, for example, should always keep their heads covered in the worship assembly; no vestments or adornments should be used in worship; oaths should never be taken; and the term sacrament, absent from Scripture, should not be used.

On the Catholic side, Tradition was looked upon as a second source of revelation. It included the information Christ entrusted to the apostles during those forty days following his resurrection when, according to Acts 1:3, he spoke to them about the Kingdom of God. This in turn, said the church, was passed down to the successors of the apostles, the bishops, first among whom was the bishop of Rome who succeeded in the ministry of Peter. The pope with the bishops, not only had this source to call upon in leading the church, but when the need arose the official and definitive interpretation of Scripture came under their care.

The dissemination of the Bible among the people in their own language (thanks to the printing press and Luther's translation), along with the Reformers' challenge to Rome's authority, set the stage for the division between Catholics and Protestants down through the ages. In the ecumenical climate following Vatican II, however, great strides have been made in overcoming these problems. We will examine this breakthrough, but first we must look further into the questions of New Testament's origins and the true meaning of Tradition.

How Did the New Testament Come into Existence?

Christianity, along with Judaism and Islam, is a religion of the Book. Each of these world religions holds in esteem its Holy Book, its Scripture, its record of God's revelation. For Christians the Old and New Testaments—the Hebrew and Christian Scripture—make up the Bible. Jews hold in special esteem the Torah, the Law, but the Hebrew Bible also contains the Prophets and the Writings. The Writings include the Book of Psalms, Proverbs, Job, among others. (The Talmud—consisting of the Mishnah and the Gemara—an authoritative compilation of rabbinic traditions and discussions about Jewish life and law, is also given a special place in Judaism. It is not, however, considered God's revelation.)

Both Christians and Jews look upon their Holy Book as having been mediated to their respective communities through human agents, inspired by God but acting on their own. In other words their Holy Writings were not dictated directly by God. The Muslims, on the other hand, hold that the Qur'an (Koran) was inscribed in heaven and revealed word-for-word to the prophet Muhammad, who memorized it and then later copied it down. Another religious group that claims its Holy Book came directly from God is the Mormons. Let us turn for a moment from our examination of the formation of the New Testament and look briefly at the Mormon religious community.

Focus:
The Mormons

The Mormons (divided today into two groups: the Church of Jesus Christ of the Latter-Day Saints and the Reorganized Church of Jesus Christ of the Latter-Day Saints) believe their Holy Book, the Book of Mormon, came directly from God. Golden tablets that had remained hidden for a thousand years were discovered in 1827 by Joseph Smith, the founder of Mormonism. With the help of an angel he transcribed the message of the tablets word-for-word as the Book of Mormon. The tablets then disappeared.

Mainline Christians do not accept Mormons as fully Christian. This is to take nothing away from their exemplary life and work on behalf of Jesus Christ. The reason rests on what was discussed in the previous chapter about Jesus being the ultimate and final revelation of God. Mormons believe that additional public revelation came through the prophet Joseph Smith. This additional public revelation com-

pletes and even supersedes the New Testament. The
Book of Mormon, therefore, takes its place alongside
of, and even above, the Bible. Mainline Christians
cannot accept further public revelation after the coming of Jesus. Mormons, in turn, believe that early in
its history the Christian church abandoned its principles and was lost until Joseph Smith founded the true
Christian church in 1831.

Mainline Christians do, however, accept Mormon
baptism. If a baptized Mormon were to seek membership in the Catholic, Lutheran, Presbyterian,
Methodist, United Church of Christ/Congregational,
or Baptist church (the so-called mainline Christian
churches), they would not be rebaptized. Mormons
baptize with water using the trinitarian formula, "In
the name of the Father, the Son, and the Holy Spirit,"
even though their understanding of the Trinity
diverges greatly from mainline Christian doctrine.
Mormons do believe that they are saved through the
death and resurrection of Jesus Christ and consider
themselves the true Christians.[1]

Focus:
The Mormons

In our examination of the process by which the New Testament
came into existence we should begin by saying that the Hebrew
Scripture—what Christians call the Old Testament—came into existence in an analogous way but over a much greater span of time. Let
us then consider the one without whom we would not have the New
Testament—*Jesus Christ*. In a series of seven steps we shall outline
the process by which the New Testament came into existence. If any
of the following steps had not occurred, we would not have the New
Testament as we know it.

1. Jesus was born, preached, and attracted followers. Had he been
born but never preached, we wouldn't have the New Testament.
Had he preached but not attracted followers, we would not have
the New Testament, etc.

2. Jesus was put to death but his followers experienced him alive, and it changed their lives. Throughout human history many wandering preachers have attracted disciples, but upon their deaths the followers drifted apart and back to their former homes and ways of life. The followers of Jesus did likewise. Despondent and afraid, they fled. Peter had even denied he knew Jesus. Only some of the women, including his mother, along with the John the beloved disciple, stayed with him to the end. But then something happened that changed everything. He had arisen! He was alive! He had appeared to the women, to Peter, and to the disciples back in Galilee. They received the Spirit of the living Christ, the Holy Spirit, and they were no longer afraid. Had this not happened we would not have the New Testament.

3. The disciples began to preach, and communities of faith arose. Jesus came preaching the Kingdom of God. Like John the Baptist he called people to change their lives and to believe the Good News. What God wanted for the people was wholeness, health, salvation. Luke's gospel records Jesus' inaugural sermon back home in Nazareth. Jesus identified with the prophet Isaiah proclaiming his task was to bring good news to the poor, proclaim release to the captives, recovery of sight for the blind, to let the oppressed go free.

Jesus preached not himself, but the Kingdom of God. The disciples, however, began to preach Jesus as the inbreaking of the Kingdom. He was the Good News; he was salvation and liberation. The shift here is vitally important for Christianity: *the preacher (Jesus) became the preached one (the Message—the Good News).*

Peter among the Jews, and Paul among the Gentiles, along with many others including women, began to spread this message, and large numbers responded. They, too, experienced new life in the risen Christ through the power of the Spirit. Without this shift—preacher become the preached one—made possible because of the disciples' experience of the risen Christ, we would not have the New Testament.

4. Questions and problems arose in these new faith communities and letters were written. Here we have the first writings of the New

Testament. At this step we have passed from the *oral* (preaching) to the *written* (letters) form of evangelization. When someone like the great missionary Paul visited a city and by his preaching established a new community of faith, he would keep in contact with them by means of letters. The earliest of these, and the earliest New Testament writing that we have, is Paul's first letter to the Thessalonians. Scripture scholars tell us that it was probably written in the year 51 C.E.*

The problem that Paul was dealing with in this letter to the Thessalonians was one of the first big questions that early Christian communities had to face. It has to do with the delay of the return of Jesus. In 1 Thessalonians 4:13–18 we read:

> But we do not want you to be uninformed, brothers [and sisters], about those who have died, so that you may not grieve as others do who have no hope. For since we believe that Jesus died and rose again *[here we have the earliest written summary of our faith—a creedal formula]*, even so, through Jesus, God will bring with him those who have died. For this we declare to you by the word of the Lord *[Other translations say, "as if the Lord himself has said it." Because the early Christians believed prophecy was alive again within the community, Paul felt confident to teach in Jesus' name. The gospel writers likewise felt free to put their own teachings and interpretations into the mouth of the historical Jesus as we shall see.]*, that we who are alive, who are left until the coming of the Lord, will by no means precede those who have died. For the Lord himself, with a cry of command, with the archangel's call and with the sound of God's trumpet, will descend from heaven, and the dead in Christ will rise first. *[Here we see Paul using apocalyptic language.]* Then we who are alive, who are left, will be caught up in the clouds together with them to meet the Lord in the air *[the so-called rapture that is so pop-*

---

*C.E., the common era; and B.C.E., before the common era, are used in scholarly writing today instead of A.D., *anno domini*—the year of our Lord; and B.C.—before Christ. Ecumenical sensitivity has led to this change. Non-Christians accept the Christian calendar but should not have to speak of "the year of our Lord" and "before Christ" when they accept Jesus neither as Lord nor as the Messiah.

ular in televangelists' preaching]; and so we will be with the Lord forever. Therefore encourage one another with these words.

Here in the earliest New Testament writing we find Paul assur-
ing the Christian community in Thessalonica that they need not
worry about those who are dying before the return of the Lord. Paul
still expects Jesus to return within his own lifetime, but those who
die before the second coming will be brought back from the dead
upon Christ's return. We will see this apocalyptic expectation of the
imminent return of Christ slowly be defused in the process of the
formation of the New Testament.

As far as Paul's own letters are concerned, the seven that he most
assuredly wrote—1 Thessalonians, 1 and 2 Corinthians, Galatians,
Philippians, Philemon, and Romans—were all probably written
within the decade of the fifties. Those letters associated with Paul
but probably written by his pupils—2 Thessalonians, Ephesians,
Colossians, 1 and 2 Timothy, and Titus—span a much longer period. Second Thessalonians, for example, does not see the end as
coming soon, but sees many things that must happen before the
end time. The letters to Timothy and Titus show a church that has
settled into fixed structures, doctrines, and forms of leadership.

*5. In certain communities the sayings and deeds of Jesus were col-
lected and written down.* Paul made use of the letter or epistle form.
Paul was not one of the original apostles. It is highly unlikely that
he knew the historical Jesus. Indeed he had persecuted the early
members of the Christian communities. But he had a religious
experience on the road to Damascus in which he encountered the
risen Christ, and everything changed for him. His preaching and
letters centered around the new life he had experienced in the risen
Christ and how he wanted others to share in that same new life.
There is little material in Paul's letters about Jesus before his death
and resurrection. If one were to attempt to construct a biography of
Jesus from Paul's letters it would amount to little more than this:
Jesus was born of woman (he is fully human like you and I), and

he died on a cross. There is a bit more. In his first letter to the Corinthians, Paul gives the earliest account we have of the Last Supper. Familiarity with Jesus' ministry and teachings is not absent from his letters, but overall, Paul's gospel was of the liberating effects of Jesus' death and resurrection.

In other communities, however, especially among those in Galilee and its surroundings who had known the historical Jesus, as the early followers began to die and Jesus had not returned, his sayings and deeds were collected and written down. (Scholars call one such collections of sayings of Jesus the Q source. We shall refer to it later.)

6. *Certain teachers arranged the sayings and deeds of Jesus (and their own teachings and interpretations) in particular ways to meet the needs of their communities. The result is what today we call the gospels.* The gospel is a unique literary genre or form. It is not biography but it contains biography; it is not history but it contains history. It is a proclamation of Jesus' message to his disciples, the gospel writer's proclamation of Jesus' message to his or her own community, and the community's (the church's) proclamation of Jesus to the whole world, including us. In addition to proclamation, the gospels contain ethical direction or exhortation (parenesis) for those who hear and accept the proclamation. Finally the gospels contain metaphor and myth.

Each of the four gospels has its own particular slant (theological perspective) on the one central figure, Jesus Christ. Matthew, for example, presents Jesus as the teacher of the new law, the new covenant. Jesus is the new Moses. As the law of the old covenant is contained in the first five books of the Old Testament, so Matthew arranges the sayings of Jesus in five great sermons, the first being the Sermon on the Mount. As Moses went up the mountain to get the old law, so Jesus goes up the mountain to give the new law. (Luke, who presents Jesus from another perspective, has Jesus come down the mountain to a grassy plain to give that first sermon.)

Matthew alone has Mary and Joseph fleeing into Egypt with the child Jesus and remaining there until after the death of Herod. All of this, Matthew reminds us, took place to fulfill what the prophet had spoken, "Out of Egypt I have called my son." According to Matthew, Jesus, like Moses, was called from Egypt. The Moses parallel is not, of course, the only theological perspective presented by Matthew. That Jesus is in the line of David and the legitimate heir to the royal house of David is another theme that Matthew emphasizes more than the other gospel writers.

Mark's gospel is apocalyptic in form. Written during the Jewish uprising of 66–70 C.E., Mark is encouraging his community to remain faithful during severe persecution. To follow Christ means to pick up the cross of martyrdom. Yet there is glory in the cross, for very soon "the Son of Man" is coming on the clouds, and angels will gather the elect. The terrible tribulation of the last days is described in the "Little Apocalypse" in chapter 13.

Luke is more the historian. He says at the beginning of his gospel that he wishes to present an "orderly account." He does this by what is called a periodization of history. One epoch or time must end before the next begins. This causes Luke to have John the Baptist jailed before the baptism of Jesus (3:18–22). Luke alone has the account of the twelve-year-old Jesus remaining behind in the Temple while his parents start for home (truant son? negligent parents?). John the Baptist may have preached before Jesus, but Jesus was teaching when just a boy! Luke alone has Jesus remaining forty days after the resurrection before his ascension.

Luke also presents Jesus with a special sensitivity to women (the widow of Nain, 7:11–17; the poor widow's offering in the temple, 21:1–4) and to the poor (the rich man and Lazarus, 16:19–31). In Luke's gospel Jesus is also a faithful Jew who prays before every big decision he makes, often praying through the night.

Perhaps Luke's attempt at an orderly account becomes most evident in his sequel to the gospel, the Acts of the Apostles. Luke begins volume two where volume one leaves off. Here Luke presents a time or epoch for the church as depicted in the ministry of

Peter and the missionary journeys of Paul. This period begins with the ascension of Jesus and the coming of the Holy Spirit upon the apostles. It will extend until Christ returns to usher in the final age, the eschaton, or the Kingdom in its fullness. For Luke the imminent return of Christ, the apocalyptic expectation has been postponed. In "calming things down" Luke reflects the changing condition and perspective of the early church. It is the time of the Holy Spirit dwelling within the followers of the Risen One through baptism and in the community as the Body of Christ. A small but significant addition that Luke makes to one of the sayings of Jesus captures this development in early Christian thinking on the end time. In Mark's gospel Jesus says, "If you want to be my disciple you must...take up your cross and follow me." Luke says, "you must take up your cross *daily.*" Discipleship does not necessarily mean martyrdom but being filled with the Spirit, enduring the daily tribulations while being witnesses of Christ "in Jerusalem, in all Judea and Samaria, and to the ends of the earth" (Acts 1:8).

We have been examining the basic theological perspectives of Matthew, Mark, and Luke. These first three gospels are closely related. For this reason they are called the *synoptic* gospels (*syn* — "together or with one another"; *optic*—"they can be seen or viewed"). The question arises, how are they interrelated? Before we consider the theological perspective of John's gospel, let us briefly review what is known as the *synoptic problem.*

The Synoptic Problem

Matthew, Mark, and Luke share a substantial amount of traditional material about Jesus in their respective gospels. They present the events of Jesus' life for the most part in the same sequence. A number of theories have been proposed about the interrelationship of the three. In the late nineteenth century what has become known as the *two source hypothesis* was proposed, and it has held up through the years as the best solution to the problem.

According to the two source hypothesis, Mark is considered to be the first of the gospels. Both Matthew and Luke must have used

Mark in the composition of their own gospels. Therefore Mark becomes the first source. Matthew and Luke, however, have a considerable amount of material in common not found in Mark. Because this material (primarily sayings or teachings of Jesus) is so similar in both of the gospels, the hypothesis is that Matthew and Luke must have had another common source. Scholars call it Q, from the German word *Quelle*, which means *source*. This hypothetical source of sayings called Q becomes the second source in this two source hypothesis.

We do not have the Q source, but scholars have reconstructed it from the common material in Matthew and Luke not found in Mark. One theory on why the Q source did not survive on its own is because it apparently did not have an account of the passion and death of Jesus. In this pivotal event in all of the gospels, Matthew and Luke closely follow Mark with no common material from another source.

Matthew and Luke each do have additional material that does not appear in either Mark or in Q that is called *special Matthew, special Luke*. Over one-third of the Gospel of Luke is special to Luke. If we did not have Luke's gospel, for example, we would not have the stories of the Prodigal Son, the Widow of Nain, or the Poor Man Lazarus.

The most obvious *special* material in Matthew and Luke is the birth stories. Mark begins his gospel with John the Baptist's preaching and Jesus' public life. There is no birth story in Mark. In the Gospel of John the writer tells the "Christmas story" or birth story succinctly: "And the Word was made flesh and dwelt among us." No star, wise men, or camels, no angels, shepherds, or stable. Matthew and Luke employ them, but each writer tells the story from his particular theological perspective. We intertwine them as we recall the lovely story of the birth of Jesus, and that is fine. But a brief examination of the birth stories in Matthew and Luke will uncover another aspect of theology that needs to be understood.

In the first two chapters of Matthew and Luke the story of Jesus' birth is told (often called *the infancy narratives*). Matthew relates the story from Joseph's perspective, Luke from Mary's.

According to Matthew, Joseph, of the house of David, was told in a dream to take Mary as his wife even though she was pregnant before their marriage. It appears they were living in Bethlehem at the time, for when the wise men found the place of birth (with the help of the star and the advice of religious leaders in Jerusalem—Jeremiah had prophesied Bethlehem as the birthplace of the Messiah), *they entered the house* and presented the child with gifts of gold, frankincense, and myrrh.

Joseph was then warned in a dream to take the mother and child into Egypt in order to save the child's life from Herod's death threat. After Herod's death another dream informed Joseph it was safe to return home. However, a further dream told him it still wasn't safe in Judea under the rule of Herod's son, so they avoided Bethlehem and went to Galilee and settled in a town called Nazareth.

That is the story from Joseph's perspective as Matthew presents it. No stable with its animals and grubby shepherds to witness the birth of the Messiah, but a house with wise men bearing gifts fit for a king.

Luke, on the other hand, tells the story from the woman's point of view, from the perspective of a poor family. Mary was told by the angel Gabriel that she was to have a child through the power of the Holy Spirit. Mary questioned, but then agreed. She then went to visit her cousin, Elizabeth, who in her old age was blessed with a pregnancy that removed the disgrace of being unable to have a child.

Mary then made the long journey with her husband from Nazareth to Bethlehem. Joseph had to register, together with Mary, in his hometown because of a decree by the Roman Emperor Augustus. While they were there Mary gave birth, and she "wrapped him in bands of cloth, and laid him in a manger, because there was no place for them in the inn."

Shepherds in the region were informed by angels of what had taken place and where they would find this newborn Messiah. They were to look for a child in a manger wrapped with bands of cloth. The shepherds told the parents what they had been told about the child, and "Mary treasured all these words and pondered them in her heart."

Eight days after Jesus' birth he was circumcised and named Jesus, "the name given by the angel before he was conceived in the womb." The couple went up from Bethlehem to Jerusalem for the purification of Mary and the presentation of their firstborn to God in the temple. In the temple they encountered Simeon, who was awaiting the birth of the Messiah. He blessed the child and told Mary that Jesus would be opposed by many, and "a sword will pierce your own soul too." Also in the temple was a prophet, Anna, who began to tell those "looking for the redemption of Jerusalem" all about the child. (A woman again is included in Luke's story.)

Then, we are told, the couple returned to Nazareth with their child, and he "grew in wisdom; and the favor of God was upon him."

Two stories of the birth of Jesus. They don't exactly mesh. Where did the couple live before the birth of Jesus? Where did the birth take place? Who came to see the newborn child? How did those who came find out about the birth? Who got to name Jesus? What was Joseph's role in all of this? Did they live in Egypt? Was there a Roman census at this time? Was there a wholesale murder of male children under the age of two in and around Bethlehem? Are there any records outside of the Bible that testify to this?

The first two chapters of Matthew and Luke present stories whose purpose is to get across a deep theological truth. Jesus, born of Mary, is special. He is Emmanuel, God with us. He is the Messiah, the Savior. He is special from his very birth, his very conception. The details of the story, as they were passed on in the community of Matthew and Luke, are not so important. One account is not correct and the other in error, as we might judge them today.

This type of theologizing—telling a story that gets across a deep theological truth—is called *theologoumenon*. The word itself is not so important. We can recognize in it *theos*, "God," and *logos* "word." Literally it means "that which is said about God." Something that is taught not because it can be verified or refuted on the basis of historical evidence (a dream or a message of an angel) but because it is closely connected to some defined doctrine about God. The Holy Spirit was involved with the very beginning of the life of this One in whom we have experienced new life. He fulfilled the expectations of the prophets of the coming of a Messiah. He was born of woman and has full humanity like you and I. His mother was graced from her very beginning as the bearer of God's very Son, yet she freely responded to this grace. God truly acts in human history.

When we turn to the fourth gospel, the Gospel of John, we find a presentation of Jesus quite different from those in the synoptic gospels. John begins not with a birth story but with the pre-existence of the Word—*Logos*—from all eternity. Jesus as the incarnate Word of God performs *signs* instead of miracles and thus "revealed his glory, and his disciples believed in him" (John 2:11). Folksy parables and sermons are presented in the fourth gospel as finely worked out *discourses*. Sharp contrasts of light and darkness, above and below, good and evil are frequently employed, along with much symbolism—life, bread, water, vine and branches, lamb of God.

Symbolic priority may explain one of the obvious contrasts between John's gospel and the synoptics. In Matthew, Mark, and Luke the Last Supper is described as the Passover meal. In John, Jesus is dying on the cross at the same time the Passover lambs are being slaughtered in preparation for the feast. In the opening chapter, John the Baptist first recognizes Jesus with the phrase, "Look, here is the Lamb of God!" The symbolism of Jesus as the sacrificial lamb is, perhaps, more important to John than the symbolism of the Last Supper as a Passover celebration. Theologically, John presents Jesus as the descending and ascending redeemer figure who can say, "And I, when I am lifted up from the earth [both on the cross and in resurrection], will draw all people to myself." John shows the strong influence of the Wisdom tradition in his presentation of Jesus. (This neglected tradition that presents Jesus as the incarnation of Wisdom [*Sophia*—a feminine personification of God] has been resurrected by feminist theologians in very creative and challenging ways.)

The sixth step in the process of formation of the New Testament has been lengthy, but the gospels also form the core of the Christian Scripture. We now proceed with the final step of the New Testament formation.

7. *Through a process of discernment over an extended period of time the Christian community decided which writings or books should be included in the New Testament.* The New Testament did not drop out of heaven in completed form. Nor did it come into existence in a precise and orderly way because Jesus or the Holy Spirit designated certain ones to be the official recorders or archivists. As the apocalyptic expectation of the end time "cooled down" and the early communities realized they were going to be around for a while, numerous writings circulated among the communities. Some were quickly accepted by all. The second letter of Peter, written at the end of the first century or early in the second, already refers to Paul's letters as Scripture (2 Peter 3:16). Other writings had a difficult time being accepted—the Gospel of John, for example, the letter to the Hebrews, and especially the book of Revelation. Still others were rejected—*The Shepherd of Hermas* and *The Teaching of the Twelve Apostles* (the *Didache*) were popular in some communities, but did not make the final list.

Some second-century writings about the early life of Jesus—how he helped Joseph in the carpenter shop, miraculously lengthening, stretching with his hands, boards too short for furniture old man

Joseph was asked to make; fashioning clay pigeons and then blowing on them and watching them fly away—were rejected. The Good News is about salvation in Jesus, not about Jesus the boy-wonder. At the end of the *Gospel of Thomas,* a second-century collection of sayings of Jesus strongly influenced by *gnosticism* (a perspective that understood revelation as secret knowledge given only to a few whereby they could escape the evil of the material world and return to the realm of the spirit), we find this conversation between Jesus and Peter: "Mary should leave us," Peter says, "for females are not worthy of life." Jesus replies, "See, I am going to lead her to make her a male so that she too might become a living spirit that resembles you males. For every woman that makes herself male will enter the kingdom of heaven."[2] (Any wonder the *Gospel of Thomas* didn't make the cut!)

The criteria for inclusion was not primarily based on authorship. Except for Paul's letters, most of the writings were circulated anonymously. Only later were they associated with prominent personages in the tradition to facilitate their acceptance. Rather the primary criterion was how well the particular writing reflected the new life that the congregations experienced in the risen Christ. Technically this is called the process of *connaturality*—one comes to recognize that which is one's own. Let us look at an example of connaturality found in the Bible.

In the first chapter of Genesis, God creates man and woman in God's own image—male and female. This equality of imaging God in both male and female needs to be stressed today. But for the sake of an analogy of connaturality let us look at the second account of the creation of humans in chapter two of Genesis. God first made Adam and then realized that it was not good for him to be alone. So God made every animal of the field and every bird of the air, and brought them to the man. But Adam did not find among them an apt partner. God then made woman from a rib of Adam, and when God brought her to him Adam exclaimed, "This at last is bone of my bones and flesh of my flesh...." They then became one, for they recognized their common humanity.

So analogously the early Christians recognized the writings that were truly "their own." As today, in spite of ethnic, cultural, and racial diversity, we recognize all other humans as "our own," so the early Christians, in spite of the diversity between Mark's gospel (Jesus very human) and John's (Jesus very divine), between Paul's letter to the Romans (salvation by faith alone) and the letter of James (faith without works is dead), still they recognized certain writings as *inspired*, as reflecting their new life as a part of a Spirit-filled community, the Body of Christ.

If God willed the community to continue the word and work of Jesus (God is "author" of the Christian community), then God must also have willed ("authored") the writings that became the foundational literature of that community. God "in-spirited" the community within which the human authors found their inspiration to produce the New Testament writings that we as the Christian community recognize as our own.

In 367 C.E., Athanasius, bishop of Alexandria, wrote an Easter letter to his people. In it he listed the twenty-seven books that his community accepted as constituting the New Testament. Gradually other communities began referring to this list, and eventually it was accepted in both the East and the West. The official list became known as the *canon* of Scripture—a word referring to a reed that was used as an instrument of measure—a type of yardstick. These writings "measured up," one might say.

If theology is *our attempt to express in words what we believe to be the ultimate revelation of God in Jesus,* then after our review of the New Testament material above, we could substitute *the early Christian community's attempt* for *our attempt,* and have a theological definition of the New Testament.

> *The New Testament is the early Christian community's attempt to express in words what they believed to be the ultimate revelation of God in Jesus.*

The New Testament itself is theology (or the product of theologizing), but a very special, *privileged* theology. The New Testament is privileged theology because it came into existence at the time the Christian community was being formed. It both was formed by, and helped to form, the community. The New Testament became constitutive and normative for the Christian community.

In this limited way, the New Testament has parallels with the Constitution of the United States. Born out of the experience of this nation's founders (formed by, but helping to form, the emerging nation), the Constitution became constitutive and normative for our country.

The same interpretative questions asked of the Constitution are likewise posed of the New Testament: What does the particular passage mean? What was the intent of the original writer? How is it to be applied today? (One distinguishing difference is, of course, that the Constitution can be amended.)

As the foundational, constitutive, and normative literature for the Christian community, the New Testament will continue be proclaimed, preached, studied, and meditated on as long as the Christian church continues to exist. It is, as the Second Vatican Council says, the *soul* of theology.

Before turning to the meaning of *Tradition*, the second part of the main question of this chapter, it is worthwhile to consider briefly the matter of the *canon* (the official list of books) of the Old Testament.

Because the Christian community accepts the Hebrew Scripture as a part of its foundational literature, it is of some ecumenical importance that Protestants and Catholics do not agree on the Old Testament canon. There is agreement among Catholics, Protestants, and Orthodox on the twenty-seven books of the New Testament. In this case the discernment process has been successful. The reason for the disagreement in the Old Testament is historical, and although most Christians do not see it as an ecumenical roadblock, still it results in the distinction between the Protestant and Catholic "versions" of the Bible that we know today.

Focus:
The canon
of the Old
Testament

Focus:
The canon
of the Old
Testament

Catholics accept forty-six books in the Old Testament. Protestants (and contemporary Jews) accept thirty-nine. There are seven disputed books (and parts of two others). The disputed books are Tobit, Judith, Wisdom, Ecclesiasticus or Sirach, Baruch, 1 & 2 Maccabees—and parts of Esther and Daniel. A popular reading at a Catholic funeral liturgy is from chapter three of the book of Wisdom. It begins, "But the souls of the just are in the hands of God, and no torment will ever touch them." This reading would not be heard at a Protestant funeral. Not that they would find anything against it, but to them it is not a part of Sacred Scripture.

The problem comes with a longer Greek canon or list of books that Catholics use, and a shorter Hebrew canon followed by Protestants. The historical explanation takes us back to about 250 B.C.E. Jews living outside of Palestine (in *diaspora*), especially those living in Alexandria, Egypt, having accepted Greek as their language, wanted the Hebrew Scripture translated into Greek.

According to legend, seventy-two scholars (six from each of the twelve tribes of Israel) did the translation in seventy days—each working separately, yet all agreeing perfectly on the final product. Regardless of the details, the translation was made, and it was nicknamed the *Septuagint,* from the Greek word seventy. This translation included certain later writings, some of which were originally written in Greek. The total number of books that came to be included in the Greek translation of the Hebrew Scripture, the Septuagint, was forty-six.

The early Christian community, having spread quickly into Greek-speaking culture (the gospels and Paul's letters were all written in Greek) understandably used the Septuagint with its forty-six books.

After the destruction of Jerusalem and the Temple by the Romans in 70 C.E., a group of Pharisees gathered in the city of Jamnia and began to reorganize the Jewish faith now that the Temple was gone and there was no longer a place to offer sacrifice. Of the Jewish sects at the time of the destruction, the Pharisees were the ones who survived for the most part. They were popular teachers associated with the synagogues and bent on making the Jewish faith, as embodied in the Law, a religion the people could practice. The Sadducees, the wealthy sect who controlled the Temple and had collaborated with the Romans, got wiped out in the uprising. The Zealots, the revolutionaries who instigated the Jewish revolt against Rome, also were eventually eliminated. A small group of them, about one thousand, including women and children, took refuge in a stronghold in the desert near the Dead Sea, called Masada. There they withstood the Romans for three years. When it became clear that the Romans, who had built a ramp up one side of the mountain, were going to knock down the gates with a battering ram, the Zealots divided themselves into groups of one hundred and then into tens. The leader of each group of ten killed the other nine and then himself or herself. When the Romans arrived, they found only the dead. The Jewish people look upon Masada as a monument to martyrdom, not a mass suicide. The motto of the modern Israeli army is "Never Again Masada!"

Another Jewish sect, the Essenes, had earlier withdrawn from Jerusalem to Qumran, also near the Dead Sea. There in a monastic type of life they awaited the apocalyptic coming of the Teacher of Righteousness. They too were destroyed by the Romans, but some of their writings survived in caves where they had hid them. These writings were found in 1947 by a shepherd boy of the area. One of the great archeological finds of this century, they are known as the Dead Sea Scrolls.

Meanwhile the Pharisees, who met outside of Jerusalem to pull together the badly wounded Hebrew faith, drew up a list of books they considered acceptable and sacred for their worship and study. This list or canon contained 39 books.

Focus:
The canon of the
Old Testament

Focus:
The canon
of the Old
Testament

Later, in the fourth century, some Christian leaders, including the great Scripture scholar Jerome, began using the shorter Hebrew canon, but the Christian church generally followed the Septuagint.

We jump now to the sixteenth century and the Reformation. Luther, himself a Scripture scholar, accepted the Hebrew canon, or the shorter list, as definitive. This became the practice of the Protestant tradition. Whether Luther had any ulterior reasons for favoring the shorter canon is not clear. But he did have a problem with the Roman church's teaching on purgatory. The only place that a scriptural basis might be found for that teaching is in the second book of Maccabees. At the end of chapter twelve the traditional translation reads, "It is a holy and pious thought to make atonement for the dead, that they might be delivered from their sin."

In the sixteenth century the Council of Trent, which was the Roman Church's response to the Protestant challenge, taught officially (after much heated debate) that the forty-six books of the Greek canon were all inspired and constitute the Old Testament. Protestants call the seven disputed books, along with seven others, *apocryphal* (those for which divine authorship is falsely claimed). Catholics call the seven disputed books *deutero-canonical* (of the second canon) and agree with the apocryphal designation of the additional books.

Today the disagreement/division remains, but at least we agree to disagree. Modern Protestant versions of the Bible often include the disputed books but carefully label them *Apocrypha*. Catholics, on the other hand recognize that the seven disputed books are not at the center of Old Testament teaching. The *New Revised Standard Version of the Bible with the Apocrypha* provides a good explanation of the current situation and the historical background surrounding the apocryphal literature.

Tradition

We turn now to Tradition, the second part of our general discussion on the relationship between Scripture and Tradition. Because of the emphasis of the sixteenth-century reformers on *Scripture alone,* in the post-Reformation period, extending up until the Second Vatican Council, the Catholic church put most stress on the "second source" of revelation, Tradition. Also, because all authority was challenged by the Enlightenment period and because of rationalism's effect on Catholic theology, Tradition became identified, or at least closely associated, with doctrine. Tradition, at least in theology, became narrowly identified with the post-biblical reflection on Scripture or, in a more catechetical formula, the sum of the truths outside of Scripture revealed by God and necessary for salvation. Discussed above as the doctrinalist approach to theology, this approach robbed Tradition of its dynamic character. It became the *traditionalism,* described so succinctly in the epigram: *Tradition is the living faith of the dead, traditionalism is the dead faith of the living.*[3] The Second Vatican Council recaptured the dynamic, living character of Tradition, broadening it from a *positivistic* understanding to an *existential* one. Tradition becomes the lived experience of the faith community down through the ages. Tradition is a dynamic and living concept. It includes all those various ways that the risen Christ, through the power of the Holy Spirit, affects his followers through the faith community. Tradition is something that we become a part of through liturgical celebration and worship, through profession of faith, and through adhering to and following the gospel way as a way of life. A sign of the development of the understanding of Tradition can be found in its treatment by the Council of Trent (1545–1563) and Vatican II (1962–1965):[4]

Trent indicated that the starting point of Tradition is the preaching of Christ and his commissioning of the Apostles to preach the gospel "as the source of all saving truth and moral teaching." Vatican II added to this last phrase, "and thus communicate to them divine gifts." Therefore Tradition is more than a matter of the

Focus:
The development of the understanding of Tradition.

Focus:
The development
of the
understanding of
Tradition.

handing on of defined doctrines. It is a matter of dialogue (communicating) and grace (divine gifts).

Instead of Christ's commission to preach being fulfilled by carefully repeating and interpreting the original statements of Christ and the Apostles (Trent), Vatican II teaches that: "This commission was faithfully fulfilled by the apostles who, by their oral preaching, by example, and by pastoral practices, handed on what they received." Therefore Tradition was communicated and guaranteed by the whole living out of the gospel within the Christian community by the leaders and the people.

Trent said the Holy Spirit "dictated" what was to be passed on; Vatican II said that it is through the "prompting" of the Holy Spirit that Tradition is passed on. Tradition is more than doctrine, formulae, or statements of faith. One might say that Tradition is not just the candle or the wick, but the burning.

Traditions, sometimes designated with a small "t"—traditions or customs—also form part of the community's life. While important, they are not at the core of the Christian way of life. The rosary, for example, has been a powerful private devotion for many Roman Catholics since the thirteenth century. While the "mysteries" that are meditated upon during its recitation—Jesus' birth, his passion and death, resurrection and ascension, his sending of the Holy Spirit upon the Apostles, along with the special role of Mary as Jesus' mother—are part of Tradition proper. (The "mysteries" associated with Mary, as found in the birth stories of Matthew and Luke—the annunciation, visitation, birth, presentation, finding Jesus in the temple—provide deep theological truth for meditation rather than detailed factual material.) The particular prayer form of the rosary itself is tradition or custom.

One might wonder how the accidental (tradition, custom) is to be distinguished from the essential (Tradition). The norm of Scripture certainly becomes part of the discernment process, but the lived experience of the Spirit-filled community as articulated through its legitimate leaders and teachers also has a role. Some of the traditions were unworthy of the name—the crusades, the inquisition, the condemning of Galileo, the witch-hunts, the plunder and oppression of indigenous peoples by the conquistadors, the economic imperialism in the name of Christendom, the treatment of the Jews and of racial minorities and of women. Only slowly, and with the help of prophetic voices and lives, do the unworthy traditions get rooted out and distinguished from Tradition.

Focus:
The development of the understanding of Tradition.

We are now ready to propose an ecumenical solution to the questions posed in this chapter, the relationship between Scripture and Tradition. Having examined the process of the formation of the New Testament, how the writings came out of the lived experience of the early faith community, and having examined how the notions of Tradition must be widened from a narrow dogmatic perspective, we can say this: *The New Testament is itself a part of the Tradition* (the early disciples first having followed and experienced new life in the risen Christ and only later having reflected on that experience in writing), *although a privileged, irreplaceable part of the Tradition* (as the foundational, constitutive, and normative writings of the community founded on the apostles, it is spirit-filled literature *[inspired]* arising out of a spirit-filled community). Both the holy Scripture and the Tradition flow from the single source, God's gracious self-disclosure in and through the Word who continues to live among us through the power of the Holy Spirit within the community of faith. We must now turn to an examination of this community that is called together in the Spirit to continue the word and work of Jesus the Christ.

Questions for Reflection and Discussion

1. Does an examination of the process by which the New Testament came into existence help you understand the different perspectives or theologies found there? Why or why not? Identify two different theological perspectives on salvation found in the gospels that don't

seem to mesh with each other, and may indicate there are many ways to the Kingdom.

2. How do you explain the difference between a "Protestant" and a "Catholic" version of the Bible? What does it mean that on the *canon* of Scripture we have agreed to disagree?

3. Does the birth story of Jesus told from two different perspectives that cannot be reconciled in detail bother you? How would you explain it to your grandmother or grandfather? What is the deep theological truth that both accounts attempt to convey?

4. How does a dynamic understanding of Tradition help you appreciate its essential place in the Christian faith? From a broad understanding of Tradition, explain how Scripture itself becomes a part of the Tradition.

5. How would you explain the difference between Tradition (capital T) and tradition (small t)? Can you identify instances when the two have been confused in your own church community?

Suggestions for Further Reading

Blenkinsopp, Joseph. "Canon of the Scriptures," in *The HarperCollins Encyclopedia of Catholicism*, ed. Richard P. McBrien. New York: HarperCollins, 1995, pp. 221–223.

Brown, Raymond E. "Scripture and Dogma Today," in *The Catholic Faith: A Reader*, ed. Lawrence Cunningham. New York: Paulist Press, 1988, pp. 7–15.

Meier, John P. *A Marginal Jew: Rethinking the Historical Jesus.* New York: Doubleday, 1991. See chapter 8, "In the Beginning... The Origins of Jesus of Nazareth," pp. 205–230.

Schneiders, Sandra M. "The Bible and Feminism: Biblical Theology," in *Freeing Theology: The Essentials of Theology in Feminist Perspective*, ed. Catherine Mowry LaCugna. New York: HarperCollins, 1993, pp. 31–51.

Sheard, Robert B. *An Introduction to Christian Belief: A Contemporary Look at the Basics of Faith.* Mystic, CT: Twenty-Third Publications, 1996.

Chapter Four

Church:
Its Meaning and Mission

Being caught up in the Spirit of the Risen Christ is captured by a young university student who wrote three letters "home" as if he were an early disciple of Jesus. Can you put yourself in the place of the young disciple?

Letter I

Dear Father,

The teacher is dead. I guess you can now say, "I told you so." He was crucified at Jerusalem, the city he loved. I did not see it, but some of the women who travel with us did. They said he suffered greatly, hanging for three hours until death offered him the mercy which the Romans denied. Some have died harder on the cross, hanging for days until they suffocated from their own weight being pulled back into the earth. None have died more blameless, for none have lived more blameless a life. He taught by his own life what it is to be truly and fully human. That was his only crime against our people.

I know it didn't seem right, leaving like I did. It has been hard on the family without me to help in supporting you. There is never enough money. In spite of all that, I had to follow him. If only you had known him. Heard him speak. His face beamed as he announced the news of the coming of a new era. A broad smile and a voice robust with an authority never before known filled the people with hope. His message of love touched the heart of all who would have it. In them great faith could be found. Everywhere people would seek him out. His dark eyes could look into a person's heart. Once at Temple, we were watching some people pay the temple tax. Most had much money. One woman did not appear so rich and, indeed, she offered a coin or two of little value. The Teacher wept. We tried to comfort him, but he would have nothing to do with it. Instead he went to the woman and hugged her! Later we learned that she had offered all she had to live on for that day.

Why did a good man have to die? He was not a Zealot. He did not preach revolution. He preached reconciliation. All who sought his comfort found his peace. Is that bad? He asked for love. Does that deserve the cross? All he had was a dream—a city of love. All that is left us is reality—a city of hate.

I will be at your home soon. I am done chasing the wind. It is as you said, a fool's holiday. I hope you can forgive me, or at least allow me to be in your employment if you no longer can call me a son. The Teacher said we must forgive each other. I wish you could have heard him.

Your son,

Letter II

Father,

Something is happening here. Some of the women went to anoint the Teacher's body. They came back on the run, wailing that he is alive! Do not think that I have lost my mind completely! This is what was told me. Perhaps it is the grief at the loss of the Teacher. Surely that can affect the mind, especially of women.

We asked them for details of their encounter. They could offer few. It is an experience for which humans have no words. It is a new reality— a feeling in the heart that can't be seen with the eyes or heard with the ears. It is the fear of standing on the edge of forever and the fascination in wanting to fall. His face was aglow in colors that cannot be remembered.

Could this be? The women, in spite of what they said, spoke in a confidence that made me think of the Teacher. I fear you are distressed, Father. You believe that I am off again to chase the wind. Not at all; who can catch the wind? But, just the same, I will be delayed in returning to you. Not so much because of this story. I have other reasons that I cannot explain. There is also the matter of caring for the women. The Teacher instructed us to care for each other.

What if he is alive? To experience that would be to experience what it is to be truly and fully human, for that is how he was. To experience that would be to know that only love is real and not just a word that is heard when things are being said. To experience that would be to find the city of love that he promised.

I will be along soon. Please do not tell of this. It would only add to the great price you have already paid.

Your son,

Letter III

Dad,

I am sorry, but I won't be home. The Teacher is alive! Don't worry, Dad. Just tell everyone you can find. I am not chasing the wind, because the wind has caught me.

Your son,

(Timothy Irwin,
Unpublished manuscript, 1981)

It was in such a spirit that the birth of the church took place. We will now examine the church's meaning and mission.

What Is the Church?

Up until this point we have been discussing the early Christian community, the first disciples who had known the historical Jesus, who, with the exception of a few, fled when Jesus was arrested, put on trial, and crucified, but then experienced the risen Christ and reassembled in the power of the Spirit. The new life they experienced through the power of the Holy Spirit removed their earlier fear and they boldly began to spread the good news and attract others to this new "way" as it was called. The contemporary Dutch theologian Edward Schillebeeckx has suggested that the whole Christian message can be expressed in the words Jesus used so often in his appearances to the disciples after his death and resurrection: "Be not afraid!" Even the darkness of death had been overcome in Jesus' sacrificial death for the love of his brothers and sisters.

Karl Rahner has suggested three appeals of Jesus as the ultimate redeemer that made the message of the early community so contagious to those searching for the Messiah[1]:

1) *We long to love another human being with the absolute love of God*—with a love that holds nothing back, confident that our love will be accepted and returned without measure. In Jesus, fully one with us and one with God, we find our answer. He is the human whom we can love with the absoluteness reserved for God alone.

2) *We long to be able to face death with absolute confidence that we will fall helplessly into the hands of a gracious God.* In Jesus who loved and forgave his own who abandoned him, and even those who put him to death, and who was vindicated by being raised up in glory, we gain that confidence to face death with assurance.

3) *We long to face the future with an indomitable hope that in spite of the disappointments and sufferings in this life, goodness is victorious in the end.* In Jesus, who endured suffering and still loved, disappointment and still trusted, death and still believed, we are given hope that justice, peace, and healing are possible, and that the Reign of God, our absolute future, is secured.

The church is built, as the letter to the Ephesians says, "upon the foundation of the apostles and prophets, with Christ Jesus himself as the cornerstone" (2:20). We need not think that Jesus during his lifetime set about establishing the church as a continuing institution complete with its hierarchy, liturgical/sacramental system, and distinctive ethic. Jesus, like many other Jews of his time, was caught up in the apocalyptic movement. In his preaching, Jesus looked for the imminent coming of the Kingdom. It does appear that he associated closely the acceptance of himself and his message with the coming Kingdom. Although the late nineteenth-, early twentieth-century French theologian Alfred Loisy, condemned by the Catholic church as a Modernist, was wrong on a number of things, there was truth in his statement that, "Jesus came preaching the Kingdom of God and what happened was the church."

Historical-critical studies today point out that Matthew's account of Jesus telling Peter that it was upon him (*Petrus, Rock*) that he was going to build his *church*, was reflective of the time when Matthew was writing (about 85 C.E.) rather than of Jesus' own words. For one thing, the word church (*ecclesia*—those called out or called together) appears in the gospels only in Matthew (16:18 and 18:17). Paul's letters, also reflecting the post-resurrection period, understandably use it often. We have examined in the previous chapter how there is a development of an understanding of "church time" as Matthew and Luke reinterpret Mark's gospel. Likewise there was a development from Paul's first letter to the Thessalonians, in which Paul thought the end was coming in his lifetime, to the second letter to the Thessalonians, probably written by one of Paul's pupils, which states that many things had to take place before the end would come. Also, as pointed out in the previous chapter, in the so-called Pastoral Epistles (we discussed Timothy and Titus) a rather clear church structure of presbyter-bishops and deacons was developing. Their task was to defend church doctrine and enforce church discipline. Institutionalization had begun early in the second century.

A theological and ecumenical definition of church follows. (As in previous chapters, we formulate a working definition phrase by phrase.)

The church is the community,

[The church is first and foremost the people, not the structure. Certainly it is not the building that for some has to "look like a church" with steeple, bell, stained-glass windows, and holy smoke coming out the chimney. Nor is the church primarily an institution or a hierarchy—pope, bishops, presbyters, deacons. Rather the church is the people of God of the New Covenant.]

called together in the Spirit,

[The church is not our doing but God's. Therefore it is unlike any social or welfare organization.]

that professes Jesus as Lord,

[This is the distinguishing characteristic of the Christian community. Jesus is the Messiah, Redeemer, Savior, Emmanuel—God is with us. This profession of faith sets the Christian community apart from the people of the synagogue or the mosque.]

that ratifies its faith through baptism,

[From the beginning it has been through the waters of baptism that one enters the community, dying and rising to new life in the name of the triune God—Father, Son, and Holy Spirit.]

(Definition of church continues on page 87)

Focus: Models of baptism, models of church

Some churches practice infant baptism, others adult baptism. A case can be made for either. Those who practice infant baptism have an understanding of church (an *ecclesiology*) modeled on the family. As the infant becomes a member of the family through the parents', siblings', and extended family's acceptance, yet when reaching adulthood must personally affirm (or deny) what has been done on her or his behalf, so the baptized infant, claimed for Christ by the congregation through the parents and godparents, must at adulthood accept or reject what has been done on his or her behalf. This adult acceptance is often celebrated through a ceremony known as *confirmation*.

Those churches that practice adult baptism look upon the community as a voluntary society to which an adult commitment is necessary for membership. One must be personally called, and personally accept. However, many of these churches have a ceremony of *dedication* of the child as an infant.

Focus: Models of baptism, models of church

that celebrates its faith in the Lord's Supper,

[From the earliest time the Christian community gathered to "eat bread and drink wine" in remembrance of Jesus, as he asked the disciples to do at the Last Supper. St. Paul in his first letter to the Corinthians (about 54 or 55 C.E.) recounts the Last Supper as already being part of the Tradition, "I pass on to you what I also received...." (1 Corinthians 11:23–26). At the end of the second chapter in the Acts of the Apostles (about 85 C.E.) Luke says that the early Christians "broke bread at home (or from house to house) and ate their food with glad and generous hearts..." (Acts 2:46).

Although there are many divergent ways of understanding the Lord's Supper, the majority of Christians, when they gather to eat bread and drink wine in Jesus' name, believe that Christ becomes present in some special, unique way. Christians believe that Christ is present where two or three are gathered in his name, Christ is present in the preaching of the word, and Christ is present with the Father and the Spirit dwelling within those who love and obey him. But there is a special presence of the risen Christ in the meal in which he said the bread and wine are his very body and blood.

In this ecumenical age when young people especially no longer want to continue the "old battles," it will be helpful to describe the attempts of various Christian traditions to explain the mystery of Christ's presence in the celebration of the Lord's Supper with the hope of moving toward a common understanding. Along with being "radically ecumenical," many young people are also woefully lacking in knowledge about their own tradition. Ecumenical progress is made when the participants bring with them an awareness of the gifts their own tradition has to offer.

Concerning the name of the celebration itself, the Lord's Supper, which is scriptural, is perhaps the best term to use today. The Eucharist, a Greek word meaning *thanksgiving*, is also an ancient and revered name. (Actually the Greek word *eucharist* was used by the early Christians to translate the Hebrew word for *blessing*, the basic form of all prayer for the Jews.) Communion or Holy Communion is also used to designate the celebration. In the Roman Catholic tradition Mass has been the common name. The word Mass is actually a nickname and not a very good one at that. It comes from the Latin phrase used for the dismissal of the congregation once the service has been completed: *Ite, missa est*—"Go, it has been sent or offered." It is usually rendered, "Go, *you* have been sent," but that is a free translation.]

(Definition of church continues on page 91)

Focus: Understanding Christ's presence in the bread and wine

• *In the Catholic tradition* the classic way of explaining Christ's presence in the bread and wine, using Aristotelian/Scholastic terminology, is *transubstantiation*. The very *being* (substance) of the bread and wine becomes, through the power of the Holy Spirit and the prayer of the celebrant, the very body and blood of Christ. Although appearances remain, it no longer *is* bread and wine. Moreover, the blessed or consecrated elements *remain* the body and blood of Christ. Any blessed bread remaining is therefore reserved with special care in a tabernacle or tent-like reservoir where a burning candle reminds people of the reverence they should show the consecrated bread. This explains the genuflection or bowing gesture Catholics, Orthodox, and Anglicans use when they enter a church. This blessed bread is used for communion at a later service. (Some churches also reserve the consecrated wine.)

• *In the Lutheran tradition* the word *consubstanti-ation* is employed in attempting to speak of Christ's presence in the blessed bread and wine. Luther and his followers hold that the blessed elements *are* the body and blood of Christ, but they also *are* bread and wine. In other words, the very being of the bread and wine is not changed but the being of Christ's presence is *joined with* the bread and wine—*con*substantiation. Therefore, once the liturgical service is over, any remaining elements are once more bread and wine. At a future service they would be blessed again.

Ecumenical discussions between Lutherans and Catholics have been very fruitful especially in the United States. In a joint document on the Eucharist, Lutherans have reminded Catholics that the primary reason for reserving the blessed bread is for food (communion) for the sick or those close to death. Devotions and pious practices that have grown up around the reserved bread (the Blessed Sacrament, as it is called) should not lose sight of this primary purpose. Catholics, on the other hand, have reminded Lutherans that they should have more respect for the bread that has been blessed. But both churches recognize on the theological level one another's basic belief in the real presence of Christ in the bread and wine of the Lord's Supper.

The attempts to *explain* this *mystery of faith* (to theologize about it, and we must) by employing philosophical terms such as *consubstantiation, transubstantiation,* or in even more recent Catholic attempts, *transignification* and *transfinalization,* must be understood for what they are—*attempts.* In times past, once young Catholics could pronounce the word *transubstantiation,* it was assumed the *mystery* was solved. Today a deeper understanding of the biblical concept of *memory* has helped to put the mystery of Christ's presence in the Eucharist in perspective. When the Hebrew people would remember or renew the promises of the covenant, and through the power of God those promises were made present for the people,

Focus:
Understanding
Christ's presence
in the bread
and wine

Focus:
Understanding
Christ's presence
in the bread
and wine

their memory made present the past. So too, when early Christians followed Jesus' command to "do this in memory of me," they understood it as a living memorial filled with the events commemorated in the original event—the sacrificial death and resurrection of Christ. Therefore, just as Moses established the Old Covenant in the blood of ritual sacrifice, so Christ on the cross and in the Eucharist seals the New Covenant in a similar way. Yet Christ's sacrifice of love for his brothers and sisters was not just another ritual sacrifice. Because of who he was, it became the point of convergence of the ancient sacrificial system and the focal point of all future worship in the Christian community. The sacrifice of Christ can only be understood properly through the eyes of the resurrection—the victory over evil and death and the new life open to all of us through the power of the Spirit of the risen Christ. The Eucharist signifies what we are capable of becoming—friends with God and one another.

(One small indication of a growth in liturgical practice between Lutherans and Catholics is found in the most recent Lutheran hymnal and service book. In a communion rite for the homebound, the blessed bread can be taken directly from the communal celebration of the Lord's Supper to the one who is sick by a member of the congregation. This is an extension of the understanding of eucharistic presence. Formerly the minister would have had to go to the home of the sick person and celebrate the rite of the Lord's Supper there.)

• In the Presbyterian (Reformed or Calvinist) tradition the receptionist understanding is the way of speaking about the eucharistic presence. Presbyterians believe that as they receive the blessed bread and wine Christ becomes present to them. It is in the eating and the drinking that the presence of Christ is experienced. The presence of the risen Christ is not "out there" in the elements of bread and wine on the altar. It is a more spiritual understanding of presence, and yet this tradition too speaks about the real presence of Christ in the celebration of the Lord's Supper. There

would, of course, be no concern to reserve as consecrated any elements that might remain.

Although officially there is not yet an open invitation for intercommunion among those Christians
who understand the mystery of Christ's presence in
the Lord's Supper in the above three ways (Lutherans
and Anglicans are very close), from a theological perspective, while admitting the differences, there is a
basic agreement on a *unique* presence of Christ in the
Lord's Supper.

• *The Baptist (Free Church or sectarian) perspective:* A fourth example will be given but it differs sub-
stantially from the three above because it does not
choose to speak of a special or unique presence. This
perspective stems from the Radical Reformation, the
Anabaptist or Free Church tradition. We will use the
Baptist church as the representative of this tradition.
When Baptists gather to celebrate the Lord's Supper
and share the bread and wine together as Jesus did
with his disciples, they do it as a commemoration and
nothing more. They do not employ the sacramental
understanding common to the Catholic, Lutheran,
and Presbyterian models—the outward sign (ritual
celebration) carries with it an inward reality (Christ's
real presence). They believe that Christ is with them
in the gathered community and through the preached
word, but it is this general presence rather than a specific eucharistic presence that they emphasize. The
Lord's Supper is a sign of fellowship, of sisterhood and
brotherhood among the gathered followers of Jesus.
No theology of eucharistic presence is called for.

*Focus:
Understanding
Christ's presence
in the bread
and wine*

We return now to give the final phrase of our working definition
of church: The church is the community

> *that joins in a common mission to preach, witness, and serve.*
> [The church has a mission, a purpose, a vocation. Each
> aspect of that mission must be examined.]

To sum up, then, here is our definition of the church:

The church is the community called in the Spirit that pro-
fesses Jesus as Lord, that ratifies that faith through bap-
tism, celebrates it in the Lord's Supper, and joins in a
common mission to preach, to witness, and to serve.

What Is the Mission of the Church?

1. The church is *called to preach*. The community of the followers of Christ are to go out and tell the Good News that the Kingdom of God—what God wants for us and for all of creation—has broken into human history in the life, death, and resurrection of Jesus. The disciples of Christ were never meant to just "sit at the feet of the Master," but rather to invite others to share the new life they had experienced in and through the Spirit-filled community, the very Body of Christ, this living structure in which each member is a living stone with Christ as the capstone.

2. The church is *called to witness*. By its communal life and celebration the church is to be a believable sign (a sacrament—an outward sign of an inward reality) of what God wants for everyone—the Kingdom of God. The Christian church is not only to "talk the talk," so to speak, but also to "walk the walk." "By the way they love one another you will recognize them," Jesus said of his followers. Because we are called to be a sign of reconciliation and hope, joyfully anticipating in our worship the heavenly banquet, it is clear that we fall short of our calling, both as a community and as individuals. We are in continual need of reform and reconciliation. The scandal of our divisions within the church cries out for healing so that we might fulfill our call to be the "light of the world" and the "salt of the earth." Mahatma Gandhi, a Hindu, was fascinated by the life and message of Jesus. "Why don't you became a Christian?" he was supposedly asked one day. "Because," he replied, "I have never met one."

3. The church is *called to serve*. As Jesus came to serve and not be served, so the community of his disciples must join with others of good will in the socioeconomic and political realm to remove those things that stand in the way of God's Kingdom. The basis on which we will be judged by Christ is spelled out powerfully in chapter 25 of Matthew's gospel: "I was hungry...thirsty...a stranger...naked...sick...imprisoned...and you gave me food...drink...you welcomed me...clothed me...took care of me...visited me." Working for justice is an integral part of the mission of the church. That means involvement in matters of society, the economy, ecology, the political realm. It does not mean that the church has the solution to so-called "worldly" problems, much less a program for civil or political society. But it does mean the church as church is obliged to speak out with a prophetic "no!" against injustice, oppression, exploitation, greed, violence, racism, sexism, and consumerism.

We cannot build God's Kingdom, the perfect society, here, as Marx would have us believe. The Kingdom is God's gift. We pray, "Your Kingdom come." But we can build and prepare for it, facilitate its coming, and work to remove those countersigns standing in the Kingdom's way.

God's Kingdom—what God wants for us and all of creation—extends to every realm and every relationship. The church has no earthly ambition, as Vatican II pointed out, nor as a pilgrim people are we to identify earthly life with the Kingdom. Still, to the extent that earthly progress can contribute to the better ordering of human society, it is of vital interest to the Kingdom of God. Political theology, liberation theology, black theology, Asian and African theology, feminist theology, environmental theology, all have their place within the mission of the church.

What Is the Relationship between the Church and the Kingdom of God?

The common goal tying together the three aspects of the mission of the church is the Kingdom. The church must preach Jesus as the Kingdom, witness to the Kingdom, and serve the Kingdom. The church, therefore, is not an end in itself but rather an instrument of the Kingdom. All are invited to God's Kingdom. God our Savior "desires everyone to be saved and to come to the knowledge of the truth," as 1 Timothy 2:4 assures us.

This universal call to salvation has been the dominant Christian perspective through the ages. There have been exceptions. John Calvin, claiming to trace the predestination of Paul and Augustine to its logical conclusion, taught what is called double-predestination. God, from all eternity, has not only destined some to eternal happiness, but also from all eternity has destined others to damnation. God can do what God wills, and we are unable to fathom divine purpose. Luther, on the other hand, taught that if we find ourselves as believers, we must have been predestined for faith, because we could not achieve this gift on our own. But he does not make a judgment about the others. Karl Barth, the great twentieth-century theologian in the Reformed or Calvinist tradition (but also an ecumenical theologian), did not follow Calvin's harsh teaching of double-predestination.

All are called to God's Kingdom, and some are called to membership and mission in the church. The second part of this statement can be made on the basis of historical observation. There has never been a time when all were members of the church, and it does not seem that there ever will be that time. Christianity today, while growing in numbers is, nevertheless, shrinking in proportion to the growth of the whole human family. Some see the church as an "Abrahamic minority," dwelling in an alien land. As we get to know the other world religions better, and deepen our mysterious relationship to the Jewish community who are still people of the promise, we come to realize more deeply our role as described in the second aspect of mission. We as church are called to be a witness to, and a sign or sacrament of, what God wants for everyone.

Our call or vocation is not one of privilege (not that there are not many blessings that come with it) but of responsibility. It is not that God loves us more and those outside the church less. Nor do we have some "hotline to heaven." But having been called or invited, we must respond by participating in the common mission of the church. Those who have not been called to discipleship in the church may still be a part of the Kingdom. It is true that one can cite Mark 16:15–16 where Jesus, after commissioning the disciples to go into the whole world and proclaim the good news, warns, "The one who believes and is baptized will be saved; but the one who does not believe will be condemned." One can cite as well Acts 4:12 where the prisoner Peter, boldly testifying before the Jewish rulers about Jesus Christ of Nazareth crucified and raised up, proclaims, "There is salvation in no one else...." But we must also recall Matthew 25, cited above, where judgment is based on neither faith nor baptism but on meeting the needs of the least of the brothers and sisters in whom Christ is not even recognized.

There are many paths to the Kingdom, but for those mysteriously called to discipleship in Christ, the call brings with it responsibility. The warning to the church in Laodicea in chapter 3 of the book of Revelation may well be an admonition to all in the Christian church: "I know your works; you are neither cold nor hot. I wish that you were either cold or hot. So, because you are lukewarm, and neither cold nor hot, I am about to spit you out of my mouth." One might be tempted to think of the call to membership and mission in the church as a "holy rip-off."

If others are invited to salvation as well as we Christians, why should we have to proclaim, witness, and serve the Kingdom through the church? Recall Jesus' parable of the workers in the vineyard. Some were hired at the beginning of the workday for "the usual daily wage." (We can assume it was a just wage.) They labored throughout the day. Others began working at mid-morning, midday, and even in the late afternoon. When pay-time arrived the owner instructed the manager to pay the last to the first the same day's wage. When those who worked all day complained, the owner reminded them that he had given them the daily wage agreed upon. "Am I not allowed to do what I choose with what belongs to me? Or are you envious because I am generous?" This parable might be applied to those who work as disciples in the community of the Lord. As Augustine has noted, "Many the Father has that the church does not have, and many the church has that the Father does not have." Augustine did have a very pessimistic view on the number who would be saved, but here he warns church members not to be presumptuous about their position. God's ways are not our ways.

The consolation comes when we consider the words of the father of the prodigal son (or daughter) addressed to his elder son (or daughter) who, coming in from working in the fields, refused to take part in the celebration the father had prepared for the delinquent one. "Son [or daughter], you are always with me, and all that is mine is yours." We who are blessed with the gift of a faith and respond through baptism to a life of discipleship, must continue to share the good news with others, inviting them through dialogue to consider Jesus, on the chance that God has chosen them also to participate in the church's saving mission. Nevertheless, we Christians are confident that anyone who reaches out to a brother or sister in selfless love or seeks to know the deepest of truth has already somehow encountered the living God whose Word, present in the world from the time of creation, was concentrated uniquely in Jesus Christ. This same Word continues to be available through the power of the Holy Spirit in the community called church. Although the term has its shortcomings, Karl Rahner's use of *anonymous Christianity* does capture the Christian understanding of those who are hearers and doers of the Word of God outside the Christian community. In this sense we profess that Christ has saving significance for all peoples and religions, indeed for the whole cosmos.

Can We Say without Qualification that Any Particular Church Is the "One," "True" Church?

This question might seem strange to some people. Would a particular church or denomination claim that they alone are the true church and all others are false, or not churches at all? The Roman Catholic church, for one, did make such a claim. The *Baltimore Catechism*, an instruction manual for United States Catholics up until the Second Vatican Council, answered directly, "The Roman

Catholic Church is the one, true Church established by Jesus Christ." Other churches, denominations, or congregations have made similar claims. The story is told about a Catholic high school student who was dating a young Baptist woman. One day she said to him, "Joe, you're a great guy and I love you very much, but you're going to hell." When he asked, "Why?" she replied, "Because you don't belong to my Faith Baptist Church!"

In the Roman Catholic tradition, in wake of the splintering of the Christian church in the West at the time of the Reformation, clear and uncompromising boundaries were established about church membership. To be a Catholic one had to profess the true faith, share in the same sacraments (seven, not two as the Reformers held), and be in union with Rome—the pope, the vicar of Christ on Earth. As late as 1950, Pope Pius XII, in his encyclical (a letter meant for the whole Catholic church) *The Mystical Body of Christ,* taught that the Body of Christ *is* the Roman Catholic church.

Vatican II, meeting a little more than a decade later, after much serious debate on the nature of the church, changed one word that Pius XII had used and set a whole new course for the Catholic church in relation to other Christian denominations. Instead of using the copulative verb *is*, "the Body of Christ *is* the Roman Catholic church," the Council members used the qualifying phrase, *subsists in.* The "unique Church of Christ" the Council taught, "*subsists in* the Catholic Church...."[2] The clear implication of this statement is that the one church of Jesus Christ extends beyond the boundaries of the Roman Catholic church.

In the *Decree on Ecumenism,* for the first time since the Reformation the Catholic church recognized that "ecclesial communities" separated from Rome could be recognized as churches, related in various ways to the one church of Jesus Christ. The Roman Catholic church does see itself as the model of faithfulness and truthfulness to the Apostolic Tradition. Other churches have, however, developed aspects of the church's mission beyond that of the Catholic tradition. One need only consider the richness of the gift of preaching that is found in many churches of the Reformation

tradition and the gift of healing in some of the denominations in
the Free Church tradition.

Are There Any Criteria by which We Can Evaluate the Truthfulness and Faithfulness of our Own Church or Denomination?

If no one church can claim without qualification that it is the
"one," "true" church, then are all churches equal in faithfulness to
the Apostolic Tradition founded on the risen Christ and empow-
ered through the centuries by the Holy Spirit? If Christ were to
return and enter our congregation would he feel at home and recognize us as truly his body? Is your church *being* the church of
Jesus Christ? What criteria, if any, can we use to see how well we
are doing, or perhaps better, how well we are *being*? The following
four criteria are proposed:

1. Does your church work and pray for the unity to which Christ has called us?

Christ prayed that we might be *one*. And yet the Christian church
is divided into often competing and bickering parts. The divisions
in the church of Christ are a scandal and a source of confusion.
How can we be the sign "that the world may believe" (John 17:21),
the sacrament of the Kingdom to which God has called us, if we
cannot get along with one another? In our time it seems the Holy
Spirit is breathing new hope into the ecumenical movement, but
often our churches are so focused on themselves that they have
"eyes that do not see," and "ears that do not hear."

The ecumenical movement, that search for mutual understanding, cooperation, and respect among the Christian churches separated by doctrinal, social, ethnic, political, and institutional factors,
is fostered by prayer, dialogue, and common witness in those areas
where we already share and experience gospel values.

An overview of the modern ecumenical movement will help us
put this question in perspective.

(Criteria for evaluating denominations continues on page 100.)

The beginning of the modern ecumenical movement is usually associated with the 1910 World Missionary Conference held in Edinburgh, Scotland, where delegates from 122 Protestant denominations declared that "a unity in Christ and fellowship in the Spirit is deeper than our divisions." Further dialogue and cooperation ensued in the formation of the Life and Work movement in 1925 and the Faith and Order movement in 1927. The first of these called for practical collaboration in the secular order, and the latter began dialogue on church teaching, sacraments, and governance. In 1920 the Orthodox patriarchy in Constantinople called for a permanent institution of all churches to promote dialogue and cooperation.

Focus:
The modern
ecumenical
movement

In 1948, after the scandal of the Second World War in which more than five million Jews lost their lives in the "Christian West," leaders from Protestant, Anglican, and Orthodox national churches came together in Amsterdam and formed the World Council of Churches. Member churches profess "the Lord Jesus Christ as God and Savior according to the Scriptures," and together seek to fulfill "their *common calling* to the glory of the one God, Father, Son and Holy Spirit." As further elaborated upon in a later world assembly (Nairobi 1975), they agreed that their *common calling* is "to advance towards visible unity in one faith and in one eucharistic fellowship expressed in worship and in common life in Christ."

The World Council of Churches focuses its work in four major areas: (1) Unity and Renewal, (2) Mission, Education, and Witness, (3) Justice, Peace, and Creation, and (4) Sharing and Service. It works together with national and regional councils of churches, world confessional bodies such as the Lutheran World Federation, and other ecumenical groups. Its headquarters is in Geneva. Between the world assemblies, which meet every seven years, it is governed by a central committee and an elected president.

When the World Council of Churches was founded in 1948, the Roman Catholic church was still in its

Focus:
The modern
ecumenical
movement

pre-ecumenical period. Pope Pius XII forbade Catholics to attend the World Council of Church's program meetings and assemblies. His successor, Pope John XXIII, founded the Secretariat for Promoting Christian Unity in 1960 and sent official observers to the 1961 world assembly (New Delhi).

The Second Vatican Council (1962–1965) issued its *Decree on Ecumenism* and set the stage for a new era among Protestants, Anglicans, Orthodox, and Catholics. In its introduction to that document, gladly noting the Spirit-filled movement that was already underway among Christian churches, and "moved by a desire for the restoration of unity among all the followers of Christ," it set down for Catholics "certain helps, pathways, and methods by which they too can respond to this divine summons and grace."

In 1965 Pope Paul VI approved a joint Working Group, an official consultative forum of the World Council and the Catholic church that initiates, evaluates, and sustains collaboration between its respective organizations and programs. Although not a member church, the Catholic church participates in various ways in almost all of the Council's programs. Perhaps at this point in the ecumenical movement it is best that the Catholic church is not a full member of the World Council because with its enormous size and the Council's proportional representation, it would dominate the World Council's governing bodies.

Numerous dialogues continue to take place between and among various churches and denominations. The goal is not to establish some kind of super-church with complete uniformity. Rather, the goal is a mutual recognition of ministry and a sharing at the table of the Lord. Can we say that our sister churches are legitimate expressions of the gospel of Jesus Christ? More will be said about this in the following chapter.

Does your church pray for the unity to which Christ has called us? Does it participate in the Church Unity Octave, eight days of prayer for the religious unity of all Christians and all people? In your local community, does your church join with other churches in a common Thanksgiving service commemorating our national celebrations of thankfulness? Does your church join with other churches on the local, national, and international level in organizations and groups working for mutual understanding and unity, for justice and peace? If it does none of these things, to what extent *is your church truly being the Church of Jesus Christ?*

2. Does your church foster and promote the holiness of its people?
Holiness is *wholeness,* and *wholesomeness.* In his life and mission Jesus displayed a wholeness and wholesomeness that attracted people to him. He had a wholesome attitude toward life and human relationships. He enjoyed friends, sympathized with the sorrowing, and healed by his love those whose lives were broken through sin. He was at home with himself, at home with others, and at home with God. He was holy, a saint. He invited and enabled others to share that wholeness, that holiness. The church, holy because Christ is holy and because the Holy Spirit dwells within it, should continue to bring that holiness to its people.

Does your church have any teachings or practices that are anti-human, anti-family, anti-social? Does your church have a healthy perspective on sexuality, on relationships among men, women, and children, on healthy and wholesome recreation, and an appropriate appreciation for all of God's creation—the earth, the air, the water, as well as animal and plant species? St. Francis of Assisi, admired by all Christians, showed us a model of holiness close to God's creation. Healthy asceticism—prayer, fasting, a simple life of self-sacrifice for our brothers and sisters—is valuable both for the individual and the community. The church should support such a holy way of life. Extreme asceticism, on the other hand, can not only bring harm to the individual, denying the goodness of the human body and of God's creation, it can also bring harm to the image of the church as a joyful people of the resurrection. Groups such as the Branch Davidians of Waco, Texas, the followers of Jim Jones of Jonestown in Guyana, or the "Heaven's Gate" cult in Southern

California, have brought not only disaster upon themselves but dishonor upon their members, their families, religion as a whole, and Christianity in particular. Individual communities or sects need the broader community, the Body of Christ, to maintain a wholesomeness and holiness to which all the baptized are called.

Does your church help to heal the pain and suffering of those whose marriages, for whatever reason, have not succeeded? Or is a mistake or failure in this area something that alienates one permanently from the community, especially if a second relationship is entered into? Where is wholeness and holiness found in these situations? How does your church respond to those men and women who come to realize in the deepest part of their being that they are attracted to someone of the same sex? They don't choose this orientation; they discover it. Is holiness in such situations to be found only in the celibate way of life? Is a charism of the Holy Spirit with which they may not have been gifted demanded of them? Are guilt and derision heaped upon those who are identified as "inherently disordered"? It should be remembered that homosexuality in the Bible is usually connected with the fertility rites of temple worship and therefore condemned as idolatry. Neither the writer of the book of Leviticus in the Old Testament nor St. Paul in the New Testament could have had the understanding that we have today of what is called "constituted homosexuality."

Holiness, wholeness, and wholesomeness must be able to be found even when the earthen vessels within which we hold the treasure of our faith are cracked or broken. Does your church foster the wholeness and wholesomeness of its people? To the extent that it doesn't, *is it truly being the church of Jesus Christ?*

3. *Is your church open to everyone, everywhere, at every level of community life, leadership, and service?* Jesus in his ministry as we know it from the gospels welcomed *everyone.* He had a special love for the poor, the outcast, and the marginalized. They felt at home with him; he gave them hope. Is there prejudice or discrimination in your church? "We don't have any of *that kind* in our church!"—the racially different, ethnically identified, those of sexually alter-

nate life-style. Is that sentiment common in your church? Did Jesus come to save the saved—and you are the saved?

When Jimmy Carter was president he would often return to his Baptist church in Plains, Georgia, and teach Sunday school. Because of the Carter family's urging from early in the civil rights movement, African Americans had been welcomed in the congregation. The church allowed them to *attend,* but when an African American wanted to *join* the congregation, to become a *member,* the covenant of the church would not allow it. Carter threatened to withdraw his membership unless the rules were changed—and they were. Is there discrimination in your church? *If so, to what extent is it truly being the church of Jesus Christ?*

Jesus wanted his message of love and reconciliation to be spread *everywhere.* "Go out into the whole world," he commissioned his disciples before he ascended into heaven. Is your church parochial—its eye set only on itself? While neighborhood churches are fine, and ethnically and linguistically united congregations were and are common among immigrant peoples, still it must be understood that the church goes beyond the local congregation. Wherever one goes, one should be made to feel at home within a Christian congregation. The story is told of a six-year-old who questioned the pastor of an ethnic Bohemian parish, St. Wenceslaus, "Is it true, Father, that ours is the one, true church?" "Ye-sss," he answered hesitantly. "Then what about St. Mary's and St. Pat's?" she exclaimed. (These were the traditional German and Irish parishes in her city.) Is your church closed in on itself? *If so, to what extent is it being the church of Jesus Christ?*

In his life and ministry Jesus was *inclusive.* Men and women, married and single, were welcome. Indeed, little children were warmly received. Jesus was born into a world, a society, and a religion that were strongly patriarchal. Peter is depicted in the New Testament as having a special role among the twelve, who were Jesus' close companions. These are often identified as the apostles, but in the New Testament the title apostle is not always limited to the twelve. Paul claims the name apostle, and he was not among the twelve.

Disciples were the larger group of followers, and among them were many women. Mary and Martha, along with their brother Lazarus, were close friends of Jesus and are prominent in the New Testament. In chapter eight of his gospel, Luke mentions Mary of Magdala, Joanna, and Susanna "among many others" who accompanied Jesus as "he went through cities and villages, proclaiming and bringing good news of the Kingdom of God." The unnamed woman in chapter 26 of Matthew who poured the costly ointment on Jesus' head, which Jesus accepted as an anointing for his coming death, received for her act higher praise from Jesus than any other person in the New Testament: "Wherever this good news is proclaimed in the whole world, what she has done will be told in remembrance of her." Elizabeth Schüssler Fiorenza has written an excellent book on the Bible from a feminist perspective. She uses as the title the last phrase of this quote, *In Memory of Her: A Feminist Theological Reconstruction of Christian Origins.*[3]

The gospels tell us that women remained with Jesus as he hung on the cross and were the earliest witnesses to the resurrection. They were commissioned as apostles to go and tell the joyous news to the other disciples. Women were present at Pentecost and received the Holy Spirit. And in the early Christian communities women were often responsible for the household churches. Paul, at the beginning of chapter 16 in his letter to the Romans, names Phoebe as a deacon of the church of Cenchreae, and he mentions many other women who shared his ministry. While radical equality and mutual sharing characterized the ministry of Jesus and the life of the earliest community with few exceptions—"neither Jew nor Greek, slave nor free, male nor female" (Galatians 3:28)— things began to go back to the strong male domination in leadership by the beginning of the second century. In Timothy and Titus women are to be submissive, to listen in silence and not act as teachers. They are to find salvation through childbearing.

Through the centuries women have been acclaimed as saints, martyrs, mystics, great teachers, and administrators. But in the Roman Catholic tradition, among others, women have been denied the leadership and ministry role that comes with ordination. When we remember the cultural world in which Jesus lived, his apocalyptic expectation of the end time and the symbolic significance of the twelve as reminiscent of the twelve tribes, the absence of women among the twelve disciples is more understandable. But in the same way that no one in the church would try to justify slavery today just because Paul said slaves should be subject to their masters, so it is difficult for many to understand the continued prohibition of equality in the church to women *at every level of community life and service.*

The same type of equality should be extended to those who choose to marry. If celibacy is a charism, a gift of the Spirit, it is difficult to understand how a gift can be demanded by the law of the church for those who feel called to ordained ministry. Celibacy is and can be a powerful sign and gift to the community, but it must be discerned and accepted freely, not as a requirement imposed if one is called to the life of service through ordination. In like manner, in Protestant churches that demand that their ordained ministers be married, in practice if not by law, does this not likewise stifle the Spirit who may be calling someone to ordained ministry and celibacy for the sake of the Kingdom? To the extent that your church continues these practices of discrimination, *is your church being the church of Jesus Christ?*

4. *Is your church faithful to the full teaching and ministry of the apostles?* The church is founded on the apostles who were chosen by Jesus as his close coworkers or who experienced him risen and were commissioned by him to proclaim the Good News by word, deed, and example. This Apostolic Tradition, according to Vatican II, "includes everything which contributes to the holiness of life, and the increase in faith of the people of God" so that the church "in her teaching, life and worship, perpetuates and hands on to all generations all that she herself is and all that she believes." Here we are speaking of the Tradition in its broad and dynamic form as discussed in Chapter Three. A privileged and irreplaceable part of the Apostolic Tradition is, of course, holy Scripture.

The teaching and ministry of the apostles does not exclude but rather requires growth and reformulation in order to meet the pastoral needs in a continuously changing world. We can ask, however, if your church ignores or downplays certain parts of the apostolic teaching and practice that find their origin in the life and ministry of Jesus. For example, does your church ignore the Lord's Supper or relegate it to the sphere of a rare, archaic ritual celebrated once in a while? Is your church a church of the word alone? "No so-called 'magical rites' in our church!" The common meals Jesus had with his disciples had great significance in his ministry, and the Last Supper that Jesus celebrated with his disciples was something he asked that we continue to do in remembrance of him. He assured us he would be with us when we did celebrate it. To the extent that your church ignores or minimizes the liturgy of the Supper of the Lord, *are you truly being the church of Jesus Christ?*

Does your church celebrate reconciliation for those who have fallen and asked again for the forgiveness of the community and of God? Forgiveness was such an important part of Jesus' ministry and the ministry of the early disciples. Some churches have a way of putting backsliders outside of the congregation, but is there not a way also of welcoming them back when they seek forgiveness? From the broadest perspective, it is not an issue of whether one has a rite that includes a strange, closet-looking box with sliding door and flashing lights, known as a confessional, in the back of the church, or even a reconciliation room, although that makes more sense. It is an issue of providing for the basic need for the ministry of reconciliation.

A group of seminarians from various denominations were beginning their clinical pastoral education as a part of their preparation for ordination. Their director, a United Church of Christ minister, addressed them with these words: "You may wonder why this pastoral education is being offered within a hospital context. When people are in the hospital and sick, they often have plenty of time to think. They may want to pour out their lives to you—and you had better be ready and able to listen and to assure them in the name of Jesus Christ that their sins are forgiven."

In the Catholic tradition such a process would be called the sacrament of reconciliation. The name and understanding may differ from denomination to denomination, but if your church has no ministry of reconciliation, to what extent *is your church being the church of Jesus Christ?* Also the church as a whole needs forgiveness for not living up to its call to proclaim, witness, and serve. A confession of sins and asking for forgiveness is often celebrated at the beginning of a liturgy of worship.

Sometimes people ask why some churches have a rite for individuals to confess their sins to an ordained minister. "I confess my sins directly to God; why should I tell them to a human being?" A brief rationale for the practice may help put things in perspective.

First two clarifications: We often hear the phrase, "To sin is human." This is not accurate in the strict sense because Jesus was human—fully human—and Jesus did not sin. Therefore to sin is to be "less" than human. We all realize that we fall short of what we were intended to be, of what God has invited us to be. Second, to "feel" guilt does not always "tell us something" about our conscience. Guilt feelings can come from another source within us that psychologists call the superego—that so-called psychic police officer within us that has little to do with conscience. More on this matter will be discussed later.

Focus: The practice of confessing sins to an ordained minister

God always offers us forgiveness, but in the mystery of our created freedom God never forces us. Therefore we have to be involved; we have to ask. But even here, God's grace engulfs us, helping us to seek reconciliation both with God and those around us.

The celebration of the Supper of the Lord is the greatest source of our reconciliation. At the penitential rite at the beginning of this celebration we ask for forgiveness and our "venial" sins are forgiven. With God's grace, which is always offered, there are numerous ways in which we are reconciled and strengthened in our friendship with God and our sisters and brothers.

In the sacrament of reconciliation we celebrate the affirmation and confirmation of what has already

Focus:
The practice of
confessing sins
to an ordained
minister

taken place. All of us confess our sins "straight to God." At least it is to be hoped that we do. According to James in his epistle, we are also to confess our sins to one another. In reconciling with our brothers and sisters we admit our sin. However, as followers of Christ and members of his church, many Christians celebrate certain pivotal moments in their lives of faith as part of the faith community.

As humans we need one another. As members of Christ's body we affect one another. When we have breached our commitment, compromised our deep relationships, failed to respond to God's call to full humanity, we come before the community through its representative, the ordained minister. In complete confidentiality and assured through God's word in holy Scripture that God through Christ in the power of the Spirit is on our side, we ask for, and are assured of, forgiveness through the grace of the sacrament. The words that we hear and the encouragement that we receive help us be and to become the person we really want to be—the one that God through Christ in the Spirit has invited us to be.

Are our sins not totally forgiven until we receive this sacrament? The Catholic church (and the Orthodox and Anglican) teaches that sins are forgiven in any number of ways but, except in extreme circumstances, if a person has completely severed his or her relationship with God and neighbor, if one has turned away from God and others with one's whole self—sinned mortally (that is in a deadly way unto death)—one must be reconciled with the community and with God through the sacrament of reconciliation.

The Catholic church also urges us to use the sacrament of reconciliation to grow in our relationship to God, neighbor, and ourselves, by discussing our serious and even slight shortcomings in these relationships with an ordained minister, opening ourselves both to God's special grace and to the encouragement of the one who speaks in the sacramental celebration for Christ and his community.

In the New Testament we find another area that was prominent in the ministry of Jesus and became a part of the Apostolic Tradition, the ministry of healing. Directed toward those who are sick in body, soul, mind, or heart, it includes the reconciliation discussed above, but goes beyond it. Without taking anything away from modern medicine, and even building on the new insights of holistic medicine, the church must continue Jesus' ministry and the example of the apostles in the ministry of healing. The close and at times even mysterious relationship between body and mind/soul encourages us to continue to pray and lay hands on the sick (and to anoint them with oil as a sign of wholeness and strength in some traditions) that they may be healed.

Some Christian churches have maintained this ministry much more faithfully than others. And while there is always the possibility of turning a ministry into a magic media machine, the basic power of faith in healing should not be overlooked. To the extent that your church completely ignores the ministry of healing, *is your church being the church of Jesus Christ?*

Many other areas could be included in the criterion of faithfulness to the teaching and example of the apostles. Care for the poor always must be a priority. Not only was this one of Jesus' primary concerns, but the great apostle Paul was continuously reminding the people to whom he preached of the collection for the poor in the church in Jerusalem. To the extent that your church does not emphasize a preferential option for the poor, and a solidarity with victims of unjust oppression, *is your church being the church of Jesus Christ?*

The criteria for evaluating one church's faithfulness and truthfulness in being the church of Jesus Christ are thus brought together:

1. Does your church work and pray for the unity to which Christ has called us?

2. Does your church promote and foster the holiness of its people?

3. Is your church open to everyone, everywhere, at every level of community life, leadership, and service?

4. Is your church faithful to the full teaching and ministry of the apostles?

These four criteria come from the Creed of Nicea/Constantinople. Traditionally they were known as the four *marks* of the church— *one, holy, catholic (universal), and apostolic.* They were considered the dimensions of the church that distinguished the true church from heretical groups. In the pre-Vatican II *Baltimore Catechism* they were listed as the definitive characteristics of the Catholic church as the one, true church. It seems more fitting, from what has been discussed above, to consider them as challenges to all the churches and denominations to truly *be, to become* that which they really are. One of St. Paul's pupils spoke of this "already/not yet" when he addressed the Christian congregations at Colossae: "You are God's chosen ones, holy and beloved, clothe yourselves with compassion, kindness, humility, meekness, and patience" (Colossians 3:12). In other words, You *are* holy. *Be* holy!

Husbands and wives or parents *are* what they are in fact, but they also must strive *to be* what they are. A newly ordained priest was cleaning out his desk at the seminary before returning home. In a desk drawer he found a valentine that his little nephew had sent him when he first began his studies. Proudly printed on red construction paper were the carefully formed letters: "To my Uncle Joe who is trying to be a priest." The priest looked at it and thought, "I should write, 'Ha! Ha! I made it!' and send it back to him." Then it dawned on him, he related, that all his life he would be *trying* to be a priest. Yes, he *was* a priest, but he also had to *be* a priest.

So we *are* the church of Jesus Christ, the Body of Christ, made holy and without blemish (Ephesians 5:27) by Christ giving himself up for us and sending the Holy Spirit to dwell with us. And yet we know that, as individuals and as churches, we fall short of our calling and therefore are always in need of renewal and reform. The criteria—(1) *seeking unity,* (2) *promoting wholeness and holiness,* (3) *embracing everyone,* (4) *being truly apostolic*—help to keep us focused on our call to faithfulness and truthfulness as the Body of Christ, the People of God.

This church of Jesus Christ exists in visible form here and now in the world. It is not a purely spiritual, abstract ideal, but a kind of sacrament—an outward sign of an inward reality, a mystery—sensed, felt, yielding to partial, incomplete, but true understanding through the ages. According to the Second Vatican Council this one church of Jesus Christ subsists within the Roman Catholic church, but also finds concrete expression in other churches as well.

What Is Church Polity and Why Is It at the Root of Divisions in the Christian Church?

After having examined the common faith in Jesus Christ that Christians have, the basic primacy that Scripture has within the dynamic understanding of Tradition, the growing theological consensus on major doctrinal differences, and considerable ecumenical convergence through dialogue on matters of worship, prayer, and the Christian way of life, we can ask at this point, what is it then that divides us into various churches or denominations?

The root of the divisions in the Christian church is found in their particular understandings of church *polity*. Church polity as discussed here refers to **the understanding and exercise of authority and leadership in the church.** (Polity has its roots in the Greek word *polis* meaning city, the public realm, policy, and therefore governing structure of a state or community.)

In your church, who has the authority, and how is leadership exercised? Or, simply, in your church who decides, and upon what basis? The answers to these questions do have their effects both on the understanding of the faith and the way that faith will be lived out within the community. The three components of religion—creed, cult, and code—all are influenced by the way the churches are organized and led. Even those communities that claim that the only authority in their church or sect is the Bible must still face the question: according to whose interpretation?

We will consider here three basic church polities, three ways in which the Christian community has been organized, as evidenced even in the New Testament. We will be dealing with models.

Although models do provide a way of dealing with a considerable amount of diverse material, models are not always clearly distinguishable from one another in details. What we are doing here is a small study in the sociology of religions. The three basic models of church polity that we will consider are *(1) the episcopal, (2) the presbyterian,* and *(3) the charismatic or sectarian.*

1. The episcopal model of church polity.

We are considering models here and not particular denominations, but the Episcopal church can serve as a model. It receives its name from the church polity that characterizes it. Who is it that exercises leadership and authority in the Episcopal or Anglican church? (The Episcopal church is the name used in the United States for the Anglican communion or the Church of England.) The Anglican and Episcopalian churches are ruled by bishops. The Greek word *episcopus* means bishop or overseer.

Churches that employ the episcopal model of polity are ruled by bishops. Bishops are *ordained,* set aside for service by the ancient practice of "laying on of hands" and invocation of the Holy Spirit. Bishops are ordained by those who already are bishops. There is a "passing down" of the office, thereby creating a *hierarchical* structure. The hierarchical structure of ordained ministry consists of bishops, presbyters, and deacons. The metaphor often used in this type of organization is a biological one of body. In the body there are head and members. The head, or the bishop, claims to be in historical succession from the apostles of Jesus. This model of leadership was found in the Temple organization in Jerusalem and is described in considerable detail in the New Testament letters of Timothy and Titus.

A contemporary secular counterpart to this episcopal form of polity would be a modern corporation. The top authority in a corporation is the board of directors with its president or chairperson. Under them is the chief executive officer and various vice presidents, middle management, etc., down to the foreman in the plant. The workers on the assembly line do not decide how many units will be produced, what color they will be painted, or how a particular product will be marketed. The decisions come down the chain of command in a way similar to military procedure. We will see how this model has been somewhat modified in most churches that use it today.

Studies done during the 1950s actually compared the Catholic church to a corporation such as General Motors. Infants were born and presented to the church for baptism (the raw material). They were formed and shaped by the teachings and discipline of the church for marriage (to ensure more raw material), or priesthood and religious life (to keep the operation going). Finally they were prepared for death and eternal life as a saved soul (the final product). The mission of this vast and efficient operation (judged to be more efficient than General Motors except in the top echelon of management) was to hatch them, match them, and dispatch them.

In addition to the Episcopal or Anglican church, churches that employ the episcopal model include the Roman Catholic, the Orthodox, the Lutheran, and the Methodist. The Roman Catholic church has a particular interpretation of the episcopal model. It is ruled by bishops, but it gives special place to the bishop of Rome, the pope, the successor to the ministry of Peter. The emergence of the bishop of Rome, the universal pastor who is to be the sign and means of unity among the churches, came only slowly in the early centuries, but then developed into the great power of the papacy during the late medieval and Renaissance periods. The understanding of the church as a monarchy—especially prevalent in the nineteenth and first half of the twentieth centuries—was not a part of the Tradition in its deep sense.

Vatican II's teaching on collegiality—a church ruled by bishops in union with the bishop of Rome, but all responsible for the whole church—has attempted to put the church's episcopal model into proper perspective. This refocus has helped other churches with the episcopal model to see more possibility for dialogue with the Catholic church about future unity.

The Orthodox churches follow the episcopal model (although

they call their bishops patriarchs or metropolitans). The Orthodox are willing to accept the bishop of Rome as the Patriarch of the West and even grant him the honor "first among equals" because he occupies the *see* or local church where both Peter and Paul were martyred. The ancient patriarchies in the East (from the fifth century) were Constantinople, Alexandria, Antioch, and Jerusalem. Later, other Orthodox patriarchies were established.

The Lutheran church (the Evangelical Church in Germany) is ruled by bishops. Although Luther broke with Rome, he did not change the basic church polity. The means of selecting bishops and their authority in local congregational matters have been modified through the years (in some national Lutheran churches more than in others), and some Lutheran churches have even dropped the title of bishop but not the office. Today most Lutheran churches use the title of bishop for their leaders, including the recently formed Evangelical Lutheran Church in America, a remarkable ecumenical merger of the Lutheran Church in America, the American Lutheran Church, and the Evangelical Lutheran Church.

The Methodist church began as a prayer movement within the Anglican church. John Wesley had no thought about establishing a church separate from the Church of England. But as an organizational genius, from the beginning he employed lay preachers and circuit riders to minister to the growing number of the working class and ordinary people who found in his powerful preaching, organized prayer meetings, and concern for social justice issues, an answer to the confusion they were experiencing because of the social upheaval of the industrial revolution in eighteenth-century England. When, after the American Revolution, Wesley, himself an Anglican priest, ordained other priests and even a bishop to go to minister to the fledgling congregations in the colonies, his break with the Anglican church seemed assured. Although many elements of the presbyterian polity (which we will examine next) have been incorporated into Methodist polity in the United States as the result of the evangelical revival connected with the Great Awakening, the Methodist church still retains its episcopal polity.

For example, a prospective pastor may be interviewed by the local congregation and voted on by the church committee or council; nevertheless, the appointment of that pastor would come from the Methodist bishop of the area.

2. The presbyterian model of church polity.

The Presbyterian church can be used as an example of this model of polity. It is the largest denomination in the United States representing the Calvinist/Reformed tradition. The Presbyterian church is ruled by *presbyters* (from the Greek word *presbyteros*—meaning *elder*). Elders are not ordained; they are laypeople. There is no hierarchy. The elders govern by consensus based on a previously accepted covenant. A sociological rather than biological metaphor describes this model—a community of people with a common goal. We can see a striking difference between this way of organizing a church and the episcopal model. A more democratic understanding of leadership will in turn affect the way this community interprets and lives out the gospel.

A contemporary secular counterpart to this form of church polity is the modern university. In a university there are a number of legitimate centers of power—the board of directors, the president, the deans, the faculty, the students. If it is a state university there is a board of regents or governors; if church-related, there is the local bishop, other church authorities, or a religious community. Alumni and alumnae also have their say, and if it is a private institution its benefactors also have input. The role of the president is to attempt to get these various power groups to work together toward the fulfillment of the goals set out in the university's charter.

A minister in the Presbyterian church has a similar task. He or she must attempt to get the presbyterium (the council of elders) to work in harmony with the pastoral team, including those various groups in the church—the choirs, the committees for education, evangelization, social justice, finance, etc. At the same time the minister must preach the prophetic word of God within the congregation. The origins of the presbyters or council of elders are found in the leadership organization of the Jewish synagogues. In the New Testament churches founded by Paul, we find the presbyterial model evident, although Paul continued to exercise considerable influence in these communities as an apostle. (Calvin did the same in the church in Geneva.) In some of the early church communities the bishop-presbyter roles were not always clearly distinguished. Also, in the church of Corinth, we find evidence of the third model of church polity, the charismatic model.

3. The charismatic model of church polity.

Those who follow the charismatic model of church polity would say that it is the Holy Spirit who has authority in their churches. "Charismatic" comes from the Greek word *charis,* meaning *gift.* In church polity it refers to the gifts of the Holy Spirit poured out on a community, as evidenced in Paul's first letter to the Corinthians, and usually exercised through some charismatic leader. These groups, arising at times throughout the history of the church, are often known as *sects.* Many trace their roots to the *radical* branch of the Reformation, to the Anabaptist and Free Church tradition. The Anabaptists held that those baptized as infants—before they had freedom of choice and a clear call from the Holy Spirit—had to be rebaptized. (The prefix *ana* in Greek means *again.* Therefore they were called Anabaptist because they were baptized again.) Also they believed that Luther and Calvin had not gone far enough; they wanted the church completely free from any association with, or dependence on, the state. Thus they are also known as the Free Church tradition.

In a sense these sects want no church polity. They are anti-institutional (no ordained bishops or hierarchy) and anti-liturgical (no set calendar or order for worship). They are what might be called the "minority report" in the church, always challenging the more "established" churches by insisting that Jesus never intended a structured community. They want to be free to "praise the Lord in the Spirit!" In a sense religious orders have fulfilled a similar role in the Catholic tradition, although they are usually brought under the direction of the official leadership of the church when they are granted a charter.

The metaphor that would describe the polity of the sects would be *movement,* finding its roots in the field of spirituality rather than biology or sociology. A modern secular counterpart to the charismatic church polity would be the civil rights movement. A movement has a spontaneity to it with more emphasis on enthusiasm and dedication to the "cause" than on organization. In the religious realm one could point to the popular charismatic movement that cut across traditional denominational boundaries in the form of charismatic prayer groups during the 1960s and 1970s. Some of these groups have continued. We should note that most people who have participated in charismatic prayer groups have still maintained their membership in their original churches.

It is difficult to maintain a free church or charismatic polity over a period of time. Once the charismatic ruler is gone either the sect or movement dies or the initial charism is institutionalized and the movement moves toward some presbyterian form of polity.

There are a number of sects that have survived for a considerable time, however. These include groups such as the Amish, the Mennonites, the Amananites, the Hutterites, and the Quakers. More recent sects would include a number of the Pentecostal and Holiness churches, Fundamentalist churches, the Christian Church (Disciples of Christ), and those apocalyptic-oriented sects that look for the imminent end of the world. The Assemblies of God, the Adventist churches, and the Church of the Foursquare Gospel would come under this category.

The Baptist church is one large Christian denomination in this country that is not easy to classify. The Baptists find their roots in the Anabaptists/Free Church sect tradition, but they also have many of the more established characteristics of the presbyterian church polity.

Former president Jimmy Carter, as mentioned above, was a dedicated Baptist. When he was running for president in 1976, Carter spelled out clearly how Baptists view the church:[4]

One thing Baptists believe in is complete autonomy. I don't accept any domination of my life by the Baptist Church, none. Every Baptist church is individual and autonomous. We don't accept domination of our church from the Southern Baptist Convention. The reason the Baptist Church was formed in this country was because of our belief in absolute and total separation of church and state. These basic tenets make us almost unique. We don't believe in any hierarchy in church. We don't have bishops. Any officers chosen by the church are defined as servants, not bosses. They're supposed to do the dirty work, make sure the church is clean and painted and that sort of thing. So it's all very good, democratic structure.

Carter mentions each Baptist church being autonomous. The churches in both the presbyterian and charismatic model of church polity follow this principle of the autonomy of the local congregation. It is also called *congregationalism*. The Congregational church, the church that grew out of the Pilgrim/Puritan/Separatist groups of the New England colonies, had that name because of their insistence on local autonomy. (In 1957 the Congregational church joined with the Evangelical and Reformed church to form the United Church of Christ). Churches that follow this principle of local autonomy do belong to regional and national associations, conferences, or synods that coordinate education of clergy and missionary work, but any decisions made at a level above the local congregation (for example, by the Southern Baptist Convention, as mentioned by former president Carter) are limited to descriptions and recommendations.

We can compare the episcopal and presbyterian and charismatic models of church polity by using an analogy with the development of three school systems—the United States pioneer model of public schools, the Latin American regent model of government schools, and the nontraditional model of private alternative schools.

Imagine the owner of a Latin American plantation deciding it would be good to have a school on his land to teach the indigenous children to read so they will remain docile and learn about God and religion in Spanish. He contacts the mayor who contacts the governor who contacts the viceroy who sends a messenger to Spain to speak with the king. If the king approves, the information goes back through the same channels until finally, by the decree of the all powerful king, a school shall be erected on the plantation according to specific directions, including what will be taught. That is similar to the episcopal model of polity.

Now imagine a group of pioneers who settle down and establish a number of farm homesteads in a particular area. Some, concerned about the education of the children, spread the word around that there will be a meeting at the crossroads to discuss the possibility of establishing a school. When the families gather they decide to start a school. They choose a site and a day to build a one-room school. Someone volunteers to provide firewood for heating the school, another to dig a well. They select a teacher from among those who are especially good at reading, writing, and arithmetic. Finally, a board of directors is elected, the curriculum is decided, and the school is given a name. This is similar to the presbyterian model of polity.

Finally, imagine a person with a charismatic personality, filled with ideas and a facility with languages, who arrives in an area where the education system is dull and rigid. This person sets up shop in an abandoned building and before long the word is out that he or she has a nonconventional way of teaching that is not only easy but exciting. There is no accreditation but what difference does it make if one learns what one needs to know. It is easy to get into the class, but staying demands total dedication. Being part of the group affects every aspect of one's life. This is education by total immersion. Freedom abounds as long as one does not question the whole process. This is similar to the charismatic model of polity.

Focus:
A school system analogy to the three models of church polity

We have examined three basic models of church polity, the episcopal, the presbyterian, and the charismatic or sectarian. The differences among them concerning the understanding and exercise of leadership and authority in the church should be clear. In the episcopal model the threefold ordained ministry of bishop, presbyter, and deacon—a hierarchy—stands out. Within this same model the Roman Catholic understanding of the role of the bishop of Rome as the universal pastor heightens the hierarchical and institutional aspects of this model, making it difficult at times for those from other traditions to see how it protects gospel values. In the presbyterian model a broad decision-making process and quest for consensus is laudable, but prophetic leadership, while maintaining unity, is sometimes difficult to achieve. The charismatic/sectarian model brings with it an enthusiasm and dedication to the gospel way of life, but elitism lurks as a danger, making the common quest for unity more difficult.

With all these various churches and sects, with their various understandings of leadership and authority, which in turn have their effects on the interpretation, the teaching, and the living of the faith, does the movement for Christian unity have any chance at all? It is to this question that we now must turn.

Questions for Reflection and Discussion

1. When you think of the word "church" what is the first thing that comes into your mind? How has your understanding of church changed after reading this chapter?

2. Can you imagine yourself as an early disciple of Jesus writing the "three letters home" as the university student did? How do your views of discipleship differ in today's church, and why?

3. How do you react to the statement, "Young people today are radically ecumenical but woefully lacking in knowledge of their own church tradition"? How would you summarize the particular gifts that your church or denomination brings to the broader church of the followers of Jesus Christ?

4. What are your thoughts on receiving communion in a Christian church other than your own? Do you believe that guidelines are helpful? Is "table fellowship" (intercommunion, or sharing communion in one another's churches) something that you believe is important in the quest for church unity? What has been your experience?

5. How do your react to the statement, "All are called to God's Kingdom; some are called to membership and mission in the church"? What are your thoughts on who will be saved? Are other world religions also a way to God's Kingdom?

6. How well does your church live up to the challenges of being *one, holy, catholic* or *universal, and apostolic*? Give examples of where your church still needs to grow.

7. Do you find your church within one of the three models of church polity discussed in the chapter? Do you feel "at home" with that particular polity? How might it be modified to achieve an ecumenical church polity?

Suggestions for Further Reading

Brown, Raymond E. *The Churches the Apostles Left Behind.* New York: Paulist Press, 1984.

Carr, Anne E. *Transforming Grace: Christian Tradition and Women's Experience.* New York: Harper & Row, 1988. See chapter 9, "The Salvation of Women: Christ, Mary, and the Church," pp. 180–200.

Boff, Leonardo. *Church Charism and Power: Liberation Theology and the Institutional Church.* New York: Crossroad, 1985. See chapter 9, "The Base Ecclesial Community: A Brief Sketch," pp. 125–130, and chapter 10, "Underlying Ecclesiologies of the Base Ecclesial Communities," pp. 131–137.

Coll, Regina A. *Christianity and Feminism in Conversation.* Mystic, CT: Twenty-Third Publications, 1994.

Hines, Mary E. "Community for Liberation: Church" in *Freeing Theology: Essentials of Theology in Feminist Perspective.* ed.

Catherine Mowry LaCugna. New York: HarperCollins, 1993, pp. 161–178.

McBrien, Richard P. *Catholicism: New Edition.* New York: HarperCollins, 1994. See chapter 19, "The Church in Contemporary Theology and Doctrine," pp. 691–737.

Schillebeeckx, Edward. *Church: The Human Story of God.* New York: Crossroad, 1990. See chapter 4, "Towards Democratic Rule of the Church as a Community of God," pp. 187–228.

Chapter Five

The Quest for Church Unity

A young married couple, the woman from the Lutheran tradition and the man from the Catholic, together attended services in both their churches on weekends. The woman had asked the pastor of her husband's parish if she were welcome to receive communion at the Catholic Mass, as her husband was welcomed at the communion service in the Lutheran church. The pastor told her that he could not give her permission to receive, but if she decided on her own to receive, he would not refuse her. Her husband, having studied the Catholic and Lutheran understanding of Eucharist, and having been convinced that theologically both churches were in basic agreement on the understanding of the Lord's presence in communion, urged his wife to receive. She declined, however, saying that she did not want to participate if she were not welcomed.

The time came when their son, who had been baptized in the Catholic church, was ready to receive his first communion. In the husband's parish it was customary for the children to receive communion for the first time with their families. After much soul-searching and prayer, the mother decided that she would receive with her husband and son. When that time came, they approached the priest, who was not the pastor, and when she extended her hands to receive, the priest reached out and gave her a blessing instead of communion. Embarrassed and shaken by the action, the woman could not return to the pew, but had to leave the worship assembly.

That serious Christians who have a grasp of their faith and a desire to live it cannot share at the table of the Lord is heartbreaking for individuals and families. It is also a scandal for the community of the disciples of Jesus, he who prayed that we might be one. The quest for church unity should be a concern for every Christian.

Is Christian Unity a Possibility?

One might respond to the question "Is Christian unity a possibility?" with another one, "Do we have any choice?" For many people, especially the young in the emerging global church, what counts is not the old anti-ecumenical spirit of the past, but the challenge of and the need for dialogue among the larger groupings of Christianity, Judaism, Islam, Buddhism, and Hinduism. Before we proceed with an examination of the possibilities of Christian unity, let us briefly examine how the one church of Jesus Christ should approach other major world religions. The process may give us some hints about dealing with differences among ourselves.

1. The larger question of Christianity and other world religions

If God is available in human experience, then we can and must approach other world religions, indeed all other peoples, with a sense of respect and a spirit of dialogue. Moreover, because all people are ultimately the People of God and called to God's Kingdom, and even here and now form a single human family, we are together responsible for our world. (Many of the following ideas are found in Vatican II's *Declaration on the Relationship of the Church to Non-Christian Religions*.)

First, *we as Christians are closest to the Jews.* As St. Paul says in Romans 9, "to them belong the adoption, the glory, the covenants, the giving of the law, the worship, and the promises; to them belong the patriarchs, and from them, according to the flesh, comes the Messiah...." We have, according to Paul, been "grafted on" to their "rich root." And Vatican II reminds us that the Jewish people remain most dear to God; God does not go back on promises made. The Jews are still God's people.

With the Muslims, along with the Jews, we share Abraham as our father, and we adore the one merciful God who will judge. Further, the Muslims accept Jesus as a great prophet and give special honor to his mother, Mary.

With Hinduism we share the thirst to contemplate the divine mystery and express it through writings (for Hindus *Vedanta* and *Puranas*) and through searching philosophical inquiry. There are also similarities to be found in Christian and Hindu beliefs—the concepts of grace and sacraments, the Christian Trinity and Hindu ultimate reality. They seek release from the anguish of our earthly condition through ascetical practices or deep meditation or a loving, trusting flight toward God. We can only admire these practices and even learn from them.

With Buddhism we are open to dialogue as they acknowledge the radical insufficiency of this shifting world. Buddhism teaches a path by which people in devout and confident spirit can either reach a state of absolute freedom or attain supreme enlightenment by their own effort or by higher assistance.

With all other religions that strive to answer the questioning of the human heart by proposing "ways" that consist of teachings, rules of life, and sacred ceremonies, the church seeks through prudent and loving dialogue and collaboration to acknowledge, preserve, and promote the spiritual and moral goods found among them.

Finally, even *with those ideologies* such as Marxism and humanism, among others, we Christians seek dialogue for the purpose of bettering the human condition and seeking truth and good will wherever they may be found.

The focus of the ecumenism of the future is bound to be with Christianity's relationship with the other great world religions. We must face such questions as the unique but not exclusive role of Jesus in universal salvation, the time-conditioned aspect of all religious teaching, and the "providential" place of other world religions in God's plan. Even beyond the ecumenism of world religions is the need for dialogue between religious faith and the new cosmology that is rapidly emerging.[1] Karl Rahner spoke of faith from a scientific and evolutionary worldview,[2] and, more recently, theologians are speaking of the need for faith to come into dialogue with quantum physics and chaos theory.[3] But that takes us beyond the parameters of foundational theology. Our attention here is more modest, but equally important—the possibility of the Christian churches coming together in unity.

2. *Unity and lawful diversity*

It seems to be an impossibility, but we can still have hope that the Holy Spirit is urging and pointing the way to Christian unity. A starting point may be the Second Vatican Council's spirit of ecumenism, its teaching on collegiality, and its recognition of the gifts of the Spirit poured out on everyone. Through dialogue and mutual respect, our churches can and must seek to heal the divisions that handicap the effectiveness of our common mission. What the Second Vatican Council said about lawful diversity within the Roman Catholic communion should be applicable to the wider Christian community as well:

> Such a mission requires in the first place that we foster within the Church herself mutual esteem, reverence, and harmony, through the full recognition of lawful diversity. Thus all those who compose the one People of God...can engage in dialogue with ever abounding fruitfulness. For the bonds which unite the faithful are mightier than anything which divides them. *Hence, let there be unity in what is necessary, freedom in what is unsettled, and charity in every case.*[4]

This last statement reflects what the Vatican Council called a "hierarchy of truths," and the World Council of Churches calls a "sense of proportion." That is, there is a center or core of truth on which we all as Christians can agree, and this is vital. As we move further from that center, there is going to be less agreement, but there also should be more toleration for diversity.

3. Conciliar denominationalism

If church polity is at the root of what divides us, some type of conciliar denominationalism might be a way of finding common ground in this matter. Drawing on the strongest elements of each of the models of church polity discussed above—the corporate element of the episcopal model, the covenantal element of the presbyterian model, and the charismatic element of the sectarian model, we shall attempt to formulate an ecumenical church polity.

Remarkable progress has been made through bilateral dialogues among the churches that have the same polity—the Anglican/Episcopalian, Lutheran, Orthodox, and Catholic. Indeed they have more features in common. Dialogue between the churches of the episcopal and presbyterian polities has achieved considerable agreement also. An example would be the dialogue called COCU—Consultation on Church Union—taking place within a group of Protestant churches in the United States. Trying to agree on the threefold ministry in the church—bishop, presbyter, deacon—the Presbyterian church within the consultation has agreed to consider, in a limited sense, the role of bishop, an office that has had no place in the Calvinist/Reformed tradition from its founding. There are four churches in a proposed Lutheran-Reformed Formula of Agreement and two churches in the proposed Episcopal-Lutheran Concordat.[5]

The Catholic-Orthodox union is one much hoped for by many, but it faces many obstacles. One is the presence of Uniate churches in the East. They are eastern in their liturgy, tradition, and church polity, but are in union with Rome. The Orthodox church wants the question of the Uniate churches, which they see as western church imperialism, settled before further dialogue toward unity proceeds. In 1993 a joint international commission between Roman Catholics and Orthodox issued a communiqué on the results of their theological dialogue.[6] It is hoped this will facilitate further movement toward Orthodox-Catholic unity. The great strides toward union achieved in the Catholic-Anglican dialogue came up against a stumbling block when the Anglican communion began ordaining women. However, dialogue continues.

On a broader scale, one of the most significant results of the ecumenical movement has been the 1982 Lima Document of the Faith and Order Committee of the World Council of Churches (in which Catholics were participants). Entitled *Baptism, Eucharist and Ministry*, it was able to express remarkable consensus on these three major issues in the Christian church even though the Vatican was critical of many of its conclusions.[7]

Since the Second Vatican Council, the modification of the episcopal and presbyterian models has resulted in moving the churches of these two traditions closer together. Let us use the Catholic church and the Presbyterian church as examples.

Since the Council, Catholic churches have developed councils at the parish and diocesan levels in which laypeople participate and share responsibility with the clergy, accepting their baptismal responsibility to share in the mission of the church. Other groups have arisen advocating certain changes in the church regarding ordination, marriage, and reception of the sacraments. Catholics have begun to introduce one of the principles of Catholic social teaching—*subsidiarity*—in the area of church polity. The principle of subsidiarity states that whatever can be done at a lower level of community should be done there. This more grass-roots approach to church polity with its more democratic principles is more in keeping with the presbyterian model. But it does not deny the need for the hierarchy as exercised by the college of bishops with the bishop of Rome first among them.

The Presbyterians, on the other hand, have made the move to at least consider the role of bishop within their churches. Within their basic thrust of democracy, they are testing the possibility of a covenantal model with some central authority. Still this central authority would be responsible to the local churches. Also they have developed a deeper and broader understanding of sacraments.

Bilateral discussions are also taking place between certain churches or sects that follow the charismatic polity and the more established churches. Roman Catholic–Pentecostal dialogues have been going on for several years. This brings together the largest

Christian group in the world, the Roman Catholic church with 900,000,000 members, into conversation with the fastest growing group, the Pentecostals. The focus has been on evangelization, an area in which the two churches have much in common. This does not overlook some serious points of tension concerning methods being employed in evangelization.[8] By dialogue it is hoped that ways can be found to solve the differences, end the competition, and engage in common witness.

Incorporating the Pentecostal/charismatic tradition into a conciliar denominationalism, however, presents many challenges. First, many of these churches or sects do not wish to enter into dialogue. Also, the third model of polity, the charismatic or sectarian, is suspicious of the episcopal-corporate or presbyterian-covenantal forms of social organization. However, based upon the principle of the hierarchy of truths, the tradition of charismatic religious orders in the Catholic church, and Vatican II's openness to "various associations and organizations, both public and private," as well as the many "apostolic undertakings which are established by the free choice of the laity and regulated by their prudent judgment," should there not be room in an ecumenical church with a denominational conciliar polity for the sects with the charismatic polity?

A consensus on a few principles would have to be achieved before the Pentecostal/charismatic groups could enter into communion with the other two polities. They would have to agree to (1) remain open to dialogue with the larger church and be willing to participate in conciliar debate and abide by their consensus decisions (2) remain open in their membership and be willing to worship with other Christians (3) admit that their special concern or charism does not constitute the whole mission of the church, and (4) recognize that work for justice and peace in the world is an integral aspect of the mission of the church.

An ecumenical church polity based upon a council of all Christian churches has been proposed by Heribert Muhlen, a long-time missionary in the Third World. "What must be, can be," he declares. Such a council must have authority, according to Muhlen.

Following the model of the first council in Jerusalem in 49 C.E., "The Holy Spirit and we" must "decide" (Acts 15). How the petrine ministry (the role of the pope as the one who succeeds in the ministry of Peter) would fit into this conciliar church polity is a question of greatest importance. When Pope Paul VI visited the World Council of Churches in Geneva in 1969, he said, "I am Peter. The office of Peter, created for the unity of the Church, has become its greatest obstacle." Pope John Paul II has called for a reinterpretation of the papacy to make it more understandable and acceptable to other Christian churches.[9]

As long as the Christian church is divided it cannot carry out its mission in an effective way. One of the principal tasks of theology is to present possible ways in which growth toward unity can be achieved. Christian theology today must be done from an ecumenical perspective. Today the Holy Spirit seems to be leading us toward a renewed effort to accomplish the prayer Christ prayed for us, that we might be one. Therefore although this is an introduction to theology, the theology of church unity must be considered. What follows is one way of looking at the role of the pope in an ecumenical church polity based on conciliar denominationalism.

Focus: Rahner and Fries—The petrine ministry in a unified church

Shortly before his death in 1984, Karl Rahner cowrote a book with Heinrich Fries entitled *Unity of the Churches: An Actual Possibility.*[10] The authors propose ten theses that, if accepted by the churches, would facilitate church unity now. Thesis Four, divided into two parts, deals with the petrine ministry in a unified church. It will be worthwhile to examine it in light of the above discussion:

> *Thesis 4a: All partner churches acknowledge the meaning and right of the Petrine service of the Roman pope to be the concrete guarantor of the unity of the Church in truth and love.* (p. 8)

At first glance many Protestants would probably say "No way!" But the authors carefully explain the parts of the thesis beginning with *petrine service*. The first reason they give for the petrine service is the New Testament evidence. (The following is a summary of the material given by Rahner and Fries on pages 59–68.)

Scripture scholars in all Christian traditions admit that Peter is given a special leadership role in the New Testament. Jesus calls Simon "Rock" (Peter), which indicates a specific function within the apostolic community. The power of the keys that Jesus gives him (along with the other twelve) bestows on him a certain juridical competence in matters of leadership and order. Peter spoke for the twelve in recognizing the Messiah (Matthew 16:17–19); he is told to strengthen his brothers in faith (Luke 22:32); to tend the flock of Jesus (John 21:15–17). Peter was the one to whom the risen Christ first appeared according to Paul (1 Corinthians 15:5); he was the first leader of the original congregation in Jerusalem (Acts 1:15–22); he played a leading and decisive role in the Council of Jerusalem (Acts 15:6–11); and, according to the Acts, Peter received the first Gentile, Cornelius, into the Christian church (10:1–48). According to ancient tradition, Peter went to Rome and died a martyr's death.

Except for this last statement, it is the New Testament that describes the special ministry of Peter. Along with this, however, is the depiction of Peter as the stumbling block. "Get behind me, Satan! You are a stumbling block (*scandalum*) for me...," Jesus tells Peter (Matthew 16:22–23). Peter denied he knew Jesus at the time of the arrest, but then repented (Matthew 26:69–75). He had to be pulled from the water when he doubted (Matthew 14:28–31), and he had to be rebuked by Paul in the name of the gospel, but did not strike back (Galatians 2:11–14). Peter did not always occupy the leadership position in the first congregation—James, "the brother of the Lord" seems to have been the leader in Jerusalem (Acts 15:19), but Peter remained first. The New Testament

Focus:
Rahner and
Fries—The
petrine ministry in
a unified church

Focus:
Rahner and
Fries—The
petrine ministry
in a unified
church

points to Peter, first among the twelve, as having a *founding function*—with the other apostles—in regard to the church.

None of this New Testament evidence, however, solves the question of *succession* in the ministry of Peter. Some have claimed that it ended with the death of Peter. Others, for example the bishops at the First Vatican Council in 1870, declared that the pope as the successor of Peter has universal jurisdiction over the whole church and the individual churches. Rahner and Fries attempt to present their development of the papacy in such a way that it does not contradict the scriptural evidence.

The second reason given for a renewed openness to consideration of the petrine service in the church is the theological agreement that Protestants (Lutherans in this case) and Catholics have reached concerning justification. This was the church-dividing issue at the time of the Reformation. Luther said he would accept the office of the pope if the pope would accept what he saw as the gospel teaching on justification. While there still exists diversity on points of emphasis concerning this issue, justification is no longer considered a church-dividing issue. This opens the way for further dialogue on the question of the one who "succeeds in the ministry of Peter."

The third reason for the possibility of dialogue concerning the petrine service in the church has to do with the ecumenical climate in our era. We are no longer living in the time of interdenominational polemics. We are able to recognize the basic unity of faith that we share, and then proceed to discussion of substantive differences. "Tied to this," Fries and Rahner state, "is the effort to strive for the community of churches in faith, in truth, and in love, and, in full recognition of God's gracious freedom in history, to do everything possible to overcome the separation" (p. 67).

The question of the petrine ministry has been put into a broader perspective by Vatican II. By first reflecting on the church as the sacrament and sign of intimate union with God and of the unity of the human family, and then as the people of God who, through baptism, all share in a common mission, the Council emphasizes the communal nature of the church. This was followed by discussion of the college of bishops and then of the bishop of Rome as first among the bishops. But the function of the one who succeeds in the ministry of Peter cannot be described without the college of bishops. The collegial nature of the church includes the significance of local churches as well as the role of the laity in matters of faith.

Focus: Rahner and Fries—The petrine ministry in a unified church

That the church is not only a sacrament or sign of unity, but also a means of achieving that unity is made evident in the Catholic church's position on intercommunion with the Orthodox. Even though the Orthodox church does not accept the teachings of Vatican I on the universal jurisdiction of the pope or on infallibility as defined by Vatican I (and therefore they are not in full union with Rome), eucharistic fellowship is extended to them.

In 1965 when Pope Paul VI and the Patriarch of Constantinople (Istanbul) mutually lifted the excommunications of their respective churches (dating from 1054 C.E.), a new era of reconciliation and movement toward reunion began between these two ancient churches. Cardinal Ratzinger, the powerful head of the Roman Congregation on the Doctrine of the Faith, has suggested that, concerning the issue of universal jurisdiction of the pope and the Orthodox, "Rome must not require more of a primacy doctrine from the East than was formulated and experienced in the first millennium" (p. 70). The way the Eastern church looked upon the pope, the bishop of Rome and Patriarch of the West before the break in 1054, was, according to Ratzinger, summed up in the words of Patriarch Athenagoras when Pope Paul visited him in 1976. He greeted the pope as Peter's successor, as first in honor among the bishops, and as the presider over charity in the church. This is as much as should

Focus
Rahner and
Fries—The
petrine ministry in
a unified church

be required of the East, as long as they admit the further development of the papacy in the West as legitimate and orthodox, even as the West must admit the
legitimacy and orthodoxy of the way the Eastern
church has maintained itself (p. 70).

Although there is a different set of theological
issues involved concerning the Reformation churches and Rome (to say nothing of the free church-
charismatic tradition), still should not something
like the Orthodox–Catholic approach to shared
Eucharist and mutual recognition of ministry be possible even before the "stumbling block" of petrine
primacy of jurisdiction and infallibility is fully reconciled? The second part of Thesis 4 addresses this
issue more specifically.

> *Thesis 4b: The pope, for his part, explicitly com-
> mits himself to acknowledge and to respect the
> thus agreed-upon independence of the partner
> churches. He declares (by human right, iure
> humano) that he will make use of his highest
> teaching authority (ex cathedra), granted to him
> in conformity with Catholic principles by the First
> Vatican Council, only in a manner that conforms
> juridically or in substance to a general council of
> the whole Church, just as his previous ex cathedra
> decisions have been issued in agreement and close
> contact with the whole Catholic episcopate.(p. 8.)*

(The following is a summary of the material given
by Rahner and Fries on pages 83–94.)

Thesis 4a states that for there to be union between
the Catholic church and other Christian churches,
they must recognize the petrine office as also binding
on themselves. The communion of churches, therefore, would be something more than a World Council
of Churches. It would have collegial authority but
also a universal pastor, succeeding in the ministry of
Peter, who would serve as the sign and means of
unity among the member churches. They must

accept as a decision of faith the actuality of this office of the one who succeeds in the ministry of Peter in the one Church of Christ. They need not agree on explicit details at this time—that is, on the universal jurisdiction of the pope and a statement on infallibility as spelled out in the language of Vatican I.

Thesis 4b puts the glove on the other hand, so to speak. In its unbearably dense language, typical of certain German theologians (Karl Rahner's brother Hugo, also a theologian, swore that someday he would translate Karl's works into German!), this second part of Thesis 4 describes how the pope for his part must contribute to the more biblically oriented and ecumenically sensitive understanding and function of the papacy in the one church.

First, the pope acknowledges the permanent independence of the partner in the one church. The actual arrangement of the relationship of particular partner churches to Rome (as has been evidenced in history regarding the Eastern churches in union with Rome—the so-called Uniate churches) could be negotiated in a way similar to the agreements (*concordats*) that Rome has made through the years with secular states—recognition and respect for certain rights of nations in matters that effect church polity, but not the essence of faith.

The subtle relationship of the universal teaching authority of the bishop of Rome and that of the council of all bishops, of which he is always a part, must and can be articulated in a way both faithful to the Tradition of the One Church and the traditions of the various member churches. The pope could proscribe his right of exercise of infallibility, according to Vatican I and Vatican II, in such a way that it would entail either a joint declaration of a Council of the Church or a consensus of the bishops in union with him. The theological and practical issues involved here are obvious, but if we live what we proclaim in faith about the presence of the Holy Spirit in the church, then we can make our own the phrase iden-

Focus:
Rahner and
Fries—The
petrine ministry in
a unified church

tified with the vision of Robert Kennedy, "Some people see the way things are and ask Why? Others dreams of the way things could be and ask Why not?"

A listing of the other seven Theses will now be given (without explanation) so we can see how Thesis 4 fits into the scheme and dream that Karl Rahner, the great Catholic and ecumenical theologian of the twentieth century, and his colleague, Heinrich Fries, have proposed. (These are found on pages 7–9.)

> 1. *The fundamental truths of Christianity, as they are expressed in Holy Scripture, in the Apostles Creed, and in that of Nicaea and Constantinople are binding on all partner churches of the one Church to be.*

> 2. *Beyond that, a realistic principle of faith should apply. Nothing may be rejected decisively and confessionally in one partner church which is binding dogma in another partner church. Furthermore, beyond Thesis 1 no explicit and positive confession in one partner church is imposed as dogma obligatory for another partner church. This is left to the broader consensus in the future. This applies especially to authentic but undefined doctrinal decrees of the Roman church, particularly with regard to ethical questions. According to this principle only that would be done which is already practice in every church today.*

> 3. *In this one Church of Jesus Christ, composed of the uniting churches, there are regional partner churches which can, to a large extent, maintain their existing structures. These partner churches can also continue to exist in the same territory, since this is not impossible in the context of Catholic ecclesiology or the practice of the Roman church, as for example, in Palestine.*

> 4a. [discussed above]

4b. [discussed above]

Focus:
Rahner and
Fries—The
petrine ministry in
a unified church

5. All partner churches, in accordance with ancient tradition, have bishops at the head of their larger subdivisions. The election of a bishop in these partner churches need not be done according to the normally valid manner in the Roman Catholic church. (The new Roman Canon Law also mentions ways of appointing a bishop other than through the pope's free choice. See can. 377, par. 1.)

6. The partner churches live in mutual fraternal exchange of all aspects of their life, so that the previous history and experience of the churches separated earlier can become effective in the life of the other partner churches.

7. Without prejudice to the judgment of another church concerning the theological legitimacy of the existing ministerial office in the separated churches, all partner churches commit themselves henceforth to conduct ordinations with prayer and the laying on of hands, so that acknowledging them will present no difficulty for the Roman Catholic partner church either.

8. There is pulpit and altar fellowship between the individual partner churches.

Certainly the above theses need further explanation, and they do not solve all the difficult problems involved in discussing church unity. But we should keep in mind that for the first three centuries the Christian church survived without one dominant theological system or a rigid church polity. It was during that chaotic period that the New Testament canon took form, and even then tensions among different groups within the one church continued. Scripture scholar Raymond Brown has noted that by bringing the gospel of John into the same canon as Mark, Matthew, and Luke, the latter three implicitly advocating a position contrary to John, means that

the Great Church...has chosen to live with tension....In this day
when Catholics quarrel about how much respective authority pope,
bishop, priest, and lay person should have, and when Christians
quarrel about whether a woman should be an ordained minister of
the Eucharist, John's voice cries out its warning. The greatest dignity to be striven for is neither papal, episcopal, nor priestly; the
greater dignity is that of belonging to the community of the beloved
disciples of Jesus Christ.[11]

When we discussed "What Is Theology?" in chapter one of this
book, we insisted that it is *our* attempt to put into understandable
words our faith and commitment to Jesus Christ. That reflection
and profession come out of our experience of the new life that we
find through baptism into the Body of Christ as disciples of the
Risen One. Our examination of God's gracious invitation (*revelation*) to new life (*salvation*), and our acceptance and response
through the Spirit's prompting to that invitation (*faith*), calls us to
discipleship in the community called out in the power of the Spirit
(*church*). Being church demands that we spread the good news of
Jesus as the Kingdom of God (*preach*), that we be an example of the
Kingdom by our life and worship in community (*witness*), and that
we participate with others in preparing for the fullness of God's
Kingdom (*serve*).

Divided, the One Church of Jesus Christ cannot carry out this
mission effectively. Therefore we are called to work and pray for the
unity to which Christ has called us (*ecumenism*). Although the
work of the unity we seek—shared communion and mutual recognition of ministry—is the gift of God, still the words of 1 Peter
3:14–15 urge us to participate in the task: "Always be ready to give
*reason...*for this hope of yours *[theology]*; yet do it with gentleness
and reverence *[ecumenical dialogue]*."

Having presented the essentials of foundational theology—*What
do we believe and why?*—we must now turn to the second part of
our study, to moral theology and the question, What are we to do
and be as Christians?

Questions for Reflection and Discussion

1. What has been your experience with people from other world religions? Do you see a need for Christians to be familiar with the basic tenets of Judaism, Islam, Hinduism, and Buddhism? Explain why or why not.

2. What are your thoughts on baptism, Eucharist, and ministry in your own church tradition? How do you see agreement on these three tenets important for church unity?

3. Do you see a way of reinterpreting the role of the "one who succeeds in the ministry of Peter" (the pope) as universal pastor and sign of unity in the broad ecumenical church that would make that position acceptable to most Christians?

4. How realistic is the hope for church unity? What does the principle, *unity without uniformity,* mean to you in relation to the distinction between *Tradition* and *traditions*?

Suggestions for Further Reading

Desseaux, Jacques. *Twenty Centuries of Ecumenism.* New York: Paulist Press, 1984. (Original French version, 1983.)

Dunn, Edmond J. *Missionary Theology: Foundations in Development.* Lanham, MD: University Press of America, 1980. See chapter 7, "An Ecclesiology for the Theology of Development: A Prospectus," pp. 351–375.

Edwards, Denis. *Jesus and the Cosmos.* New York: Paulist Press, 1991.

Hellwig, Monika K. *Jesus, The Compassion of God.* Wilmington, DE: Michael Glazier, Inc., 1983. See Part III: "The Believer's Christ in a Pluralistic World," chapter 9, "Buddha and the Christ: Detachment and Liberation," pp. 127–133; chapter 10, "Moses, Jesus, and Muhammad: Law and Liberation," pp. 134–141; chapter 11: "Jesus and Marx: Social Justice and Redemption," pp. 142–150; chapter 12, "Jesus and Gandhi: Salvation and Non-violence," pp. 151–155.

Küng, Hans. *Theology for the Third Millennium: An Ecumenical*

View. New York: Doubleday, 1988. See Part C, "A New Departure Toward a Theology of World Religions," chapter II, "Is There One True Religion: An Essay in Establishing Ecumenical Criteria," pp. 227–250.

Marty, Martin E. *The Public Church: Mainline-Evangelical-Catholic.* New York: Crossroad, 1981. See chapter 5, "Unity and Mission," pp. 70–93

Rusch, William. *Ecumenism: A Movement to Church Unity.* Philadelphia: Fortress Press, 1985.

Stransky, Thomas F. "Ecumenical Movement," in *HarperCollins Encyclopedia of Catholicism,* ed. Richard P. McBrien. New York: HarperCollins, 1995, pp. 456–457.

Tillard, J.M.R. *Church of Churches: The Ecclesiology of Communion.* Collegeville, MN: A Michael Glazier Book. The Liturgical Press, 1992. See especially chapter 4, part II, "The Bishop of the Church of Rome," and part III, "Outside of Visible Communion," pp. 284–318.

Part II
Moral Theology

Chapter Six

Moral Theology: A Definition

After a month and a half of sharing a dorm room, Tom, a freshman college seminarian, told his roommate, Jeff, that he was dropping out of the seminary because he was gay. Jeff later spoke about this with the seminary rector. "If I had known I was going to have a homosexual for a roommate," Jeff said, "I never would have come here to school. But now I'm confused. I don't know exactly how to feel. You see, Tom is a good person. He's my friend. I like him...and, you know, he never tried to...get me. I've got to do some rethinking. It is a lot different when you know someone."

To live the moral life is not just a matter of following some kind of "rule book" in which everything is clearly spelled out. In this chapter the term "premoral" will be introduced, and will be further developed in succeeding chapters. The distinction between moral and premoral values and disvalues should help to clarify the confusion Jeff was going through when his preconceived ideas were challenged because he "got to know someone."

What Is Moral Theology?

In chapter one we began our inquiry into theology by looking at the word itself, *theos logos,* *"God talk."* We shall do the same here. The word *moral* comes from the Latin word *mors* meaning "manner," "custom," or "habit." From the words themselves, therefore, we can say that moral theology is *God talk about manners, customs, and habits.* We saw, however, that although theology defined as God talk was accurate, it was not adequate. It did not say enough. The faith dimension must be included in theology. In a similar way, while it is accurate to define moral theology as God talk about manners, customs, and habits, it is not adequate. Not only does it not take into consideration the faith dimension from the theological point of view, it does not take into consideration the human dimension from the moral point of view. Non-humans can have manners, customs, and habits. We usually refer to such characteristics as instincts.

We humans have instincts as well. But when it comes to our manners, customs, and habits, something more is involved. Freedom, choice, and decision, both personal and communal, come into play, and we judge our manners, customs, and habits as good or bad, right or wrong, virtuous or sinful, just or unjust.

> *Moral theology, therefore, is our attempt to know and understand how we are to live and what we are to do (or not do), to be (or not be) from a faith perspective* [and as Christians we would add] *as disciples of Jesus Christ.*

Moral theology carries with it obligation, what we *ought* to do and be. These obligations are sometimes stated as norms or commands. Foundational theology is *descriptive.* It describes what we believe and why. Moral theology is both descriptive and *prescriptive.* It not only describes but prescribes what we ought to do.

Let us pause here for a moment and take a brief look at words associated with the word *moral.*

If *moral* has to do with what is good, right, and virtuous, then *immoral* is what is evil, wrong, and sinful.

A number of other words are associated with the word moral.

Amoral refers to acts (or persons) in which rightness or wrongness don't seem to enter the picture. One who operates a prostitution ring, for example, and looks upon his or her business as so much flesh to sell, seemingly is oblivious to the human lives being manipulated and abused.

Sometimes moral terms are used in a *nonmoral* context. A "good" car or a "bad" shot in sports is not a comment about the moral condition of the object or the act. The dog that defecates on the living room rug or even the infant who fills its diaper is not bad in the moral sense. The one who acts must have sufficient knowledge and freedom to perform a moral (or immoral) act. A "good" hit in dropping a hydrogen bomb on a civilian populace, however, is a moral issue.

Another term that is associated with the word moral and is used frequently in moral theology today is *premoral*. This term will enter our discussion later, but for now it can be described as the way things are according to nature. It is the situation before moral rightness or wrongness apply. Organic material exposed to the sun will eventually rot and smell. The bumper sticker "Shit happens" expresses a premoral fact. The human body eventually wears out with aging. Human beings, endowed not only with intellect and will, but also with emotions and the subconscious, experience certain urges, yearnings, and feelings that in themselves are neither good nor bad. They, like the other examples cited, are just part of creation as we know it. Later we will distinguish between premoral and moral values.

Foundational theology and moral theology are, of course, deeply intertwined. Both are concerned with our relationship to God through Christ in the life of the Spirit. Foundational theology focuses on *knowing* (what do we believe and why?) while moral theology focuses on *loving* or *willing* (what ought we to do and be?) In the same way that the intellect and the will are intimately intertwined in the human, so the mind and the heart are intimately intertwined in our relationship to God and all of God's creation.

We find a parallel in the relationship between foundational theology and moral theology in the terms *orthodoxy* and *orthopraxis*.

Focus: orthodoxy and orthopraxis

The Greek prefix *ortho* in both words means "straight" or "correct." (An orthodontist corrects or straightens teeth). *Doxy* comes from the Greek word *doxa*, which means "praise." We have the word doxology—exclaiming praise (to God). *Orthodox* means "correct praise." It also means correct opinion or doctrine. The Orthodox church claims that it has preserved the correct doctrine and therefore is able to praise God correctly. The word orthodoxy with its combined meanings—correct praise/correct doctrine—reflects an ancient Latin axiom, *lex orandi, lex credendi* (the law of praying is the law of believing). We seek the truth (law/doctrine) that we might worship God as we ought (prayer), and, in turn, our worship is one of the primary norms for our doctrine.

Orthodoxy, correct doctrine, is related to foundational theology—what we believe and why. Orthopraxis, correct practice or action, is related to moral theology—what we are to do and be. The word *praxis*, however, so popular in liberation theology, means not just practice but reflective practice or action. Praxis is action that arises out of reflection on one's concrete situation and experience. Moral theology relates to reflective action arising out of our concrete situation and experience.

The continual challenge of the Christian life is to keep in creative tension orthodoxy and orthopraxis—right belief and right action. But often we experience situations where the balance is lost. On the one hand, someone might say, "I'm a good Christian! I don't abuse my wife, I let the kids have the car on Friday nights, and I pay my taxes." And someone else might respond, "I don't care what you do for your wife or kids or Uncle Sam. If you don't go to church, join your fellow Christians in worshiping God and taking part in the Supper of the Lord, you're no Christian! You've got to proclaim what you believe." And the comeback: "Yeah, I know those people who parade to church each Sunday just to be seen. But what do they do all week? Actions speak louder than words!"

Foundational theology and moral theology are intimately intertwined. There is truth in the old saying, "Don't talk the talk if you can't walk the walk," but the inverse is also true. To be a disciple of Jesus one must talk as one walks. One cannot have faith without expressing it—both in words and actions. Also, Christian faith from beginning to end is communal—*our* attempt to express *our* lives in relationship. In moral theology we will be examining these relationships.

Focus: orthodoxy and orthopraxis

How Is Moral Theology Related to Ethics?

Moral theology is our attempt to understand what we are to do and be as people of faith and followers of Jesus Christ. To *understand* involves *reason*. As the great theologian Anselm says, theology is faith seeking understanding. It is our attempt to reason about our faith. Moral theology also involves "God talk." And God talk, or theology, involves our attempt to express in words what we presume to be the self-disclosure of God in Jesus. This self-disclosure is what we call *revelation*. Moral theology, therefore, is our attempt to understand what we are to do and be in light of *reason* and *revelation*. (Note the *our* and *we* in the preceding statement). Moral theology, as part of the broader field of theology, is also done from within the community of faith.

Ethics, on the other hand, is an attempt to understand what human beings ought to do and be according to right *reason*. Ethics is a branch of philosophy, not theology. Philosophy (*philos*, " love" and *sophia*, "wisdom"), the love of wisdom, investigates the deepest meaning of existence from the point of view of reason. There is a close relationship between philosophy and theology. Especially in the Catholic tradition, philosophy has provided one of the principal foundations for theology. From philosophy, more particularly from Aristotle, the Stoics, and Cicero, Catholic moral theology has developed its *natural law* tradition. (More will be said about this later.)

In everyday talk we interchange the terms *ethics* and *morals* regularly. To say that something is ethically right or wrong, or morally right or wrong, is basically to say the same thing. Further, if one speaks of *biblical ethics* or *Christian ethics,* then one is speaking of moral theology. The distinction between moral theology and ethics, therefore, with their respective foundations in theology and philosophy, is real, but in practice often blurred. According to the definition of theology presented in this book, an unbeliever could not do moral theology—based as it is on reason *and* revelation. But when revelation is understood as being available to everyone in human experience, the distinction fades. The unbelieving ethicist, seeking the good according to right reason, can already be said to have been touched by God, even if that person denies the possibility.

The question often arises whether there is such a thing as *Christian* ethics. If ethics is right conduct based on reason, and every human being (if well) has the faculty of reason, then what would the faith perspective add to the ethical or moral decision making? Moral theologian Timothy O'Connell[1] suggests that one can speak of a distinctive Christian ethic or morality from four points of view—*obligations, sources, vision,* and *motives.* Christian ethics or morals has its special characteristics, according to O'Connell, but in a specific, limited sense.

Christians have different *obligations* because of the religious commitment they have made within the faith community. Discipleship does not change the rightness or wrongness of particular acts, of course. Unfaithfulness in marriage, for example, is not wrong just because one is Baptist, Catholic, or Lutheran. On the other hand, a Christian couple undertakes the obligation to make their marriage, as St. Paul says, a sign of Christ's love for his people, the church (Ephesians 5:32).

Concerning *sources,* Christians do look to the Bible and the traditions and teachings of their particular faith communities in forming their conscience and making moral decisions. The wisdom of these sources is often very helpful. Again, however, this must not be understood in a narrow, fundamentalistic way. Something is not right or wrong because the Bible says so, but the Bible says so because something is right or wrong. Even here one must be careful in using the Bible as a rule book, attempting to apply specific ethical directives found there to life today in an uncritical way.

For example, in 1 Corinthians 7, when St. Paul suggests it would be better not to marry, it does not mean that celibacy is a higher calling than marriage. Rather, Paul is convinced that the end is coming very soon, and he wants the people to be free from worldly obligations. For this same reason, according to Paul, slaves are to remain slaves. They are already free in the Lord, and since there is so little time before the return of Christ, all people should remain as they are. Even husbands and wives are not to engage in sexual intercourse! The ethical insights found in Christian sources should, in principle, be available to all people through the use of human reason. Moreover, there is no single ethical system to be found in the Bible. Christians should, however, be able to find inspiration and guidance in the Bible (and in other church sources) without falling into the trap of legalism or literalism.

Christians approach ethics and morals with a different *vision.* As followers of Christ we are gifted with a particular view of the meaning of the world. This is found especially in a deeper understanding of the dignity of the human person. God through Christ became flesh—one of us (*incarnational theology*)—and therefore our bodies and all matter have been touched by God. Moreover, the intended destiny of every person and all creation is salvation through Christ in God's Kingdom (*Christian eschatology*). Our vision enables us to see God in and through other persons (*theological anthropology*), and all creation as good and imbued with meaning and purpose

(*Christian cosmology*). We hold this vision in spite of the sin and suffering in the world and our own brokenness and failure to live up to our calling. Ours is a vision filled with hope because of the victory won for us through the cross and resurrection of Jesus Christ.

Christians also approach ethics and morals with different *motives*. While our outward actions may be indistinguishable from others, as Christians our motives for acting may be very different. One may be acting in a particular way, or doing a particular thing, because he or she has had a personal experience of Christ, who loves everyone and wants us to do the same. One may want to do what the church asks because through the church he or she has experienced the joy and challenge of the Christian community as the Body of Christ. One may be doing a particular deed because it reflects the ideals found in the Bible. The Christian way of life involves Eucharist—thanksgiving—for all that God has done for us in Christ. Our vision and motives are intertwined with those of the One we call our brother and our savior. Christian discipleship is a love affair in which losing one's life means finding it.

Why Do "Good" Christians Disagree on Basic Moral Questions?

With our common faith in Jesus Christ and a shared notion of discipleship, we Christians still disagree on basic moral questions. We question one another's vision and motives and even accuse each other of bad faith, of being unchristian. A question that continues to tear at the very fabric of the Christian community is that of abortion. Others, such as the death penalty, euthanasia, birth control, nuclear arms, welfare, and aid to the Third World, also continue to divide us. Christians disagree on basic moral questions because of their *different approaches to moral decision making*. It comes down to a question of method. The way one approaches moral decision making usually will predetermine the outcome. What is allowed or not allowed is often built into the presuppositions of the method.

We shall be examining three basic methods of moral decision making in the following chapter.

Questions for Reflection and Discussion

1. Moral theology and fundamental theology are closely intertwined. How would you explain the terms *descriptive* and *prescriptive*, *orthodoxy* and *orthopraxis* in relationship to these two branches of theology?

2. How would you make the distinction between moral theology and ethics? How does it tie into the question asked in the first part of the book, "Can one do theology without faith?"

3. Do you agree that there is something distinctive about *Christian* ethics? Explain.

4. What are your reactions to the statement, "Christian discipleship is a love affair in which losing one's life means finding it"? How would you explain such a statement to a friend?

Suggestions for Further Reading

Cahill, Lisa Sowle. "Feminism and Christian Ethics: Moral Theology," in *Freeing Theology: The Essentials of Theology in Feminist Perspective*, ed. Catherine Mowry LaCugna. New York: HarperCollins, 1993, pp. 211–231.

Gustafson, James M. "Can Ethics Be Christian? Some Conclusions," in *Readings in Moral Theology No. 2: The Distinctiveness of Christian Ethics*, eds. Charles Curran and Richard McCormick. New York: Paulist Press, 1980, pp. 146–155. See also chapters by Josef Fuchs, Charles Curran, and Richard McCormick in this same volume.

Keane, Philip S. "Why Ethics and Imagination?" in *The Catholic Faith: A Reader*, ed. Lawrence Cunningham. New York: Paulist Press, 1988, pp. 128–145.

O'Connell, Timothy E. *Principles for a Catholic Morality*. rev. ed. New York: HarperCollins, 1990. See chapter 1, "The Meaning of Moral Theology," pp. 3–10.

Chapter Seven

Method in Moral Theology

It is time for sexually active believers to proclaim in the Lord's name, and without fear, what they have learned in bed, confident it is, when communally funded, as authoritative as any episcopal letter or papal encyclical.

Dick Westley
(from Address given in Waterloo, Ontario, 1987)

"Communally funded" in the above quote refers to the lived-experience of married couples, shared and tested within the faith community. As we examine in more detail why it is that good Christians disagree on basic moral questions, we will find that the expected answers are often built into the way the questions are asked, or are based on presuppositions behind the questions. The focus of this chapter will be moral decision making based on lived experience within responsible relationships.

What Are the Three Basic Ways
of Approaching Moral Decision Making?

Following theologian and Christian ethicist H. Richard Niebuhr,[1] we shall look at the *goal-oriented*, the *rule-oriented*, and the *responsible/relational-oriented* approaches to moral decision making. The particular perspective on the human person, on sin, and on the law will be examined in each of the approaches.

What Is the Goal-oriented Approach to Moral Decision Making and What Are Its Strengths and Weaknesses?

All human acts are directed toward some goal, purpose, or end. That is the basic position of Aristotle and Thomas Aquinas. Human acts have "built within them," one might say, a purpose, a goal, an end. (This approach is sometimes called the *teleological* approach, from the Greek word *telos* meaning "end.") From the faith perspective the ultimate goal of all of our actions or deeds is to be fully human, that is, to be saved, for that is what we are invited to be. Heaven, union with God, would be the traditional way of expressing this ultimate goal.

This built-in purpose of human actions is known to us through what is called *natural law.* This term has been understood in various ways with various emphases both by its proponents and opponents from its inception among the Greek philosophers. St. Paul in his letter to the Romans speaks of the requirements of the law that are *written on the hearts* of the Gentiles who do not have the law of Moses. In Christian philosophical and theological development there was a tendency toward a rigid conception of natural law. It is this rigid understanding of natural law—every human act has built within it a proper goal—that is operative in the goal-oriented approach under discussion here.[2]

In the goal-oriented approach *the human person* is seen as a master builder or craftsperson who by the decisions he or she makes constructs a life worthy of one invited into the friendship of God. The person is capable, with God's grace, of making right decisions and cooperating with God in the plan of salvation.

In the goal-oriented approach *sin* means missing the mark or substituting some less worthy goal for the intended one. It is acting against the way things ought to be according to nature.

In the goal-oriented approach *law* is meant to assist one in making decisions that are in keeping with nature. Law here is utilitarian. If it directs people toward the proper goal it is a good law. If it does not, it is a bad law.

To observe how this goal-oriented approach works let us use as an example the act of human sexual intercourse.

The goal or purpose of human sexual intercourse is procreation. According to nature it is the way by which the human race continues in existence. In Catholic teaching up until the Second Vatican Council, procreation was seen as the primary purpose of sexual intercourse within marriage. Recent teaching has emphasized the dual purpose of sexual intercourse—not only is it for procreation, it is also for the expression and growth of the love of the couple. Both the procreative and unitive aspects of sexual intercourse are emphasized and intimately joined. In other words, both must always be present in every act of intercourse.

In the goal-oriented approach this is the place where the problem of artificial contraception arises. Every act of intercourse is meant to express the love of the couple, but every act of intercourse must also be open to the possibility of new life. To prevent the latter by artificial means is to disrupt the purpose of the act itself. It is contrary to nature and therefore always gravely sinful. The use of the pill, condom, or diaphragm is wrong. Natural family planning by use of the rhythm method, on the other hand, is not against nature because it is built around the natural menstrual cycle in the woman. Refraining from sexual intercourse during the few days of the month when the woman is fertile does not violate the purpose of the sexual act and therefore is acceptable according to the goal-oriented approach.

From this perspective, the prohibition of artificial contraception is not just a law of the church binding on its members, but something that should be understandable by all according to the natural law. Such contraception violates the very goal or purpose of the marriage act.

Other sexual issues follow this same pattern of reasoning. Masturbation, for example, is always wrong because it frustrates the purpose of the sexual capacity in humans to procreate and express married love. In the medieval understanding of sexuality, it was believed that the whole of life was present in the male semen. The woman merely provided the ground in which the seed could grow. Therefore, masturbation was solely a male problem and it involved destruction of potential life. A sperm count to test male fertility is also wrong because it would have to involve masturbation. The same is true of in vitro fertilization. Even though it involves the egg and the sperm of the married couple, and the fertilized egg is implanted in the womb of the wife, the whole process is unnatural—the marriage act is not performed according to nature, and getting the sperm again involves masturbation. (The practice of fertilizing a number of eggs in case implantation is not successful in the first attempt, and the disposition of those fertilized eggs, only adds to the seriousness of the moral problem according to the goal-oriented approach.)

In the matter of abortion, removal of the fetus from the womb is against nature, besides destroying a human life. Because we do not (and cannot) know when *human* life begins, we must respect and protect the fetus as human from the moment of conception.

The goal-oriented approach seems to be preoccupied with sexual issues, but examples from other areas pertaining to the moral life could also be cited. Lying, for example, is always wrong because it violates the human faculty of speech, which is meant to express the truth.

The goal-oriented approach puts emphasis on the act itself and the purpose of the act according to nature. On the one hand, there is a clarity in this method, but on the other hand, there is a tendency toward rigidity and what some see as an excessive emphasis on the biological or physical. If we put so much emphasis on the goal, then the circumstances and the means, and the effects of those means on human relationships, are in danger of being slighted. The danger of utilitarianism—the end justifies the means—is always lurking in the shadows when so much emphasis is placed on the goal or the end, but utilitarianism is a modern development, not part of the traditional goal-oriented approach.

What Is the Rule-oriented Approach to Moral Decision Making and What Are Its Strengths and Weaknesses?

According to the rule-oriented approach to moral decision making, the human person, so injured by original sin, is capable of little more than obeying the rules or commandments given by God in the Bible, or by God's representatives, the leaders in the church, through official doctrine. (The rule-oriented approach is known in its classic form as the *deontological* approach. The Greek word *deon* means duty or obligation.) In order to live the moral life one is to be obedient to the rules.

The perspective on the *human person* in this approach is not very optimistic. The human person is not called to fashion or build his or her life by discerning the universal law written by God in the hearts of all humans, as in the goal-oriented approach. Rather, he or she is to follow what God has called for in the commandments given to Moses, the new law of Christ as it is spelled out in detail in the New Testament, or in the rules and regulations laid out by the church leaders, who are Christ's representatives here on earth.

In this rule-oriented approach, *sin* is disobeying the law. And the understanding of *law* in this approach is that which is to be followed in every circumstance without question. To observe how the law-oriented approach works let us again turn to the act of human sexual intercourse.

Sexuality in the Old Testament, and the Rule-oriented Approach

The rules or commands that govern sexual relations can be found in the Bible and the teachings of the church. As one begins to read the Bible, it is striking to find that in the "garden of paradise" where Adam and Eve find themselves and where there is an abundance of all that sustains life, one thing that is missing is children.

Focus: Procreation and the accounts of creation in the Bible | Although in the first account of creation (chapter 1 of Genesis), after God formed man and woman in God's own image, and after blessing them, telling them to be fruitful and multiply, still there is no mention of children. Then in the second account of creation (chapter 2 of Genesis), Adam is incomplete without a partner with whom he can share fully, so God fashions woman from a rib of Adam, and he is delighted. They are to cling to one another and become one flesh. They are naked, but not ashamed. Still, there are no children.

Then comes the temptation and the fall. God puts the fruit of one tree out of bounds for Adam and Eve and warns them that if they eat the forbidden fruit they will die. Tempted by the serpent's claim that if they eat the fruit they will be like God and know good and evil, Eve eats and then gives the fruit to Adam. He eats and their eyes are opened. They now recognize they are naked, and they cover themselves. When God confronts them the snake is first cursed and made to crawl on its belly. Eve is told she will suffer pain in bearing children, that she will have desire for her husband, and that he will rule over her. Adam in turn is told that the ground he will cultivate is cursed, thorns and thistles will grow with his crops, and he will have to labor hard all his life for a livelihood. Finally, he will die and return to the ground from which he was taken. God drives the couple out of the garden. Adam then *knows* Eve, and she conceives and brings forth a child, Cain. Thus the children arrive outside the garden.

The deep theological meaning of this story is, first of all, what God creates is good. If there is evil in the world—pain and toil and death—it is not God's doing, but ours. The order in relationships that God desired is frustrated by what later is called *original sin.* Like the great creation myths of all civilizations, the Hebrew story of the creation and fall attempts to help people understand why things are as they are.

"Why do snakes crawl on their belly and why don't people like them?"

"Let me tell you a story. You see there was this beautiful garden and...."

"Why do women have such pain in giving birth?"

"Let me tell you a story...."

Focus: Procreation and the accounts of creation in the Bible

"Why do we have to work so long and hard and often have so little to show for it?"

"Let me tell you a story...."

"Why do people die?"

"Let me tell you a story. In the garden no one died. Death came because Adam and Eve disobeyed the commandment God gave them. They were driven out of the garden and that's when death became a reality for them."

"But why didn't they have any children in the garden?"

"Didn't I say that no one in the garden died? If people kept having children and no one died, what would eventually happen?"

"You mean overpopulation?"

"Look, we don't know how God would have handled it. All we know is that children weren't mentioned in the story about Adam and Eve in the garden. What we do know is that we do have children, and we die. No story can answer all the questions. Just obey what God tells you to do and you'll be all right. Adam and Eve messed things up for us."

"How do you suppose that evil serpent got into the garden?"

"Don't mess up the story! Obey. That is what you're supposed to do!"

Sexual intercourse within marriage was something taken for granted among the Hebrews. The restrictions placed on sexual intercourse were directed primarily toward adultery, incestuous relationships, homosexuality, and bestiality (Leviticus 18:6–23). Concerning the latter two, Leviticus calls them both abominations. The Hebrews also had regulations related to ritual uncleanliness that forbade sexual intercourse during a woman's menstrual period.

There is one instance in the Hebrew Bible that some identify as a prohibition against birth control or punishment for masturbation. In Genesis 38:8–10 there is the story about Onan. According to the ancient custom of levirate marriage, if a married man dies without having produced an offspring, his living brother is to take the dead man's wife and beget a child by her. In this way the name of the dead brother will be perpetuated.

Onan's brother died childless. But Onan did not want to beget a son that would not be his, and so, "he spilled his semen on the ground whenever he went in to his brother's wife." God found this displeasing, the Bible tells us, and put Onan to death for his sin. Most Scripture scholars today do not consider the sin of Onan a sexual sin, but rather a sin of refusal to fulfill the law of levirate marriage. In the past, however, the "sin of Onan" was referred to as a biblical condemnation of masturbation as well as of birth control by means of interrupting the sexual act. The traditional Latin term for the latter was *coitus interruptus*.

Sexuality in the New Testament and the Rule-oriented Approach

Jesus' teaching on sexuality is minimal. It may be that he wanted to avoid any possible association with the fertility cults so common among the pagan religions of the time. He also was caught up in the apocalyptic movement and expected the imminent coming of the Kingdom. When told about a woman married successively to seven brothers and asked whose wife she would be in the Kingdom, Jesus said, "in the resurrection they neither marry nor are given in marriage, but are like angels in heaven" (Matthew 22:30). He does speak forcefully on adultery, however, even warning that "anyone who looks at a woman with lust has already committed adultery with her in his heart" (Matthew 5:27–28). On divorce and remarriage Jesus has some harsh things to say. We will examine how this teaching can be interpreted from the rule-oriented approach to moral decision making.

Within rabbinical teaching at the time of Jesus, we find three positions on the matter of divorce and remarriage. They can be identified as the strict, the moderate, and the liberal. In Mark 10:2–9, Jesus is asked if a man may divorce his wife. He asks in turn what Moses' command was. The questioner responds that Moses allowed a divorce as long as the man presented a certificate of dismissal (the moderate position). Jesus' response was that Moses allowed that because of the people's hardness of heart. He then refers to the teaching of Genesis—what God had joined together no one should separate (the strict position). In this exchange Jesus took the strict position rather than the moderate one. The liberal perspective on divorce stated that a man could dismiss his wife if she displeased him. Burning the meat was sufficient cause.

When the disciples later asked Jesus about his teaching on divorce and remarriage (Mark 10:10–11), Jesus tells them that the man who divorces his wife and marries another commits adultery. (In verse 12 he turns this teaching around and says that the woman who divorces her husband and marries another also commits adultery. It is highly unlikely that this teaching was Jesus' own. In the Jewish society at the time of Jesus, a woman could not divorce her husband. Mark must have added this in light of the practice among the Gentiles.) Matthew complicates this teaching by adding an *exception clause*. In Matthew 5:32 Jesus first refers to the law of Moses and then says, "But I say to you that anyone who divorces his wife, *except in the case of unchastity*, causes her to commit adultery; and whoever marries a divorced woman commits adultery."

This exception clause in Matthew has caused the Christian church no little problem. Protestant churches on the whole allow divorce and remarriage based on the exception clause. The Catholic tradition, on the other hand, has held that divorce and remarriage is forbidden for those who have been baptized and have properly celebrated the sacrament of marriage.[3] (An *annulment* of a marriage in the Catholic tradition means that convincing evidence is presented to a church court that a *sacramental marriage* never in fact was effected. For some identifiable reason—for example the psychological inability of one or both of the parties to make a permanent commitment—the couple never became "one in mind, one in heart, and one in affection." The indissoluble sacramental union was absent from the beginning.)

The Orthodox tradition, which like the Catholic tradition looks upon marriage as a sacrament, allows a second marriage if unfaithfulness occurred in the first marriage. A famous case of an ecumenical dilemma arose between the Catholic church and the Greek Orthodox church a few years ago when Jacqueline Kennedy and Aristotle Onassis wanted to be married. Jacqueline Kennedy, a Roman Catholic, was free to marry in the Catholic church because her husband, John Kennedy, was dead. Aristotle Onassis, a Greek Orthodox, was free to marry in the Orthodox Church because infidelity occurred in his first marriage. Both were free to marry in their respective churches; both churches recognize the validity of each other's sacrament of marriage, and yet the couple were not free to marry each other. The Catholic church would not recognize that Onassis was free to marry because his first wife was still living.

Cardinal Cushing, the archbishop of Boston, and a close friend of the Kennedy family, told Jacqueline Kennedy to go ahead and marry Onassis in the Greek Orthodox church. Other Catholic church leaders protested Cardinal Cushing's advice to such an extent that the ever-colorful Cushing even threatened to resign. Jacqueline Kennedy did marry Aristotle Onassis in the Greek Orthodox church, and the cardinal did not resign. Although his pastoral decision didn't please the canon lawyers, it solved the dilemma caused by the pesky exception clause in Matthew's gospel.

In the New Testament it is Paul who speaks most on the question of sexual morality. In the first chapter of his letter to the Romans, he decries those who have given up worship of the true God

> for images resembling a human being or birds or four-footed animals....Therefore God gave them up to degrading passions. Their women exchanged natural intercourse for unnatural, and in the same way also the men, giving up natural intercourse with women, were consumed with passion for one another. Men committed shameless acts with men and received in their own persons the due penalty for their error. (Romans 1:23–27)

Paul's first letter to the Corinthians (6:9–10) lists among those who will not inherit the Kingdom, fornicators, adulterers, male prostitutes, and sodomites. Again in Galatians 5:19 fornication and impurity are included among the works of the flesh. Paul makes use of catalogues of vices (and virtues) that were common in the Greco-Roman world. Those who are *biblicists* and follow the rule-oriented approach to moral decision making point to these passages as God's unchanging law condemning homosexuality.

Those who are *doctrinalists* and employ the rule-oriented approach to moral decision making will look to the teachings of the church as the sure norm. The authority given to Peter and the apostles to bind and loose (Matthew 16:19 and 18:18) has been passed on to the pope and the bishops to teach authoritatively in matters of faith and morals. Although the official teaching of the Catholic church on human sexuality is rooted in the goal-oriented approach (the natural law should be evident to everyone on this matter), still those following the rule-oriented approach would insist that artificial means of birth control and related sexual issues are wrong because the pope, following the teaching of his predecessors, has declared that they are wrong. To belong to the Catholic church, they say, means you follow its rules. When Rome speaks on a matter, the question is settled. While conscience is the ultimate norm, the task of the individual is to bring his or her conscience into line with the thinking of the church. "Church" in this instance is understood as the hierarchy. This outlook has led one moral theologian, schooled in this perspective to the extreme, to declare that a condom *in itself* is evil—intrinsically evil—whereas a nuclear bomb could be good in itself if used as a deterrent.

Strengths and Weaknesses of the Rule-oriented Approach

The strength of the rule-oriented approach is that it makes moral right or wrong very clear and explicit for people. Moral doubt exists only for those who refuse to listen and obey. Its weakness is its tendency to reduce the moral life to a juridically determined list of dos and don'ts. There is a danger that the Bible will be reduced to a fundamentalistically interpreted rule book and the gift of leadership in the church reduced to juridical and legalistic decisions of a patriarchal hierarchy.

There certainly is a place for norms, laws, and commandments in the faith community. But moral decision making based primarily on rules can produce a self-righteousness on the one hand ("I've kept all these rules, now you owe me, God") or a moral minimalism on the other ("How far can I go before I break the law?" or "How much do I have to do to fulfill the law?") The latter is contrary to the gospel maximalism that challenges us as disciples of Jesus to go the extra mile, give the shirt as well as the coat, turn the other cheek, and love even our enemies.

What Is the Relational/Responsible Approach to Moral Decision Making and What Are Its Strengths and Weaknesses?

Humans are by nature relational beings. They come to be who they are through dialogue and sharing. From the very beginning of life, relationships exist that call and invite us to respond, and, little by little, we grow in our ability to respond. We are "response-*able*" so to speak. For the newborn the dialogue begins with facial and vocal imitations of the parent or caregiver. Words and the naming of things follow—"Dada," "Mama," "eye," "nose," "toe." Moral decision making takes place in the ever-expanding world of relationships and responsibilities that constitute community. When parents come home in the evening and are greeted by their child who proudly announces, "I shared, Mommy," or "I shared, Daddy," an important step toward the moral life has taken place. From the world of "mine"—"my book," "my ball," "my house," "my Dad"—the child begins to realize that the gift of giving, of sharing, of loving, is the way to become truly a member of the human family.

There are a variety of relationships in which we are invited and called to participate. Most obviously we have a relationship with other human beings. From the faith perspective, of course, we are invited and called into a relationship with God, and for Christians this relationship comes through Jesus Christ in the power of the Holy Spirit. Also, in a unique way, we humans have a relationship with ourselves. We are not only aware, but we are aware of ourselves being aware. We can, figuratively speaking, step outside of ourselves and take a look at ourselves. Statements like, "There I go again!" "Isn't that just like me?" or "I can't believe myself!" indicate this *self*-awareness or the relationship we have with ourselves. Statements from others such as, "He was his own worst enemy," or "She needs to pull herself together" also indicate this relationship we have with ourselves.

There is much truth in the little description of salvation as "being at home." The word salvation itself comes from the Latin word *salus,* meaning health or wholeness. If we can be at home with others (socialization), and be at home with ourselves (self-integration), then we will be at home with God (salvation). Here we have an example of the need for moral theology to be in dialogue with the human sciences, in this case sociology and psychology. If we can't get along with others and be at peace with ourselves, how can we hope to be at home with God? Saint Irenaeus of Lyons, a great second-century theologian and church leader, expressed the idea of salvation as full humanity in the phrase, "The glory of God is the human person fully alive."

In addition to the relationships we have with God, ourselves, and others, we humans have a relationship with the earth, the cosmos—all of God's creatures and all of God's creation. We are part of the "stuff" of the universe, and therefore we have a responsibility in relationship to it. If the origin of the cosmos began with God's "big bang" and if we all have our roots in that initial "star dust," if we humans—with our senses, minds, and wills—*are* the earth seeing, knowing, and loving, and if, according to God's infinite wisdom, in the fullness of time God chose to become one with us in Jesus Christ our true brother, then our relational responsibility to the land, the air, the water, and all of God's creatures is vital. Because of our belief in the full humanity of Jesus Christ—that in him God's gracious invitation to friendship and our response was complete, that in him spirit and matter became one in a unique and irreversible way—the Christian perspective on environmental matters includes a moral responsibility. Not only is our focus on theological anthropology (God in relationship to us humans) but on theological cosmology (God in relationship to the material world of which we are a part).[4]

These relationships involve a mutuality that leads to interdependence and reliability. At the same time, the way and extent of our responding changes as our situations change. The child's dependence on parents may be reversed when the child reaches adulthood and the parents old age. Likewise a child's relationship to God should mature as the child grows. The relationship between husband and wife changes as their marriage matures and their responsibilities vary. The same can be said about our relationship to ourselves and to nature. All of our relationships change, and we can change them. We have that freedom, and it is out of that freedom that moral responsibility arises. As will be discussed later, our freedom as human beings is limited. Still, by our free choices in particular situations, we determine the person we are and are going to be.

The relational/responsible method of moral decision making is closely related to the correlative method in foundational theology. Functioning out of this approach, we attempt to correlate the message and the values that have come to us through the community of faith, with the moral situations that present themselves within our relationships in everyday living. This dialogue includes prayerful consideration of sacred Scripture and the lived-experience or Tradition of the church, as well as consideration of our own life experience. In attempting to respond to the responsibilities found in various relationships, we make our moral decisions. All of the circumstances of each moral decision must be taken into account in judging the right thing to do. The analysis used in the process of determining the objective moral rightness or wrongness of actions when our obligations and responsibilities conflict with each other is called *proportionate reason* or *proportionalism*. More will be said about this and about *values* and *norms* in chapter nine.

Most moral theologians today work out of the relational/responsible method of moral decision making, or one closely related to it. The relational/responsible method is the one that will be developed in the following chapters. The Roman Catholic church uses this approach in formulating its social teaching.[5] Reflecting the method used in the Vatican II document *The Church in the Modern World,* the relational/responsible approach attempts to read the signs of the times and interpret them in light of the gospel. The goal-oriented approach, however, continues to dominate in the Catholic hierarchy's official teaching on human sexuality, as is evidenced in recent papal teaching, Pope John Paul II's *The Splendor of Truth*[6] (1993), and in *The Catechism of the Catholic Church*[7] (1992).

The *human person* in the relational/responsible approach is one who is always seen as responding (or refusing to respond) within relationships. The person comes to be who he or she is through dialogue and sharing within community. The person has the freedom to determine the person he or she will be.

Sin is turning in on oneself, refusing to respond to the invitation or call to our various relationships. Sin is selfishness. It is saying no to full humanity, to the salvation to which we have been invited.

The *law* from this perspective is the cumulative wisdom of the faith community that enables and requires us to develop our personal and social responsibilities. It is a type of road map that indicates the general route to human fulfillment or salvation, but also allows for the exercise of human freedom in choosing, and for detours in case a particular path is closed to us.

To observe how the relational/responsible approach to moral decision making operates, let us turn again to the question of human sexual intercourse. We shall use a hypothetical situation for our example.

A happily married couple is entering the later years of the wife's childbearing period. They have five children, two in college, two in high school, and one in junior high. The woman is told by her doctor that because of her age and certain health problems it would be most unwise for her to have another child. The husband too has been experiencing some health problems. The parents of both spouses are alive and living independently, although they require a growing amount of the couple's attention and care. The couple has always had a happy and fruitful sexual relationship in their marriage. The woman had missed her period twice during the past six months, and both times the couple was terrified that they might be pregnant. They had tried natural family planning early in their marriage and it just had not worked for them. After long discussions about their own love relationship, about the obligations they have for their children's education and their parents' care, and at the urging of their doctor, the couple decided to begin using artificial contraception. They know there is a controversy about contraception in their church, but after talking with their pastor and after prayerful reflection on the values they cherish in their many relationships, including their church, they decide that their action does not sever their relationship and friendship with God, or cut them off from their deeply involved life in their church.

Many Catholic couples have made the decision that every act of sexual intercourse need not be open to procreation. The "act itself" should be viewed in the context of their whole marriage relationship and their attempt to respond in a loving way to each other and to the others for whom they have responsibility.[8] The danger, of course, is one of selfishness. Are they as a couple unwilling to take on the responsibility of another child? Is the husband or wife selfish in wanting his or her own satisfaction without any responsibility? Contraception for many Christians is accepted as part of married life today, and the whole discussion above may seem superfluous. However, it does help answer the question, "How can so many Catholic couples practice birth control when the hierarchy of the Catholic church says it is contrary to nature, and the pope has condemned it?" The way one approaches moral decision making, the method one uses, will affect the outcome. (The above example could have been told relating to a couple's decision for the wife to have a tubal ligation or the husband a vasectomy.)

The relational/responsible approach also is used by moral theologians in approaching related sexual issues, such as in vitro fertilization, abortion, masturbation, and homosexual relationships. Many moral theologians would find that joining the husband's sperm and the wife's egg in a petri dish, and then transferring the fertilized egg or zygote into the uterus of the wife, is morally acceptable in certain situations.[9] It is interesting that Pope John Paul I, who reigned only thirty-three days in 1978 and then died, was alive at the time the first "test tube" baby was born in England. The pope sent the parents of "baby Doe" a note of congratulations. When other Vatican officials protested his action his reply was, "But they have a baby!" That the parents did not conceive the child in the "natural" way did not seem to upset this humble successor of Peter.

Using donated eggs or sperm or surrogate parents raises a totally different number of issues regarding relationships and responsibilities. The disposition of the additional eggs—which have been removed from the woman's ovaries and also fertilized, in case the first implant is not successful—raises the question as to when *human* life begins. The official Catholic position is that we do not know and therefore we must respect life *as human* from the moment of conception. Others would argue that *human* life does not begin until the fertilized egg is implanted in the uterus wall. Still other argue that this beginning life cannot be identified as *human* for twelve to fourteen days after implantation. Up until this time the single fertilized egg can split in two and become identical twins. It is difficult to argue that one *human person* (the fertilized egg) becomes two *human persons* (identical twins) and still maintain that each individual is uniquely gifted with an immortal soul. These latter two perspectives have implications on the abortion question and the so-called "morning after pill," especially as related to victims of rape.

Thomas Aquinas had a still different perspective on the time of "ensoulment" or the time when the fetus can be declared human. He taught that the human soul was present at the time of "quickening" or the time when the woman feels the presence of the fetus in the womb. A biblical reference would be Luke 1:41, when Mary went to visit her cousin Elizabeth. "When Elizabeth heard Mary's greeting, the child leaped in her womb." Luke says Elizabeth was in her sixth month of pregnancy. The usual time for this quickening or movement that shows signs of life of the fetus within the womb is eighteen weeks or halfway through the second trimester. Aquinas was working out of the thirteenth century's limited knowledge of fetal development, of course, but his philosophical reasoning was solid. A being must be capable of receiving that which is given. If, as Aquinas thought, the intellect and the will are the distinguishing characteristics of the human being, and if the brain is the center of rational and volitional activity, then the basic formation of the cortex and spinal column had to be present before the fetus could be considered human. The Catholic church did not follow Aquinas on this teaching. Today it argues that all that is necessary for later development of the human is present in the fertilized egg.

Concerning the matter of homosexuality, the responsible/relational approach would proceed as follows. Constituted homosexuality, the discovery and realization at the deepest level of the human person that one is oriented to those of the same sex, is morally neutral. The exact origin of this orientation is not known. There is research suggesting a genetic rather than a psychological or environmental origin. Regardless, in this situation the person does not choose to be homosexual. Anyone can engage in homosexual activity, but that does not constitute that person as a homosexual. No one can cause a person to be a homosexual.

It is homosexual genital activity that raises moral questions. The response to this activity from the goal-oriented and rule-oriented approaches has been discussed above. The approach under discussion here will place the matter within the context of relationship and responsibility. Some moral theologians argue that the morality of homosexual activity between consenting adults rests on the quality of the relationship. Because constituted homosexuals are oriented toward one another not by choice but by "nature," it is their way of being human. Therefore, the morality of homosexual acts must be judged in the same way that heterosexual acts are judged.

Other moral theologians working out of the relational/responsible approach insist that heterosexual relationships are the normative ideal. The human family is perpetuated through these relationships. From the time of the creation of man and woman God has blessed the heterosexual union and it is within such union that human sexuality finds its fulfillment. However, for homosexuals this ideal is not possible. Therefore, although less than the ideal, for homosexuals in a loving and mutually giving relationship that shows signs of permanency, homosexual activity may not be wrong; it may even be grace-filled.[10]

Concerning masturbation, the relational/responsible approach would judge that such acts are incomplete as far as a relationship to others is concerned. As the saying goes, the trouble with masturbating is that you don't meet very many interesting people in the process. Still in one's relationship to oneself, it is not seen as a grave evil, as it is judged in the goal-oriented and rule-oriented approaches. In dialogue with the sciences, many theologians have come to accept masturbation as part of the developmental process of growing up. Especially during adolescence masturbation should be judged within the context of the various relationships and responsibilities with which young people are being challenged. Masturbation could be a sign of more serious problems if the young person is turned in on himself or herself, refusing to enter into relationships with adults and peers, and not responding to others in kind and helpful ways.

At any age obsessive and compulsive masturbation may be a sign of sexual addiction, which is as crippling to relationships and responsibilities as any other addiction. Professional help is needed in such cases. Masturbation at times of loneliness, tension, or discouragement may be nothing more than a premoral disvalue (this term will be discussed in chapter nine). Few moral theologians today would consider masturbation a mortal sin that completely ruptures one's relationship with God. To train a youngster (as some in the church once did) to think that every act of masturbation amounts to thrusting a dagger into the neck of Jesus is not only sad, it is sick.

The strengths of the relational/responsible method of moral decision making are that it is open to dialogue with the evolving understanding of the human person as a relational being, while still respecting the wisdom of the lived experience of the faith community. It recognizes that in light of the various relationships in which people find themselves, and the opportunity and the demand of the many responses called for, at times there may have to be compromises. It has a healthy respect for the freedom to which Christ has called us, and sees conscience as the final arbiter in the moral life. Its openness to dialogue with the world makes it able to deal with increasingly complex moral issues. It is a method that can be used in the areas of both personal and social morality.

The weaknesses of the relational/responsible approach to moral decision making are its appearance of promoting moral relativism and its seeming lack of respect for the authority of both the church and the Bible. Its perspective on the human person is perhaps too optimistic. There may be insufficient emphasis on the weakness of humans due to sin. Because of the emphasis on relationships, the matter of certain acts being *intrinsically evil* may be overlooked. This and related issues will be examined in succeeding chapters.

Questions for Reflection and Discussion

1. "'Good' Christians disagree on basic moral questions because of the particular method they use in moral decision making." Do you agree with that statement? How would you explain it to a friend?

2. The strict or narrow understanding of natural law as it is employed in the goal-oriented approach has brought the accusation that a *physicalism* or *biologism* dominates such thinking. What is your reaction to that? Explain.

3. The rule-oriented approach is based on a pessimistic perspective on the human person due to original sin. From a scientific evolutionary perspective on the cosmos, how would you explain the *truth* behind the garden story in the book of Genesis?

4. Why must the historical and cultural context in which the Bible was written be taken into consideration when applying specific biblical moral prohibitions to contemporary moral problems? Give examples.

5. Some would say that the *relational/responsible* approach to moral decision making is an "easy way out"; it denies that there are any moral absolutes; it promotes *relativism*. How would you respond to

these accusations? Is sin as *selfishness* an adequate way to describe our moral failings?

Suggestions for Further Reading

Curran, Charles E. "Method in Moral Theology: An Overview from an American Perspective," in *Introduction to Christian Ethics: A Reader,* eds. Ronald P. Hamel and Kenneth R. Himes. New York: Paulist Press, 1989, pp. 90–104.

Curran, Charles and Richard McCormick, eds. *Readings in Moral Theology No. 8: Dialogue About Catholic Sexual Teaching.* New York: Paulist Press, 1993. See especially, Bernard Häring, "The Inseparability of the Unitive-Procreative Functions of the Marital Act," pp. 153–167; John P. Boyle, "Church Teaching on Sterilization," pp. 177–200; John Mahoney, "Human Fertility Control," pp. 251–266; Margret A. Farley, "An Ethic for Same-Sex Relations," pp. 330–346; and Anthony Kosnik, et al. "Masturbation," pp. 349–360.

Macquarrie, John. *Three Issues in Ethics.* New York: Harper & Row, 1970. See Chapter 4, "Rethinking Natural Law," pp. 82–100. Also found in *Moral Theology No. 7: Natural Law and Theology*, ed. Charles E. Curran and Richard A. McCormick. New York: Paulist Press, 1991, pp. 121–145.

McCormick, Richard A. *The Critical Calling: Reflections on Moral Dilemmas Since Vatican II.* Washington, DC: Georgetown University Press, 1989. See especially chapter 17, "Homosexuality as a Moral and Pastoral Problem," pp. 290–314, and chapter 19, "Therapy or Tampering? The Ethics of Reproductive Technology and the Development of Doctrine," pp. 329–352.

Chapter Eight

A Shift in Moral Theology: From Act to Agent; From Agent to Subject

When my brother was about seven years old, or so my mother told me, he drove a big nail into the side of the old upright piano because, he said, he wanted somewhere to hang his cap. My mother was beside herself. She chastised him, took the cap, and sent him to his room. In a little while down the stairs he came, suitcase in hand, and wearing one of Dad's old hats. He announced that he was leaving home. Mother said that if he continued to act the way he had been, perhaps it was best. She did, however, offer to fix a sandwich for him to take along. He refused.

Out the front door he went, down the steps from the porch, down the walk, through the gate, and along the road leading into town. Mother watched from the dining room window. When he came to the corner he stopped, looked down the long hill leading into town, looked back at the house, kicked a few rocks into the ditch, then turned on his heel and came up the road, through the gate, and onto the porch. He opened the door, threw open his arms, and with a big smile said, "I've decided to give you another chance!"

In this chapter we will discuss some difficult moral concepts—fundamental option, grace, and sin. In the story of my "prodigal son" brother, we have in miniature form the seeds of these issues—the basic orientation and direction of one's life within various relationships (fundamental option), the strain that is put on that option and those relationships by our shortcomings (sin), and an understanding that loving relationships are not easily broken (God's grace; a mother's love). As you read the chapter see if you can identify the parallels.

Why Does Contemporary Moral Theology Focus on the Human Person?

One of the most significant statements of the Second Vatican Council concerned the basic understanding of reality. In its document *The Church in the Modern World,* after the section on how the history of the human family has become one, we read, "Thus, the human race has passed from a rather static concept of reality to a more dynamic, evolutionary one" (no. 5). Rather than looking at reality as something fixed into which we humans are to fit, this statement implies that humans participate in the continuing creation of the world. One way of picturing this is to ask what we understand by perfection. In the classical understanding of God, perfection was one of the descriptive characteristics of the divine. God, being perfect, never changes. Change would imply imperfection, and in God there is only perfection. God is immutable. Any kind of movement in God is impossible. God is at rest.

For us humans the perfection we hope for, according to this way of thinking, is reflected in our prayer for those who have died: "Eternal *rest* grant unto them, O Lord." The perfection of heaven is eternal rest. Nothing changes. While perfection as eternal rest may have been appealing to those whose lives were spent in servitude, today the question that would arise, especially among young people, would be, "You mean in heaven there isn't going to be anything to *do*? How boring!"

Today perfection is looked upon in a dynamic way. It is creative. God, as some have said, is a "verb." God is love, the first letter of John tells us (1 John 4:8, 16), and love is dynamic. Imagine the following conversation between lovers.

"Do you love me?"

"Look, I'll write down in twenty-five words or less how I love you; you do the same."

The following day: "Do you love me?"

"I thought we settled that. Please take out and read what you have written, and I'll do the same."

Love is not like that. Neither is God; nor is our understanding of perfection or reality.

From this new perspective of a dynamic understanding of reality, we humans are most like God in an act of creative love. This is most evident when husband and wife join with God in a loving act of procreation. A new being comes into existence destined for immortality. Creative love is present in a Christian couple's entire sacramental life of marriage, mirroring, as St. Paul tells us, Christ's love for his people, the church. The consecrated life of those men and women who dedicate themselves to the life of perfection in religious communities is also a reflection of God's creative love. Deep and abiding friendships are signs of God's perfection as well. Creative love as a sign of God's perfection is also revealed in works of art—the classics of literature, poetry, music, and sculpture, as well as in folk art and artifacts.

We humans are responsible for our own histories as well as the history of the universe. When humans appeared in the long evolutionary process, they began little by little to participate in that process, and—through imagination and reason, science and technology—more and more they came to direct it. Today, we have the ability to destroy life as we know it here on the earth. But we also have a growing awareness of our responsibility to preserve it. The shift that has taken place in moral theology from a cosmological to an anthropological worldview recognizes the active rather than passive role that we humans have in the future of our world. No longer is it just a matter of *acting* according to fixed laws and structures of the world "out there." It is a matter of *being* and exercising creative freedom in the evolutionary process of which we are a part. The human person can be seen as the universe having reached the stage, through evolution's marvel of differentiation and complexity, that allows one to consciously see, hear, know, and love. Therefore, in contemporary moral theology, the focus is on the human being as a *person,* not just an *agent* or one who acts. Individual acts pass, but the person remains. Personhood is the basis of moral responsibility. We do not change from moment to moment or from act to act. It is on the level of person that we are held responsible for our actions. Contemporary moral theology demands that we must examine the human person, not just the rightness or wrongness of the acts that the human person performs.

Why Do We Distinguish Between the "Outer" and the "Inner" Level of the Human Person?

While the human person is one—a unity of matter and spirit—it is worthwhile for the sake of discussion to distinguish between the *inner* and *outer* levels of the person. In this exercise we must guard against any dualism, judging, for example, that the spiritual is higher and more valuable than the material or the bodily. Our exercise, however, should help us understand and clarify the complexity of the human person. We cannot see the "person" or personhood of the individual; we only see the "acts" the person performs. But the acts reveal the person. We will examine here the differences between the outer level (the level of actions) and the inner level (the level of person). A chart may be helpful. (See pages 177–178.)

The distinctions shown in the chart will be useful as we examine sin and grace as affecting the whole person, and one's fundamental option as an expression of one's core freedom. Still it should be emphasized once again that there is no dualism intended here. The human person does not exist apart from the human as agent.

The Human Person[1]

The Outer Level

1. You are a particular instance of a universal category. At the most universal level you are male or female. You may be a college student, a biology major, and twenty-one years old. So are a lot of other people.

2. You can be categorized according to the different roles you play: you may be a college student, history major, tennis player, part-time waitress, and a single parent.

3. You are a "doer" on the outer level. You exercise reality through action. These actions can be observed. At times your actions do not reflect the person you really are. People may tell you that you are stupid or uncaring, or worthless just because you cannot perform some task in sports, in the classroom, or at work. You may act as the comic or the cut-up to be accepted, but it really is not you.

The Inner Level

1. You are absolutely unique. There is no one else in the world exactly like you. Even if you are an identical twin, the two of you are distinct.

2. You have a unity. As a person you are a unified whole. You may say you are a different person on the tennis court or at work than you are in the classroom, but you know deep down that you are the same person.

3. You are a "be-er." You exercise reality by being. At the inner level, beneath the level of objective actions, is the level of feelings, ideas, desires, and hopes. Here attitudes, outlook, virtues, and vices have their effect. You may be a hopeful person; you may be a deceitful person. At the very depths of your being is the person you are.

The Outer Level	The Inner Level
4. On the outer level you can change your life readily. You may drop out of school, give up tennis, quit your job, give your child up for adoption, or get married.	4. On the inner level you can change the person you are but not easily and not without time and effort. You have a historical breadth. You are shaped by your past as you live in the present and hope for the future.
5. You are an object of knowledge. Through observation and investigation a profile can be made of you and shared with others. This can be done even without your permission. After compiling the information the claim could be made that you are now known through and through. And yet that knowledge is only partial. You could respond, "You do not know me, and furthermore you are not going to get to know me because I will not let you."	5. You are a subject at the inner level. Subjectivity and complexity make it impossible for you to be the direct object of knowledge at this level. You can only be known if you allow yourself to be known. This comes as you choose to disclose or reveal yourself to another. (The great theologian Karl Barth held that God is absolute subject. God is knowable to us only through God's gracious self-disclosure. It is impossible to know God from the outside, from the objective point of view.) As a human being you can be known partially from the outside as an object of knowledge, but as a subject you also have a mysterious side to you, never completely knowable.
6. Freedom on the outer level is your *freedom of choice*. When we think of freedom this is usually what comes to mind. It is, however, a limiting freedom. When you choose one option you eliminate others. You can decide to get up in the morning or stay in bed. You cannot choose to do both at the same time.	6. Freedom on the inner level is the freedom to choose who you are. It is not a matter of choosing this or that, but is the freedom to be. It is an "opening" freedom. It is not limited. It is your *fundamental* or *core freedom*.

Personhood is realized in and through particular choices, although no single choice determines the "person" one is. Our core freedom is exercised in and through our freedom of choice. The challenge of the moral life is to live as authentic Christians, having our actions (the outer level) "ringing true" to the person we are (inner level).

What Do We Mean by a Person's Fundamental Option?

The phrase *fundamental option* is used in moral theology today, following the theological anthropology of Karl Rahner. It is used to describe the basic orientation that humans develop in relationship to the deepest meaning and future of their lives. It is the answer to the question, "What do you really want?" when one is focused not on this or that choice, but on the choice of one's whole existence. Although it is difficult to describe in simple terms, it is something that humans sense in the depths of their being. It is our orientation toward good or evil, toward openness or selfishness, toward meaning or nothingness, toward grace or sin. It is our orientation toward or away from God. It is the exercise of our core freedom as described above; it is the self-disposition of who we really are.

Our fundamental option might be described as the background music in our lives. The particular themes that we play in day-to-day decisions and choices are either in harmony, or in dissonance, with the background music of our lives. The fundamental option underlies all the particular choices that we make. We deepen our fundamental option when we act in accord with it (presupposing that our fundamental option is for openness and goodness), or strain it when we act contrary to it. This understanding is valuable when we turn to the matter of sin and grace.

How Is Our Fundamental Option Related to Sin and Grace?

From what we have been discussing, it should be clear that in the relational/responsible approach to moral decision making the human being as person takes priority over the human being as actor. What we *are* is more important than what we *do* or *don't do*.

Sin and grace ultimately refer to our core freedom, to the very person we are. *Mortal sin,* to use the traditional term, is deadly serious. It is, as its Latin root, *mors,* indicates, sin unto *death.* Grace is God's offer and invitation that enables us to enter into a loving relationship with God and others through Jesus in the power of the Spirit. Through grace and the practice of virtue, we are able to reach our full humanity—salvation. Grace, too, is deadly serious from the point of view of our ultimate future, but also from the point of view of responding to those other relationships that we have in both the private and political realm. God's grace is universal. God's self-offer as love is available to everyone, and is experienced by anyone who lives in faithfulness to the truth found in the depth of the heart. From the Christian perspective such a person's life is graced by God in Christ whether he or she is consciously aware of it or not.

Both mortal sin and grace involve the whole person and affect the whole person. They are the exercise of core freedom in determining who we are. From this perspective it is difficult to identify mortal sin with the doing of one specific act. Can one specific choice or action on the outer level change completely the orientation and direction of one's life? Whether one's fundamental option can be changed in this way will be discussed later.[2] If mortal sin is not to be identified with doing a specific act, still it never occurs apart from specific acts. One cannot *be* oriented away from goodness and toward evil without having *done* evil acts.

Because mortal sin (or grace) affects our inner self, our core freedom, we cannot have any objective knowledge of our moral condition. We cannot be examined or tested and then show objective proof that we are either grace-filled or morally corrupt. Certainly our outer actions give an indication of our moral condition, but final judgment has to be left to God, who can see the secrets of the heart.

If we cannot be objectively sure of our own moral condition, we are even less able to judge others. That does not mean that evil actions must be tolerated, but it does mean that the final disposition of each of us is in the hands of God. The church has never taught officially that any particular person is in hell. The church has declared that certain people deserve damnation, but final judgment cannot be made from the human perspective. The statement of Eugene Kennedy, a psychologist of religion, provides food for thought here: "If you could truly see into the heart of another person, you could never hold anything against him [or her]." We cannot see into the heart, but God can. God sees the hopes, fears, longings, disappointments, and desires, and judges us with love.

Mortal sin, the complete and persistent turning away from relationships and responsibilities, from the good, from God, is relatively rare. One does not *slip* into mortal sin; nor does one easily turn away from it. The question is often asked, "What if I try to be good all of my life and then just before I die commit a mortal sin and go to hell?" According to the relational/responsible perspective that is not going to happen. One cannot say this absolutely, because that would be presumption, but the life of moral goodness brings us into loving relationships, and relationships are not established or broken in a single instance. Our moral life is not like trying to walk down the single rail of a train track—if one walks long enough one is bound to fall. Rather, it is like growth in love within a friendship or marriage relationship that is open and mutual. Freedom grows with commitment and opens us to a sure future. God is not about to let us go after a life of trusting love that overflows in loving acts toward others.

The same is true of turning away from sin and selfishness. It is not usually a simple decision of the moment from the relational/responsible perspective. Let us use an example here of one who is caught in the life of addiction. We are not saying a life of addiction is a life of sin in a particular instance—biochemical and other reasons need to be considered—but the characteristics and the end of a life of addiction can be compared to the life of sin. Whether the addiction is to drugs or drink or gambling or sex, the person finds himself or herself compromising on responsibilities within various relationships. A parent forgets to pick up his or her youngster after softball practice. One is short-tempered with one's spouse or friends. Work begins to suffer from lack of attention. One becomes more secretive and turned in on oneself. Relationships begin to crumble. One is caught in a living hell and headed toward death.

That is what the life of sin is like. It affects one's whole being and whole life. One may "hit bottom" and realize that things must change—like the prodigal son in the gospel who "came to his senses" after a life of debauchery in which he finally found himself scrounging for food among the pigs. The gospel story shows the father (representing God) running out and welcoming the wayward child with no questions asked. The offer of God's reconciling love is always present. God's love is beyond our comprehension. But the prodigal son still had to deal with all those other relationships that had been compromised or broken. That the older brother coming in from the field refused to enter into the celebration of the return of his lost brother is just a small indication of the relationships that had to be healed. The one who turns from an addiction does so painfully. Some of the relationships may be broken beyond healing. But little by little, as one picks up the pieces and tries to put them together again, a new life begins to open. Responding within relationships again become a joy. The life of grace surpasses all the pain of the life of sin.

In attempting to respond within our various relationships, we all realize that at times we fall short. In traditional terms such shortcomings are called *venial sin*. The word venial comes from the Latin word *venia*, which mean forgiveness. A venial sin is a forgivable or excusable sin. Traditionally it was defined as a "slight offense against God," either because the matter was not grave or because the offense was done without reflection or full consent. Within the relational/responsible perspective venial sin is seen as a refusal to respond as we ought within a relationship. Since all of our relationships reflect our ultimate relationship to God, we can say that such shortcomings compromise our fundamental option toward God, who is love; they strain our relationships with others as well as with God, but they do not sever such relationships. We choose to do or not do a particular act, but we do not become the type of person the act reflects. As St. Paul says in Romans 7:15, "For I do not do what I want, but I do the very thing I hate." We all are in need of the forgiveness and reconciliation that is offered to us through Christ. The life of Christian discipleship is one of constant conversion or renewal. Yet all of this takes place with the life of grace—that confident relationship that we have with God through Christ in the Holy Spirit, made visible in our baptism. Venial sin, our shortcomings in responding lovingly within our relationships, is always there, but grace, God's overwhelming love, abounds even more.

The distinction between mortal sin and venial sin depends on the degree of our personal involvement. In mortal sin we not only tell a lie, we become a person who is not truthful. We not only steal something, we become one who is not trustworthy. When one comes to matters affecting our deep, intimate relationships, we can see how an individual act may have far-reaching consequences. If a person is unfaithful in a marriage relationship even once, although that person may not become an adulterer in his or her very person, the strain on the relationship, the rupture of the bond of trust and responsibility, can deeply affect both the relationship and the persons involved. Some theologians suggest that in addition to mortal sin (the deadly breaking off of relationships and the turning of the whole self toward selfishness and evil) and venial sin (the compromises in our relationships that strain but do not sever them), there should be a third category—gravely serious sin. While this sin may not sever our relationship to God and to others, the gravity of the offense is such that those relationships are ruptured and call for considerable time, effort, and grace to be reconciled and healed. God always forgives, but also deals with us through our relationships.

Young people sometimes argue that God will not send them to hell for having sex with their girlfriend or boyfriend (as long as there is love present!). One would hope that such an action would not break completely one's relationship with God. But in the relational/responsible approach, consideration also should be given to the stability of the relationship and whether sex merely is being used as recreation—there is nothing good on TV so…. Outside of a permanent commitment can one be sure of a true mutuality in the relationship? The old song, "You were only fooling, while I was falling in love," may have more truth in it than many would like to admit.

The following question was asked in Ann Landers' advice column: "I am a twenty-four-year-old liberated woman. I have been living with my boyfriend for the past year and a half. I am on the pill, and it is quite expensive. I think my boyfriend should share the costs but I don't know him well enough to discuss finances. What should I do?" Such a situation is not one of liberation, but of slavery! What kind of a relationship exists here? Premarital sex also raises those thorny questions about other relationships and responsibilities the couple may have with parents and grandparents, siblings, and with their faith communities.

The relational/responsible approach to moral decision making is not an easy way out. It shifts the discussion away from some abstract understanding of natural law in the goal-oriented approach (right or wrong is constituted within the act itself), or from some outside-imposed authority in the rule-oriented approach (right or wrong is determined by authoritative command), to relationships and our attempt to respond lovingly within those relationships as a part of a faith community. When conflict situations arise within our relationships, situations when a number of responses are called for and all of them cannot possibly be met, decisions involving compromise must be faced. That will be discussed in Chapter Ten. But first we must consider those things that may stand in the way or hinder our freedom to act in a morally responsible way—*impediments* and *the stages of moral development*.

Questions for Reflection and Discussion

1. How does the dynamic understanding of human existence affect theology and the role and responsibility of humans in relationship to all of creation? What does it mean that we no longer perceive ourselves as *actors* on a fixed "world stage," where all rights and wrongs are predetermined, but *subjects* or *persons* called to exercise creative freedom in shaping the future of our world?

2. Does the distinction between the *outer* and *inner* levels of the

human person "ring a bell" with your own experience? Have you experienced in your own life the challenge of being *authentic* by striving to have your outer self truly reflect your inner self, as well as the other way around? Can you give examples?

3. How would you explain to someone your *fundamental option*? Does this term help in understanding the exercise of your *core freedom*? Does the mystery of *grace* and the seriousness of *sin* make more sense when looked at from the perspective of one's fundamental option?

4. A number of years ago one of the leaders in the church made the statement, "Little children should confess their little mortal sins." What is your reaction to that? Explain.

5. How would you discuss the question of premarital sex from the relational/responsible perspective?

Suggestions for Further Reading

Carr, Anne E. "Starting with the Human," in *A World of Grace: An Introduction to the Themes and Foundations of Karl Rahner's Theology*, ed. Leo J. O'Donovan. New York: Crossroad, 1984, pp. 17–30.

Häring, Bernard. *Free and Faithful in Christ: Moral Theology for Clergy and Laity*. Vol.1. New York: Seabury Press, 1978. See pp. 189–218 for discussion of *fundamental option*.

Haught, John F. *The Promise of Nature: Ecology and Cosmic Purpose*. New York: Paulist Press, 1993. See especially chapter 1, "Ecology and Cosmic Purpose," pp. 11–38, and chapter 5, "Ecology and Human Destiny," pp. 113–42, for insights into *process theology* and a dynamic understanding of the universe.

McBrien, Richard P. *Catholicism: New Edition*. New York: HarperCollins, 1994. See chapter 5, "A Theology of Human Existence: Nature, Grace, Original Sin," pp. 157–199.

O'Connell, Timothy E. *Principles for a Catholic Morality*, rev. ed., New York: HarperCollins, 1990. See Part II: The Moral Person, esp. pp. 51–102, for discussion of the human as agent and person, and for a presentation of a theology of sin.

Chapter Nine

Human Freedom
and Its Limitations

Forthwith this frame of mine was wrenched
With a woeful agony,
Which forced me to begin my tale;
And then it left me free.

Since then, at an uncertain hour,
That agony returns:
And till my ghastly tale is told,
This heart within me burns.

Samuel Coleridge
from *The Rime of the Ancient Mariner*

Perhaps all of us have some type of an albatross that haunts us, like the ancient mariner had. Now I beg you to listen to mine.

It was a bitterly cold night in late December. I had been visiting my sister and her family and was on my way back home. The route was forty miles that wound its way up and down and around the gentle hills of Iowa farmland. As I came down into the valley where the old plank bridge crosses the Cedar River, the full moon brought my attention to the eeriness of the shadows on the ice and snow surrounding the dead trees in the flood plain adjacent to the river.

The ice was here, the ice was there,
The ice was all around:
It cracked and growled, and roared and howled,
Like noises in a swound!

As I started across the bridge, the floor creaked from the weight of the car on the planks, which had contracted because of the below zero temperature. Then, at the other end of the bridge, the headlights caught the reflection of the taillights of a car. It was a place where fishermen often parked, but no one in his or her right mind would be out here on a night like this. I slowed down as I passed the car and it appeared to be empty. Then as I glanced back in my rearview mirror I saw the turn signal flash from one side to the other. I slammed on the brakes and put the car into reverse.

As I backed up alongside the car a figure appeared, as if from nowhere, at the car window opposite me. I reached over and rolled down the window, at the same time thinking that this might be a diversion so someone could get me from the driver's side.

At length did cross an Albatross,
Through the fog it came;
As if it had been a Christian soul,
We hailed it in God's name.

"Can I give you some help?" I asked in a voice so loud that it even startled me. The man, dressed in a heavy denim jacket with a farmer's cap with the earflaps down, pointed to his head with his mitted hands and tapped it several times. "What is the matter?" I said in a louder voice. "Why won't you talk to me?" The man then began to lower his hands below the level of the window where I could see, and I thought, "He's going for a gun!" I put the car in gear and lunged forward not bothering to look back.

As I drove on at an accelerated speed I began to ponder what I had just experienced. Why was he there? Why wouldn't he talk to me? "I've got to tell someone," I thought. "He could freeze to death in no time if someone doesn't help him. Why did I leave him? What should I do?" I was entering a small town that the highway ran the length of, and I thought surely I would find someplace open. At the opposite end of the town I saw a filling station that was closed but had a light in the car repair area. Several men were there apparently working on a car. I pulled in and went up and pounded on the door. A fellow came to the door, and I blurted out what I had experienced. "There was this man by the river...He wouldn't talk to me...I left him." "You'd better come back and talk to the boss," he said. I did, and I told the whole story again, feeling smaller with each sentence I spoke. "We'd better contact the county sheriff," he said when I finished. The sheriff said I should wait there until he came. I stood by the door anxiously awaiting the sheriff's arrival. I wanted to go out to his car when he arrived. Most assuredly I didn't want to have to repeat the story in front of those men.

'Is it he?' quoth one, 'Is this the man?'
By him who died on cross,
With his cruel bow he laid full low
The harmless Albatross.

When the sheriff arrived and I began to relate the story, he stopped me about halfway through and said, "I know who you're talking about. His wife notified us that he hadn't come home from a farm sale. We picked him up. His car broke down. He's one of those, what do you call them, deaf and dumb?"

I got back into my car to continue my journey home. "He couldn't hear," I thought. "He couldn't speak. And I left him in that freezing cold. I left him! What must he have thought as my car sped away? What is that story that Jesus told? So many passed by the one who had fallen among robbers. Some good Samaritan I am."

What I experienced that night is what this chapter is about: human freedom and those things that stand in the way of our exercising it in a full and responsible way. Yes, I was afraid. But does that make the whole episode morally acceptable? At least you have listened to my story.

He prayeth well, who loveth well
Both man and bird and beast.

He prayeth best, who loveth best
All things both great and small;
For the dear God who loveth us,
He made and loveth all.

What Are Impediments,
and How Do They Affect Our Freedom To Act?

We are invited and commanded to enter into relationships. Invited because of God's gracious goodness in reaching out to us to share the very life of God. Commanded in the sense that we can reach our full human potential, become fully human, only in reaching out to others in dialogue and sharing. As humans we are not meant to be alone. As a human family we find our ultimate fulfillment in responding to God's invitation to the life of grace, to sharing in the life of God through Christ in the power of the Holy Spirit. This we are to do by reaching out and responding to those around us. The love of God and love of neighbor are mysteriously joined together.

To be a "response-*able*" people presupposes that we are free. It is only within the context of freedom that we can talk about moral goodness or evil, about virtue and grace or sin and selfishness. It is in freedom that we are able to make the choices that determine the person we are. The freedom with which we have been gifted by God is, however, a limited freedom. It is not free from influences or limits. Those freedom "blocks," which all humans have to some extent, are known as *impediments*.

Perhaps the most common block or impediment that hinders us in the moral life is fear. Not standing up for what is right or succumbing to what is wrong is often followed by, "I know, I should have...but I was afraid." Force or threat of force, ignorance, and prejudice are also common impediments. The way we were raised, our education, our family and cultural surroundings, often have built-in prejudices that we may not be consciously aware of until we are confronted with them in a specific situation. How many times do parents of minorities have to tell their children, "Don't pay any attention to what they say about you or how they treat you. Those people just don't know"?

When young people, after having been away from home for the first time and forced to interact with others of different races, religions, cultures, and ethnic backgrounds, return home to their families and neighborhoods, they often become starkly aware of the environment of prejudice in which they were raised. "My Dad, the way he talks about minorities. I had never noticed before. He wouldn't last long where I am now." Some impediments are related to personality structures, mental health, intellectual capacity, or personal history and experience. An example of an impediment resulting from personal history and experience may be helpful here.

Imagine someone growing up in a family where not only his or her basic needs are met, but whatever he or she may desire—money for nonessentials, the "in" clothing, recreation, entertainment—is given without question. In high school this person is deeply involved in sports or other extracurricular activities and has no time or need for part-time work. When this person is ready for college his or her parents establish a checking account for books, supplies, and other things students need. The student has never had to budget before, but a certain amount has been allocated by the parents for such needs. About six weeks into the semester the student writes or calls home and announces that more funds must be placed in the account.

"How could this be?" the parents ask. "That was supposed to last you a semester."

"But everybody goes out a lot," the student protests, "and we went to the mall, and there was like this really neat outfit..., and everyone is wearing these shoes..., and my roommate's microwave broke so..., will you please put in some more money? There is this rock concert coming up this weekend and...."

The young person in this example has acted irresponsibly. But he or she also has had no experience in handling and budgeting money. Another student who had to work during high school, who had his or her own bank account from junior high on from which anything "extra" came, would not have that same impediment of inexperience in handling personal finances. What the first student did was wrong and he or she was culpable, but the impediment of lack of experience must be taken into consideration in determining the indiscretion.

These freedom blocks may curtail our freedom in moral decision making and lessen our culpability, but they do not remove it. In the midst of all these impediments we still have the ability to express the person we are in the choices we make.

We can also look at these freedom blocks from a developmental point of view. Psychologists Erik Erikson and Lawrence Kohlberg have developed theories on the stages of moral development. Some of the freedom blocks or impediments that we discussed above are part of the normal development of the human from childhood to maturity. Responsibilities change as our relationships change, and both are related to our psychological, mental, social, and spiritual growth. Jean Piaget has done considerable work in the area of the stages of cognitive development, and James Fowler has made a contribution in the area of faith development. We shall limit ourselves here to Kohlberg's stages of moral development,[1] with a brief critique of his perspective by Carol Gilligan, a feminist psychologist of religion.

What Are the Stages of Moral Development and How Do They Affect Our Freedom To Act?

We are told by the depth psychologists that the earliest experience of autonomy that the infant has is when it is laid down by its parent or caregiver and then later picked up again. At first, the infant does not experience itself apart from its parent or caregiver. The first inkling of trust that is so necessary throughout our lives comes between the time when we are first placed alone and when we are later gathered up into caring arms and a loving relationship. Although the infant's earliest response may be instinctual and one of complete dependence, the mystery of love must already be at work. The growth in humanity, as was discussed earlier, begins with this early dialogue and sharing.

Prior to speaking about the *stages* of moral development, of which he enumerates six, Kohlberg identifies three broad *levels* or contexts of development—the *preconventional,* the *conventional,* and the *post-conventional.* The word conventional comes from the Latin word *con-venire,* which means "to come together." It expresses here that we are social beings, called into community, called into relationships.

The Preconventional level

The preconventional level identifies that period in the infant's life when its world is still centered on itself. Right and wrong, good and bad are understood in physical terms of either reward or punish-ment, or an exchange of favors in terms decided by the "big people" who have power and authority. This first level is divided into two stages.

Stage 1: What is wrong is what hurts.

Reward or punishment is what determines good or evil. Avoidance of punishment is why one behaves. A father may explain to a five-year-old all the reasons for not playing in the street. "You see that slight incline in the street. You see how short your legs are. If a car came up over that grade going forty miles an hour you couldn't get out of the way in time and pow! you would get hit. Furthermore, if I catch you out here in the street again it is going to be pow! and you are going to get a spanking! Do you understand?" The little child may shake his or her head in the affirmative, but what is understood is not car velocity or leg capacity but the parent's tone of voice and the threat of a spanking.

The earliest stage of moral development is the calculation of reward or punishment. As we grow through the various stages of moral development it is to be hoped that the basis of our moral deci-sion making progresses. But that is not to say that some people don't remain more or less at a particular stage all of their lives. At times all of us fall back on earlier moral reasoning on certain issues. Why shouldn't one drive a car when he or she is under the influence of liquor? "Do you want to get arrested, pay a fine, and lose your license?" It is to be hoped, however, that the fear of punishment is not the only reason drinking and driving is considered morally wrong.

Stage 2. What is right deserves a payoff.
This is the level of "you scratch my back and I'll scratch yours."

"I made my bed, picked up my room, carried out the garbage, and swept the garage. Now can I go to the movie?"

"I told you that you could not go to the movie today."

"That's not fair! See if I ever help you again!"

At this level there is always the calculation and expectation of a payoff. It is this tit-for-tat that brings the use of magic into religion and primitive faith. By doing certain rituals and using certain portents, God can be manipulated, or, if I do all of these things then God will have to let me into heaven. Faith becomes not "life insurance"—a way of living that brings joy and full humanity—but "death insurance"—a series of things that guarantees divine acceptance. Guarding against this is what St. Paul meant when he said that we are saved by faith and not by works of the law.

At the second stage of moral development, children judge right or wrong on the basis of a physical payoff. But at times in our lives we may well hear ourselves saying, "I did that for you, now you owe me one." Or, "After all those things I gave you and all the things I've done for you, you won't have sex with me. That's not fair!" It is to be hoped that there are more reasons for having or not having sex than a payoff.

The Conventional Level
The conventional level comes when the child begins to move out of himself or herself and into the world of social expectations. The child is moving beyond asking, "How well am I able to avoid punishment and get payoffs for my actions?" Now the question becomes, "How am I doing in the eyes of others, and how well am I following to the letter the norms and expectations of my immedi-

ate family, community, and nation? I am good because I obey my parents, my pastor, my teachers, and the police officer. Besides that, I am patriotic, and as a Christian I play by the rules." This level is divided into two stages.

Stage 3. What is right is what pleases your parents.

At this stage what is important is the approval of the significant ones within one's primary group—the family, the school, the parish, the state. It is the stage when what we long to hear is, "That's my little girl!" or "That's my little boy!" It is the stage where we say things like, "I'm in fourth grade, and we're the best class in the whole school! My principal told us. We sold more candy bars than any other class!" What is wrong comes with disapproval, as when someone says, "I am ashamed to have you as a son. I don't care what your friend's parents allow in their house, in our house you do not lean back and put your feet up on the table, even if the meal is finished." A look or word of disapproval from our parents, teacher, coach, or director, and our world collapses. Tears flow. We want so much to meet the expectations of others.

Young people pass through this stage in early adolescence, but for some it becomes a primary basis for moral living throughout their lives. Often at the college level students are still very concerned with meeting their parents' expectations. High school students may have been praised (and rightfully so) for achievement in a particular area of sports, art, music, math, or science. When these students get to college, they often feel that they have to major in a particular area or pursue a particular career because they can't let down their parents, teachers, or coaches.

If one were to fall in love with someone from a race or ethnic background other than one's own, and yet be convinced it would be wrong to marry that person because it would "break father's heart—to say nothing of Gramma's," one would be showing signs of being stuck in the third stage of moral development. This is not to say we ought not try please our families, but it does mean that there should be broader basis on which to make moral judgments.

Stage 4. What is right is what the law commands.
Here we find a parallel to the rule-oriented approach to moral decision making. Young people pass through this stage of moral development in adolescence, sometimes late adolescence. Rules, norms,
and social customs are to be followed if one is to live the moral life.
To challenge or question established social customs, to have a disre-
spect for authority or disregard for the laws of church or country, is
to neglect one's duty and turn away from what is good. Most beginning college students or those leaving home to seek work in the
world usually bring with them the unquestioned norms and perspectives of their families, their churches, and their communities. For
the most part, these norms or rules have not been examined critically. Things are right or wrong because that is what one has been told
and that is the way things will always be. If one were to question one
part of the whole, everything might come tumbling down. It is best
to obey, not to question. You might hear a person at this stage say
something like, "I don't know about you, but I am a Christian and I
follow what the Bible says. Who am I to question God?" or "I believe
the pope is the head of the church. If I follow what he says I won't go
wrong. Go ahead and question but it will bring you no good."

A healthy respect for laws, norms, and social customs is both
admirable and necessary. But the law cannot say everything, and
the unexamined life, as the great philosopher says, is not worth living. There must be a deeper reason for doing good and avoiding
evil than just meeting the letter of the law. We must look further.

The Postconventional Level
The postconventional level moves beyond the norms and customs
of the local community to seek reasons for living the moral life in
the more universal principles of justice and right. The value of
every human person and the solidarity of humans with all creation
determine what is good at this level. One's conscience, rightly
formed through broad dialogue and sharing, is the final arbiter of
the right and the good at the postconventional level. This level is
made up of two stages.

Stage 5. What is right is respecting the social contract that people have freely entered into after broad dialogue.

At this stage the various perspectives of different individuals and groups are examined critically, and one comes to *own* the shared moral view that has emerged. This does not mean that one renounces or denies those values and norms that have been passed down through family, church, and community; rather, one accepts or modifies these values and norms after critical examination and dialogue. Here laws, rules, and norms are seen as road maps that indicate a number of ways of reaching the destination of full humanity, of salvation. Conscience, formed through the experience of dialogue and sharing, is the final judge.

At a basic level, one example of a social contract (covenant is the preferred word today) with certain responsibilities flowing from it is the choice of a couple to enter into a marriage relationship within a community of faith. Rightness or wrongness of actions within this relationship is based on the examined and freely chosen responsibilities the couple has accepted. Some of these responsibilities may be based on an analysis of the human nature of each of the parties; some may be based on the lived experience or tradition of the community of which they wish to be a part. Finally, some responsibilities may be based on the Christian faith commitment that they share, and the particular liturgical and sacramental norms of their faith community.

Many times there is a period of confusion when one moves from the law and order stage toward the social responsibility stage. What had seemed perfectly clear as to right and wrong is challenged as one meets and enters into relationships with people of various ethnic, religious, social, and political backgrounds. The encounter with those of no faith at all can also be a challenge. Out of these experiences we can come to own the truth and beauty of our own background and tradition, discard the nonessential elements of narrowness, prejudice, and injustice, and grow more open to the solidarity, basic goodness, and graced life experience of those who may be different in many ways from ourselves.

State 6. Right is what is truly human in the broadest sense of the dignity of every individual and his or her right to justice and a share in the bounty of creation.

At this stage wrong is that which goes against one's conscience, if one's conscience is in accord with universal ethical principles (natural law) that are consistent and in accord with reason. While community is always important in moral decision making, this stage transcends community to a vision of the universe as a whole and to the value of each individual part. It would seem that few people reach this stage. Jesus did, we Christians would claim. Many would say that Francis of Assisi reached it as well. Others in our own times who may have approached this stage of universal justice and solidarity with all humanity might be Mahatma Gandhi, Pope John XXIII, Mother Teresa, and Martin Luther King, Jr.

Freedom in Moral Decision Making

The stages of moral development do not settle the question of how free we are in making moral decisions. But they can help to put things into perspective and serve as a mirror for ourselves as we attempt to grow to full humanity in grace. A disturbing example may point out the dangers when the stages of moral development and the blocks or impediments to freedom at particular times in our lives are not taken into consideration.

Focus:
How free are we in making moral decisions?

A number of years ago in the state of Texas a young college coed was beaten, raped, and killed. She was a member of a well-known family in the area; her father was a minister and two of her brothers outstanding athletes. A young man in his twenties was arrested and convicted of the crime. At the trial it was the accepted on the basis of a consensus of psychiatrists that the one who committed the crime had the mentality of a seven-year-old. The jury found him guilty of first degree murder, and he was condemned to death in the electric chair. Appeals on his behalf eventually reached the Supreme Court. The Court

Focus:
How free are we
in making moral
decisions?

concurred with the lower courts that the Texas law could stand—that chronological age rather than mental age justified the death sentence.[2]

While the crime was heinous and the perpetrator should never again be allowed to move freely in society, nevertheless, an important question arises: can a person with the mentality of a seven-year-old be held responsible for crime and given the punishment of death? The physical capability was there but the inner freedom for full moral responsibility was not. The death penalty, which more and more Christian churches are coming to recognize as cruel and inhuman punishment for our time (life sentence without parole is a humane alternative), should never be used to put to death a seven-year-old.

Before leaving the question of how impediments and the stages of moral development affect our freedom to act, we must consider a critique of Kohlberg's approach, and an alternative, feminist perspective on the matter of moral development by psychologist Carol Gilligan.[3] While Kohlberg suggests that few people arrive at Stage 6, most women, according to him, get "stuck" at Stage 4 where moral decisions are made according to norms or laws of society and family. Gilligan conducted her own studies, using many more women as subjects, and concludes that, on the whole, mature women approach moral problems in a different but equally valid way to that suggested by Kohlberg.

Gilligan finds that women approach moral problems not so much as dilemmas needing solution by abstract principles, but rather as interpersonal conflicts in need of resolution. Rather than focusing on right or wrong answers, women seek solutions based on reasoning that is grounded in maintaining the stability of interpersonal relationships.

According to Gilligan both moral reasoning based on abstract principles of right and justice and those based on maintaining relationships are important to a fully developed person and society. Some feminists go further and claim that the feminine "ethics of care" is superior and more mature than that based on abstract principles. Gilligan's insights support the relational/responsible approach to moral decision making presented here when she states that "in the different voice of women lies the truth of an ethic of care, the tie between relationship and responsibility. . . ."[4]

Freedom, although limited and at times impaired, is still the basis upon which we stand accountable for our actions. The life of grace, the life that is open to responding within our various relationships, is the life of freedom in its deepest sense. It is for this freedom that Christ has set us free. The life of sin, on the other hand, is, as St. Paul points out, the life of slavery. In such a life freedom is forsaken.

Our exercise of freedom in moral decision making calls for further examination. There are times when there are a number of responses demanded of us in our various relationships and all of them cannot possibly be met. We must explore the way in which we as individuals and as the community of the disciples of Christ can determine what the gospel demands in particular situations where there are conflicting claims confronting us.

Questions for Reflection and Discussion

1. How do you react to the statement, "Love of God and love of neighbor are mysteriously joined together"? Have you experienced times in your life when following that statement as a disciple of Christ presented special difficulties? Explain.

2. Impediments are roadblocks in the exercise of our freedom in making moral decisions. In your own life are you aware of any of your own impediments? Think back on moral decisions you have made. Can you cite, in retrospect, an example of a moral decision you made when an impediment was in operation in your life?

3. Along with impediments, stages of moral development affect our moral decision making. Are there certain moral decisions that you make when stage one, fear of punishment, is still the primary influ-

ence on your response? How strongly does the *approval of others* affect your moral decision making? Explain.

4. Do you agree that a person with the mental capacity of a seven-year-old should be put to death for a heinous crime? What are your thoughts on the death penalty in today's society in light of Jesus' command that we should not judge others?

5. Kohlberg did his study on the stages of moral development using males. From your own experience do you find that women have a different way of approaching moral issues than men? Do you believe that Gilligan's *ethics of care* can be a useful balance to the more abstract principle of justice? Give an example.

Suggestions for Further Readings

Fowler, James. *Stages of Faith: The Psychology of Human Development.* San Francisco: Harper & Row, 1991. See especially Part IV, "Stages of Faith," pp. 119–213.

Gilligan, Carol. "Visions of Maturity," in *Introduction to Christian Ethics: A Reader*, eds. Ronald P. Hamel & Kenneth R. Himes. New York: Paulist Press, 1989, pp. 281–292. Article is excerpted from *In a Different Voice*. Cambridge: Harvard University Press, 1982, pp. 151–174.

Häring, Bernard. *Free and Faithful in Christ*, Vol. 1. New York: Seabury Press, 1978. See "Contribution of the Behavioral Sciences and Philosophy," pp. 168–181.

Hill, Brennan R., Paul Knitter, and William Madges. *Faith, Religion and Theology: A Contemporary Introduction.* Mystic, CT: Twenty-Third Publications, 1997. See chapter 3, "Human Development and the Growth of Faith," pp. 67–99.

O'Connell, Timothy E. *Principles for a Catholic Morality*, rev. ed. New York: Harper Collins, 1990. Note discussion on "Impediments," pp. 53–57, and "Impediments Revisited," pp. 93–97.

Chapter Ten

The Development
of the Moral Life:
Values and Norms

A college professor who was also a priest often spent his summers working in parishes. In one parish, part of his ministry was to visit the residents of a large nursing home. He admitted that he found the ministry difficult and depressing. One day as he was finishing his visits, he was told that a young man wanted to see him. He walked into the room at the end of the hall and found a fellow in his early twenties lying on the bed. The young man wanted to tell the priest his life story.

"Father," the young man said, "I've been in bed from the time I was a little boy. I cannot get into bed or out of it without help. For many years I was at home, but they got tired of me. You know, Father, what I really want to do? I want to play guitar and write music and sing it. I want to make people happy. And you know what keeps me going every day, Father?" The young man nodded his head across the room toward a little plastic crucifix hanging on the wall. "He does, Father. Jesus. He did it. I can do it."

The priest walked out into the hallway and stopped and cried. "What the young man had said," the priest related afterwards, "was the best sermon I ever heard preached."

One of the things we will be examining in this chapter is the distinction between moral and premoral values and disvalues. In the story above, the physical disability the young man has to bear is a premoral disvalue. However, his personal attitude, courageous outlook, and desire to help others disclose powerful moral values.

What Is the Distinction Between Premoral and Moral Values?

We looked at the term *premoral* briefly in chapter six when we discussed the various uses of the word *moral*. We stated that the concept of premoral values and disvalues has an important place in contemporary moral theology. This is especially true when one employs the relational/responsible approach to moral decision making. We must now examine the distinction between *premoral* and *moral values* and how they are correlated with *material* and *formal norms, rules,* or *laws.*

Premoral values or disvalues are related to those things that are part of our world as we find it. They pertain to our human nature and to nature in general. Things like life or death, health or sickness, knowledge or ignorance, friendship or alienation, beauty or ugliness, wealth or poverty are examples either of premoral values or disvalues. *Premoral values are those good things in life that we ought to have or do to the extent possible. Premoral disvalues are those things that inhibit the fullness of life.* It is better to be alive than dead, to be healthy rather than sickly. It is good to have an education, to appreciate beauty, to have friends. Within our relationships premoral values are to be sought, preserved, and cherished. Premoral values may contribute to our moral growth, but they do not necessarily do so. On the other hand, although premoral disvalues are inhibiting, they may also enhance our moral growth. (Recall the story about the young man confined to his bed in the nursing home.)

Those things that are contrary to human wholeness and full

humanity, that are against the common good of the human family, that compromise the stewardship we have over the earth, are disvalues and are to be avoided as much as possible. Premoral disvalues likewise may or may not contribute to our moral growth. Lack of education is a disvalue. But giving up one's education plans and going to work so one's family can stay together after it has lost a parent may contribute to one's moral growth. Dropping out of school for a frivolous reason is, however, a premoral disvalue.

When we speak of *moral values,* on the other hand, we are referring to those things that are essential for living as we ought as human beings. Premoral values are good but not essential. Moral values are both good and essential. One can be fully human and still not have a college education, but one cannot be fully human and be a cheat, a liar, and a fraud. To be fully human one need not be good looking, but one must be loving and caring. Virtues such as honesty, justice, courage, temperance, and chastity (a respectful attitude toward human sexuality) are examples of moral values. Moral values are not just a matter of *doing* what is right or good, but *being* good and upright. One may abuse English grammar by using the verb "goes" for "said" (She goes, "Why did Abraham do that?" and I go, "Because God told him to"), think jet trails in the sky are the cause of bad weather, limit the treasure of Western music to country western, and prefer a psychedelic video game to a beautiful sunset, and still be a good person. But one cannot exploit children or the poor, or recklessly pollute the air, the land, or the water, and still be a good person.

What Is the Distinction Between Material Norms and Formal Norms?

Premoral and moral values are related to two kinds of norms, rules, or laws. These are *material norms* and *formal norms.* Material norms tell us what we ought to *do.* Formal norms tell us what is the right thing to *be.* Material norms are related to premoral values or disvalues. They point out what premoral values we ought to pursue or what premoral disvalues we ought to avoid. Material norms provide us direction and information in seeking what is good. They shed light on particular situations, but they do not provide the final answer to particular problems. Related as they are to premoral values, they need not always be followed. They are tentative, debatable, and open to exceptions. Life is a higher value than death. Therefore we should not kill. But there may be some situations when killing is not wrong.

Formal norms indicate the "form" our way of acting should take. Following formal norms helps "form" us into the person we are called to be. Formal norms are related to moral values, to those things we must pursue if we are to be fully human and truly Christian. Formal norms are broad in nature and do not contain much specific content. "Be honest," "Respect life," "Do not murder" are all examples of formal norms. "Love one another," and the golden rule—"Treat others as you would want them to treat you"—are also formal norms. They are universal and absolute. They allow no exceptions. The following chart will help us distinguish between material and formal norms and how they relate to premoral and moral values:

Material Norms	Formal Norms
Description:	*Description:*
•tell us what we ought to do.	•tell us the type of person we ought to *be*.
•point to premoral value to be pursued.	•point to moral values that must be pursued.
•point to premoral disvalues or evils to be avoided.	•tell us the "form" our actions should take; attitudes we should acquire.
•point to values, illuminate situations.	•point out what it means to live the gospel.
•provide concrete information, instruction.	•are general, vague, with little specific content.
•indicate factors to be considered in decision making.	•indicate goals rather than strategies; being rather than doing.

Material Norms	Formal Norms
Examples	*Examples*
•do not kill.	•respect life—do not murder.
•do not take what belongs to another.	•respect the property of others— do not steal.
•tell the truth.	•be honest—do not lie.
•pay your debts.	•act justly—give each person his or her due.
Application	*Application*
•not always applicable, not absolute.	•are universal, exceptionless; always must be pursued.
•there are times when we may have to withhold the truth, even kill.	•one may have to kill; but may never murder.
•tentative in nature, therefore debatable.	•related to the person we are, to being.
•challenge us to seek the greatest good, minimize the evil.	•challenge us to be responsible human beings, faithful Christians.

When we talk about *absolutes* in moral theology we are referring to *moral values* protected by *formal norms*, or *moral disvalues or evils* forbidden by *formal norms*. One can never be a murderer, a thief, or a liar, and still be a morally good person. Murder is the taking of an innocent life for an unjust reason. Stealing is taking what belongs to another without just cause. Lying is to utter falsehood for the purpose of deceiving. These are always wrong. They contradict the moral values of respecting life, respecting the property of others, and being honest. The condition or circumstance determining the absolute character of these values is built into the description—that these things are done for an unjust reason, without just cause, for the purpose of deceiving.

Abortion is one of those terms that admits of a certain ambigui-

ty in the matter of absoluteness. Many define abortion as the deliberate destruction of innocent life. As such it is always wrong. It is
a moral absolute. But when the fertilized egg or zygote begins to
grow in the fallopian tube instead of the uterus, resulting in what
is called an ectopic pregnancy that cannot possibly come to full
term, traditional moral teaching says that the section of the fallopian tube along with the fetus can be removed. This is a deliberate
taking of innocent life. It is not called abortion, however. The reasoning is based on what is called *the principle of double effect,* which
we shall discuss later. The same is true if the uterus of a pregnant
woman were found to be cancerous. The diseased uterus, along
with the fetus, can be removed, but it is not called abortion. The
deliberate taking of an innocent life, therefore, is always wrong—
with certain exceptions.

The moral culpability of one who violates formal norms, however, would still depend on the extent of the involvement of the whole
self. Does lying reflect one's fundamental option directed toward dis-
honesty, deceit, untrustworthiness, selfishness, and evil (mortal
sin)? Or is it an unfortunate mistake of judgment, a spur of the
moment attempt to cover one's mistake, embarrassment, or honor?
In such cases the action may not necessarily sever one's relationship
with God and others, although it could result in a rupture (gravely
serious sin) or strain (venial sin) on one's basic orientation or fundamental option toward honesty, openness, integrity, and goodness.
An example may be helpful.

A young person related an incident from his high school days.
He said that he generally got along well with others and had many
friends and a good relationship with his parents. He was not one to
get into trouble—except once. He and a group of his friends "hanging out" one night decided for some crazy reason to break into a
bicycle shop and steal a bike. They did, and they got caught by the
police. At the police station the young man called his father and
told him where he was. The father came and took his son to one
side and asked him quietly if he had really done it. The young man
said yes, and his father never said anything more about it. Of

course a fine was imposed and some community service was required, but the father basically knew that his son was not a thief and that this behavior did not fit into the basic orientation of his son toward goodness.

Because moral theology is concerned not only with our outer level of action (doing), but also with the inner level of person (being), both premoral values and material norms, as well as moral values and formal norms, are important. Moral theology not only points out what we are to *do* as disciples of Christ, but also instructs us on the kind of person we are to *be* as baptized members of the community of faith.

What Is the Role of
the Virtue of Prudence in Moral Decision Making?

There is no one tangible source that Christians can turn to to get the answer to every conceivable moral question that arises in life. We live our lives in a world of premoral and moral values and material and formal norms that express those values. From the Bible, from the lived experience and teachings of our faith communities and our families, and from our own reasoning and experience, we attempt to discern the right thing to do in particular circumstances. This discernment, and the courage and grace to act upon it, will, it is hoped, reflect and in turn enhance the type of person we really are and want to be. Our lifelong moral education, therefore, is not in learning moral norms, rules, or laws (not that they don't have their place), but in developing our character as mature disciples of Jesus. "The rudder of that course toward authentic character," as Richard McBrien points out, "is the virtue of *prudence*...."[1]

Prudence operates within the broader realm of *wisdom*—that gift of being able to perceive and place things in their proper order of importance and value, not only according to the head but also the heart. Wisdom in turn calls for *humility*—the honest perception we have of ourselves in relation to others—as well as for *justice*. Justice helps us realize that as people always in relationship, the concern of neighbor and nature must always enter our moral decisions. Justice opens our eyes to the need to discern our own moral actions and the actions of our communities, in relationship to the effects they have not only on ourselves and others, but on the structures of society and the sustainability of our planet. Prudence helps us steer a course toward full humanity in relationship to others and all that is.

What are we to do, however, when our prudent and prayerful discernment leads to conflict situations involving a clashing of values, all of which we want to respect and enhance, and to disvalues that we want to avoid, but are unable to do so? This leads us to the next question, concerning *proportionate reason* or *proportionalism,* as it is commonly called.

How Does "Proportionate Reason" Aid in Moral Decision Making?

When faced with a moral dilemma in which a number of *premoral values* (and disvalues) come into conflict, and at the same time coming up against certain specific actions that have been labeled *moral disvalues* (always evil, intrinsically evil) by church authority, some moral theologians have begun to employ *proportionate reason* in determining the objective rightness or wrongness of acts growing out of such a situation. *Proportionalism* is the name given to this analysis. In conflict situations proportionalism is used to determine objectively the moral rightness or wrongness of certain human acts as well as to establish exceptions to certain moral norms, rules, or laws.[2] This process of analysis is often misunderstood. Moral theologians employing this analysis have been accused by Pope John Paul II (in his encyclical letter on the moral life, *The Splendor of Truth* [*Veritatis Splendor*]) of subjectivism and relativism in their moral thinking. They insist, however, that the pope's letter inaccurately describes proportionalism as an attempt to justify morally wrong actions by the good intention of the actors. It is not an attempt to make immoral acts moral—that is impossible, they say. Rather, it is to insist that no moral judgment can be made without considering all the circumstances involved in the human act. When a person is *doing* something (acting), all aspects of that act must be considered together—the person's intention, the consequences of the act so far as they can be seen, and the proportion between the premoral values and disvalues involved.[3]

An example will help clarify this process. But first we need to say a word about those acts declared intrinsically evil in themselves by church authority, whether the judgment is based on the acts being contrary to nature (the goal-oriented approach), or on the teachings of the Bible or the church (the rule-oriented approach). Most of these acts are in the area of human sexuality—masturbation and contraception are two examples. Many moral theologians employing the relational/responsible approach and proportionalist analysis would say that masturbation, for example, held by the church to be always intrinsically evil, was judged so centuries ago on the basis of an understanding that self-stimulation causes evil without proportionate reason. Partly based on a limited knowledge of human physiology that placed all of potential life in the male semen, partly on the sin of Onan as related in the Bible, and partly on natural law interpretation that the sole purpose of sexual genital activity is procreation, masturbation could be judged as a more serious sin than rape or incest because the latter two at least are not "unnatural" in the sense the former is. It is difficult to make this argument from reason today.

The way that proportionate reason or proportionality helps in complex moral decision making may be seen in returning to an earlier example and analyzing it from the perspective of proportionalism. A married couple who have not been able to conceive because of a blocked fallopian tube in the woman (or a low sperm count in the man), are trying to decide whether they should attempt in vitro fertilization using her egg and his sperm. Several premoral values and disvalues come into play. Having a family is something they both want very much, and it is one of the joys of married life. As a premoral value, to the extent that it is possible it ought to be sought. On the other hand, the frustration of not being able to conceive has put emotional stress on both of them, at times leading them to blame each other and making them wonder if perhaps their marriage may fail. They have looked into the possibility of adoption, but the amount of red tape, the length of time they would have to wait without any assurance that they would ever receive a child, and the perception between them that one or the other is not fully at home with the adoption route, has discouraged them.

They ponder the route of in vitro fertilization. They cannot believe that the way the semen would have to be secured is morally sinful (a premoral disvalue). (Of course they would prefer to have followed the usual way.) They discuss it with their doctor and with their pastor. The procedure usually involves fertilizing several eggs in case the implant is not successful the first time. If fertilized eggs remain, what is to become of them (a premoral disvalue)? This causes them serious concern. They discuss the matter with their pastor. They have had a good sexual relationship in their marriage, and they decide that although the conception will not take place in the ordinary way (a premoral disvalue), their life as a couple, bound together by so many strands of love, will not be compromised by this extrinsic joining of their egg and sperm (a premoral disvalue). And the fertilized egg to be placed in the wife's womb will be their gift of love, as will be the hoped-for and prayed-for child.

In proportionate reasoning there must be a proper relation between premoral disvalues contained in, or caused by, the act (masturbation and the joining the egg and sperm outside of the marriage act in the example above) and the end of the act (the conception of a child within a loving family relationship and, it is to be hoped, the beginning of a new family), or between the end (a baby) and the premoral disvalues in consequence of the act (the possibility that more than one egg is fertilized in the procedure and the disposition of the remaining eggs). In making exception to negative material norms, proportionate reason is used to discern if the premoral disvalues contained in, or caused by, the means (masturbation, conception outside the marriage act, the possibility of having to destroy remaining fertilized eggs) stand in proper proportion to the premoral value in the act itself (a child, a family, a fulfilled marriage relationship).

Perhaps a clearer example would be the negative material norm,

"You shall not kill!" Killing another is a premoral disvalue. Yet it may be justified in the case of self-defense. Exceptions to material norms that prohibit premoral evil are made on the basis of the presence of a proportionate reason. Murder, taking the life of another without proportionate reason (a *moral* disvalue), can never be justified.

Those who employ the proportionalist analysis insist that in our actions certain premoral disvalues are bound to result. In themselves the premoral disvalues do not make the action morally wrong. (This is a fact that should be admitted honestly instead of splitting a single human act into *intended* and *unintended effects* as will be discussed below as the *principle of double effect*.) *Moral* evil results when, after considering all the circumstances in a particular case, there is no proportionate reason to justify the act. As the moral theologian and great defender of proportionalism Richard McCormick states, "Thus just as not every killing is murder, not every falsehood is lie, so not every artificial intervention preventing (or promoting) conception is necessarily an unchaste act. Not every termination of pregnancy is necessarily an abortion in the moral sense."[4]

How Does Proportionalism Relate to the Principle of Double Effect and the Doctrine of Intrinsic Evil?

One of the reasons that proportionalism has come to the fore in contemporary moral theology is the dissatisfaction with the traditional *principle of double effect* as a way of dealing with dilemmas or conflict situations in moral decision making. The traditional process in judging individual acts morally good or evil was to consider three aspects of the act—the *object*, the *end*, and the *circumstances*.

When a couple decides to attempt to have a child by in vitro fertilization, the *object* is bringing the egg and sperm together in a petri dish and then implanting the fertilized egg in the womb of the woman. That is the object of the act itself. The *intention* is the birth of a child. The *circumstances* are the inability of the couple to conceive for whatever reason. According to the goal-oriented and rule-oriented approaches to moral decision making, in which some acts (the object) are held to be evil in themselves (*intrinsically evil*)—

either because they are contrary to nature or declared evil by a legitimate moral authority—the example just cited would be wrong because to secure the male seed (a part of the object) would entail masturbation, which is always morally wrong. We will return to this example, but first let's look more closely at the principle of double effect.

When one is faced with a moral decision from which two effects will follow, one good and one evil, and the initial act itself is either good or at least morally neutral, one may proceed as long as the evil effect is not intended and is not the direct result of the act. Also, there must be a proportion between the good effect and the evil one. The examples cited earlier concerning the removal of an ectopic pregnancy or a cancerous uterus of a pregnant woman are cases that employ the principle of double effect. The intention is not to destroy the fetus but to remove the infected portion of the fallopian tube or the cancerous uterus.

Problems arise with the use of the principle of double effect. Concerning ectopic pregnancy, for example, it was not many years ago that Catholic moral teaching allowed a surgical intervention only after the fallopian tube ruptured. That meant the fetus was already dead. Later, the procedure was allowed before rupture because, the reasoning went, the fallopian tube is already poisoned by the presence of the fetus. Thus the life of the fetus is directly destroyed but, according to the principle of double effect, the destruction was only indirectly willed. It is not the *means* of saving the mother's life, but only follows simultaneously, and unavoidably, from the single action. If the act were considered from the point of view of the *means* of saving the mother, it would be immoral, because the utilitarian argument that the good result justifies the means can never be admitted. But in the exercise of the principle of double effect, the *single* human act—the surgical removal of the fallopian tube (containing the fetus), is, in effect, split in two. The single object or act is judged as partly intended and partly unintended. Although complex, the human act is a unified one.

The apparent compromises have strained the reasoning involved in the principle of double effect. There are moral theologians who have employed the principle of double effect in the case of masturbation for the sake of securing a sperm count to measure male fertility. Because the *intention* of act is a *medical* one, and therefore good, and the solitary pleasure, which is evil, is *unintended,* the act may not be sinful in this case.[5] One would think that the same principle of double effect could be applied in securing the male semen for in vitro fertilization, but the absence of the *natural* form of intercourse would still render the *object* of the act immoral.

Another strain on the principle of double effect arises in the matter of the transplant of living organs between living persons. It is morally wrong to directly and deliberately mutilate the human body. It is justified as a sacrificial gift of love, but it is difficult to argue that there is no *intention* of mutilation. Likewise there is the argument that pain medicine may be prescribed for a dying patient even to the point where the medicine may hasten death, as long as the *intention* is pain-relief—even though the *unintended,* only *indirectly willed* effect is well known. Two effects—one intended, the other not—seem to divide the single human act into two realities. Yet the human act is a structural unity.

The proportionalist argues that all aspects of the act, all circumstances, must be considered together. They cannot be isolated from one another. By admitting that certain disvalues or premoral evils are present in our conduct, we do not have to skate around unintended intentions and indirectly willed effects. By use of proportionate reason, and by admitting that some actions labeled intrinsically evil need to be reevaluated by proportionate reason, we can arrive at the objective basis for our moral decisions within the relational/responsible approach. Moral theologian Anne E. Patrick has suggested that the debate among those who insist on the traditional identification of certain intrinsically evil acts, and those who favor a proportionalist analysis, may be reconciled by developing a more adequate description of moral actions. She cites Pope John Paul II's acknowledgment in *The Splendor of Truth* (no. 53) that there is an ongoing need to discover "*the most adequate formulation* for universal and permanent moral norms in the light of different cultural contexts."[6]

We now must turn to the final arbiter of the moral life, human conscience. It is easy to say that it all comes down to conscience, but it is not so easy to explain what that really means.

Questions for Reflection and Discussion

1. Do you find the distinction between *premoral* and *moral* values helpful in clarifying our growth in the moral life? Why or why not? Can you identify in your own experience an example of a *premoral disvalue* that actually contributed to growth in the *moral virtue* of an individual?

2. Do you find the distinction between *material norms* and *formal norms* helpful in making moral decisions? Why or why not? Why are material norms that relate to premoral values *tentative, debatable, and open to exception*? Why are formal norms that relate to moral values *absolute and universal*?

3. How would you explain to someone the difference between committing a moral transgression and becoming the type of person that the moral transgression indicates? How would you relate your answer to one's *fundamental option*, exercise of *core freedom*, and *mortal* and *venial* sin?

4. Do you agree with the statement, "The rudder of that course toward authentic character is the virtue of prudence"? In your own experience have you observed how the virtue of *prudence* and the virtues of *wisdom, humility,* and *justice* are all interrelated in the growth in the moral life? Explain.

5. *Proportionate reason* or *proportionalism* is used by many moral theologians in judging the objective moral rightness or wrongness of certain human acts in conflict situations as well as to establish exceptions to certain moral norms or laws. Give an example of the use of this principle. In the relational/responsible approach, why do all the circumstances of a moral dilemma have to be taken into consideration in making a moral decision?

6. Give an example involving the *principle of double effect*. Why do many moral theologians have difficulty with this principle today? How does the understanding of *premoral values* (or *disvalues*) and the principle of *proportionate reason* help solve the difficulties with the *principle of double effect*? Does the admission that certain *premoral disvalues* or *evils* are bound to be present in our relational/responsible approach to moral decision making render the method unacceptable?

Suggestions for Further Reading

Cahill, Lisa Sowle. "Moral Methodology: A Case Study," in *Introduction to Christian Ethics: A Reader,* eds. Ronald P. Hammel & Kenneth R. Himes. New York: Paulist Press, 1989, pp. 551–562.

Fuchs, Josef. "The Absoluteness of Behavioral Moral Norms," in *Introduction to Christian Ethics: A Reader,* eds. Ronald P. Hamel & Kenneth R. Himes. New York: Paulist Press, 1989. See especially pp. 502-505 on "Moral and Premoral Evil."

McBrien, Richard P. "Christian Morality: Special Questions—Section One: Interpersonal Ethics," in *Catholicism: New Edition.* New York: HarperCollins, 1994, pp. 981-1000.

McCormick, Richard A. "Pluralism in Moral Theology," in *The Critical Calling: Reflections on Moral Dilemmas Since Vatican II.* Washington, DC: Georgetown University Press, 1989, pp. 131-146.

Westley, Dick. *When It's Right to Die: Conflicting Voices, Difficult Choices.* Mystic, CT: Twenty-Third Publications, 1995. See especially chapter 7, "For the People—Against Traditional Theologians," pp. 87–111 for a critique of the *principle of double effect,* of *intrinsically evil acts,* and of the position of O'Connell on *the direct killing of an innocent person.*

Chapter Eleven

Conscience:
The Final Arbiter
of the Moral Life

At the height of the cold war, when the arms race between the United States and Russia was running out of control, two of my former students, along with several other peace activists, formed a "plowshares" group to protest the deployment of nuclear missiles in silos in the midwest. ("Plowshares" finds its origins in Isaiah 2:4, "They shall beat their swords into plowshares and their spears into pruning hooks.") On Good Friday they approached an isolated and heavily guarded area where the missiles were deployed, cut a hole in the fence, and crawled through. With hammers they managed to do minor harm to the track of one of the silos. They also poured blood on the silo cover as the alarms began to sound. It so happened that a crew from one of the national television networks was there to catch the picture of the group lined up against the fence with arms outstretched in the form of a cross, announcing as they were arrested on this Good Friday, that they were trying to save the world from ultimate destruction.

Later, at their trial, they attempted unsuccessfully to use the situation as a pulpit for their anti-nuclear stance. They were given sentences of three years in federal prison for unauthorized entry into a high security military installation. Two of them were also told they had to pay a fine of $250 for the damage to the silo track. "How could I possibly pay to repair something that I believe is immoral to build, to stockpile, and to deploy, let alone to use?" one of my former students asked. The judged slapped on an additional three years to the young man's sentence for his refusal to pay.

Six years of a person's life is a costly price for following one's conscience. But conscience, in the end, is what counts.

What Is Conscience?

Conscience is one of those words that we all have a sense of, but may find difficult to define succinctly. Most people would say it has to do with right and wrong. Some will talk about "a little voice inside us." The word itself comes from the Latin word *sciere* (to know) and the prefix *con* (with). Therefore, to "know with"; and if we were to add the words "our whole selves," we would be getting close to the meaning. But conscience is not only knowing with our whole selves, but also knowing in relationship to others and with others. If we come to be who we are through dialogue and sharing, then this "knowing with" involves not only ourselves but others as well. Conscience is something that we share in common with others within the human community. It is a universal phenomenon. Moreover, the "knowing with" involves that deeper understanding of knowing that goes beyond just the intellect. It encompasses as well the emotions, feelings, will, and attitudes. It means knowing from the heart, so to speak.

Conscience can be defined as the moral dimension of the human person that is sensitive and responsive to values found within relationships. It is conscience that forms the link between our inner selves and the world "out there." It involves the responsibilities we encounter (many spelled out in the form of norms, rules, or laws) in our various relationships with others, with ourselves, with nature, and ultimately with God. Moral theologian Timothy O'Connell suggests that conscience is a complex phenomenon that operates on three levels.[1]

1. *Conscience can be understood as a basic sense of value and of personal responsibility.* Human beings, in whatever culture or time, have had a basic sense of right and wrong. That awareness is within each one of us. We have considered the possibility of someone being *amoral*, but such a person is still described as having his or her conscience dulled or deformed. We may not always agree in specific instances about what is right or wrong, good or evil, but we do agree that there is a difference between the two. In this first level, which is universal, conscience is part of the definition of what it is to be human. O'Connell calls it a *characteristic* of genuine humanity.

2. On the second level is the process of exercising our conscience in seeking objective moral values in particular situations. People feel obliged to analyze their own behavior and the world in which they live. They try to discover what is the right thing to do and what is not. If the first level of conscience is a *characteristic* of being human, the second level is the *process* by which the person judges the right course of action. It is at this level that conscience is subject to error. There are differences of opinion. One person may say that masturbation and artificial contraception are always gravely sinful. Another may say that neither is necessarily sinful but just a part of life. A person must seek as much information about the matter in question as possible, consulting family, friends, one's own experience, the insights of the natural and human sciences if applicable, and, as a Christian, Sacred Scripture and the teachings and lived experience of the faith community. Roman Catholics, especially, pay attention to the official teaching of the church at this level. This second level of conscience is not, however, directly accountable to the church. It is truth, wherever it may be found, that the second level of conscience is seeking. The church, the faith

community called in the Spirit to be a moral teacher, will certainly be one of the sources that a prudent person will consult.

The consultation process at this level is known as *conscience formation*. It does not mean that one merely follows what one has been told, but rather that one reflects upon, discusses, and prays over such information in an honest and open manner. An act of conscience is not just whatever one thinks or feels. It is not the glib, "You follow your conscience, I'll follow mine." Rather, it is a careful weighing of evidence, a pondering of the possibilities, a reasoning process open to grace. The second level of conscience opens the door for serious Christians to the *spiritual life* and the realization of the value of a *spiritual mentor, director,* or *counselor,* who can help one discern the path of true discipleship.

3. The third level of conscience involves the decision itself and acting on that decision. It is an act of the will based on the material pondered in the previous level. If the first level of conscience is a *characteristic* of being human—a sense of right and wrong—and level two is the *process* by which we arrive at a judgment about right and wrong in particular circumstances, then level three is the *event* in which we make the decision and act upon it. As humans we are not just called to analyze and ponder facts, we are called to intelligent action. Not unlike Martin Luther when he was called before the Diet of Worms to answer for his teachings, we must respond in a way similar to the statement attributed to him: "Here I stand, I can do no other." We may realize that theoretically we could be wrong, but we still have the sense that *this* is what we ought to do. Even if our decision were objectively wrong, if we act in good conscience, God will not hold such a decision against us. We are judged by God not on what we actually do or don't do, but on the basis of what is in our hearts.

Conscience is the final norm by which a person's acts must be guided. Conscience is inviolable; it cannot be forced either by external or internal authority. Thomas Aquinas wrote that "anyone upon whom the ecclesiastical authority, in ignorance of the true facts, imposes a demand that offends against his [or her] clear conscience, should perish in excommunication rather than violate his [or her] clear conscience."[2]

Conscience, as can be seen from the above discussion, is a complex yet vital part of each one of us. It is the place where human freedom is allowed to take its final stand. It brings us face to face with the radical, grace-filled invitation we receive to enter into a loving relationship with God through loving our neighbor. The contrast between this aspect of our lives and that of the superego, to which the conscience is sometimes compared, is worth examining. It should further clarify the meaning of conscience.

What is the Distinction Between Conscience and Superego?

Moral conscience, according to John W. Glaser, is the "recognition of an absolute call to love and thereby to co-create a genuine future." The superego, on the other hand, "springs from a frantic compulsion to experience oneself as lovable, not from the call to commit oneself in abiding love."[3] Glaser contrasts the characteristics of superego with genuine conscience as follows:

Superego	Conscience
act performed for approval, in order to make oneself lovable, accepted; fear of love withdrawal is the basis	invites to action, to love, and, in this very act of other-directed commitment, to co-create self-value
introverted: the thematic center is a sense of one's own value	extroverted: the thematic center is the value which invites; self-value is concomitant and secondary to this
static: does not grow, does not learn; cannot function creatively in a new situation; merely repeats a basic command	dynamic: an awareness and sensitivity to value which develops and grows; a mindset which can precisely function in a new situation

Superego	Conscience
authority-figure-oriented: not a question of perceiving and responding to a value but of "obeying" authority's command "blindly"	value-oriented: the value or dis-value is perceived and responded to, regardless of whether authority has commanded it or not
"atomized" units of activity are its object	individual acts are seen in their importance as a part of a larger process or pattern
past-oriented: primarily concerned with cleaning up the record with regard to past acts	future-oriented: creative; sees the past as having a future and helping to structure this future as a better future
urge to be punished and thereby earn reconciliation	sees the need to repair by structuring the future orientation toward the value in question (which includes making good past harms)
rapid transition from severe isolation, guilt feelings, etc., to a sense of self-value accomplished by confession to an authority figure	a sense of the gradual process of growth which characterizes all dimensions of genuine personal development
possible great disproportion between guilt experienced and the value in question; extent of guilt depends more on weight of authority figure and "volume" with which he or she speaks rather than density of the value in question	experience of guilt proportionate to the importance of the value in question, even though authority may never have addressed this specific value

As can been seen from the comparison above, conscience is not a *feeling* about right or wrong. Rather, it is a *sense* of right and wrong. Unlike the superego, that psychic police officer that carries over from childhood, conscience brings matters to the level of consciousness and submits them to the test of reason. The superego is a type of "unconscious" conscience, a repetitious hammering on the part of our psyche that can cause feelings of guilt when there is no reason for guilt. It is an authoritative warning that God is going to get you, or people won't like you, or this or that is very bad, dirty, naughty. An example may help clarify the matter.

Imagine that, as a youngster of age four or five, you are with some of your little friends playing in a neighbor's garage and, upon a dare, you all take off your clothes, only to have one of your parents walk in and discover you. You not only get spanked when you get home and restricted from playing with those other "bad" neighbors, but you are told again and again that what you have done is evil, that God will punish you for it, and that you should never, never take off your clothes in front of anyone else. This episode gets buried in your psyche, and as you go through school you hesitate to participate in group sports that necessitate common dressing rooms and especially group showers. Nakedness is embedded in you as something bad or evil. When you finally get married you wouldn't think of getting undressed in front of your spouse, and lovemaking, from your perspective, must be done in the dark.

What was a childhood indiscretion ends up as an adult problem because the matter has never been brought to the level of conscience and dealt with in a mature, reasonable way. It remained in the superego hammering away through the years: "this is bad..."; "my parents are not going to like me for this...."; "God is going to get me!" This is "ambush" theology. God is understood as the wily guerrilla "up there" waiting to "pick us off." But that is not the role of conscience, nor is it a healthy Christian way of life. A fixation on gender roles, racial or ethnic discrimination, homophobia, or fear of showing one's emotions can sometimes be lodged in the superego.

How Does Conscience Relate to Civil or Religious Authority and the Law?

It is clear from the above discussion that we are bound to follow our conscience. No one should be forced to act contrary to his or her conscience or prevented from acting according to conscience. An exception can be made if one's action is going to cause great harm to one's self or to others. If possible, a person should be prevented from committing suicide. A child should receive a blood transfusion if it will save the child's life even if the parents believe in conscience that the procedure is against God's will. An adult, however, may in good conscience refuse medical treatment. The government cannot force a conscientious objector to engage in military combat, although it may insist on some type of alternative service. (Whether one may refuse any kind of government service will be taken up under the discussion of civil disobedience.)

On the other hand, a person who is convinced in conscience that private business should be able to operate without any government interference may still be forced by law to give a just wage to his or her workers, to provide a safe working environment, and to not employ children.

What happens when a serious Christian disagrees with a specific moral teaching of his or her church? On matters such as birth control, abortion, use of fetal tissue in medical treatment, artificial insemination, sterilization, euthanasia, premarital sex, homosexual relationships, divorce and remarriage, capital punishment, militarism, building and stockpiling nuclear weapons, and insisting on a preferential option for the poor, may one act contrary to church teaching based on one's conscience? If conscience cannot be forced, then the answer has to be yes. But good Christians may not decide such a matter lightly. As members of the community of the disciples of Jesus, we first of all realize that on our own we, or even a group of us, cannot hope to grasp all moral truth without dialogue with the broader community of faith.

In some faith traditions, including the Catholic, special respect is given to the moral teachings and directives of those who exercise the gift of leadership in the church—bishops and bishops' conferences, the pope as universal pastor, and ecumenical councils. The United States Catholic bishops have issued important directives on moral issues such as nuclear weapons, a just economy, and immigration. The organ for such teaching varies from church to church, as does the weight and authority of such teaching. The Anglican church has the Lambeth Conference. Lutherans have the Lutheran World Federation. Methodists have issued moral directives through the United Methodist Council of Bishops in the United States. Their directive *In Defense of Creation: The Nuclear Crisis and a Just Peace*[4] attracted considerable attention. Protestants in general put more emphasis on personal decision making and formation of conscience based on biblical teaching than on authoritative church directives. Still, all Christians have an obligation to listen carefully to the authoritative teaching of their faith communities in matters that affect their moral lives, as well as the reasons given for the teaching. As Christians we are called to obedience. (The word *obedience* finds its root in the Latin word *audiere,* to listen.) Yet even Pope John II in his official letter on moral issues states, "the authority of the Church, when she pronounces on moral questions, in no way undermines the freedom of conscience of Christians."[5]

Richard McBrien offers four principles that should be followed in making a decision of conscience that is contrary to the authoritative teaching of the church.[6] They are paraphrased below.

Focus: McBrien's four principles for making a decision in conscience that is contrary to church teaching

1. The church's moral teaching is assumed to be a source of positive illumination for Christians in forming their consciences. If, however, after serious inquiry, dialogue, reflection, and prayer, a person is convinced that his or her conscience is correct, in spite of a conflict with the moral teachings of the church, the person not only may but *must* follow the dictates of conscience.

2. No church, including the Catholic church, has ever claimed to have spoken infallibly on a moral question. Some theologians have argued that the pope's teaching condemning artificial contraception constitutes an infallible teaching, but this opinion has not been generally accepted. That Catholics should accept certain directives "as if they were infallible" has been characterized as creeping infallibil-

ism. (The limits on infallibility were discussed in Chapter Four).

3. A church teaching cannot hope to account for every moral situation and circumstance. Every teaching has to be applied in particular cases. When one decides in conscience that an authoritative church teaching does not bind or apply in a particular situation, that does not necessarily mean one is repudiating the values affirmed in the teaching.

4. All teachings are historically and culturally conditioned. What may have been perceived as morally wrong in one set of circumstances, may be morally justified in another. Charging interest on a loan (usury) was condemned as immoral during the Middle Ages. Today it is one of the bases of our economic system. For a living person to donate an organ was once considered immoral. To perform an autopsy was likewise forbidden.

Focus: McBrien's four principles for making a decision in conscience that is contrary to church teaching

Not only are laws or moral teachings historically conditioned, but, especially in their negative form "you shall not...,") they tend to promote the *minimal* in the moral life. "What is the minimum I have to do to fulfill the law?" If a rigid midnight curfew is laid down by parents for their high school son or daughter, how many young people, if they arrived home at twenty minutes to twelve, would go in early knowing that their parents would get twenty minutes more sleep that night? How many would sit and talk in their friend's car until the very last minute rationalizing, "After all, they made the rule, I didn't." How far such an attitude is from Jesus' gospel admonitions to go the extra mile, give your shirt as well as your coat, and don't count the cost

Finally, we are not saved by the law, as St. Paul reminds us over and over again. If we think we can stand upright before God (be justified) by following the letter of the law, we fool ourselves into thinking we have *earned* our salvation. It is self-righteousness to think God *owes* us a place in the Kingdom. Salvation in the end is a gift that God offers to everyone. It is that mysterious and grace-filled invitation that we are free to grasp and respond to in faith.

Laws are useful road maps. They are the collected wisdom of the community that directs us and aids us in responding within our relationships in a way that facilitates full humanity—salvation for us and our communities. Laws, rules, or norms embody values. Obedience to the law is never for its own sake but for the sake of the value embedded in the law. Laws, rules, or norms are useful, even necessary, but law cannot save.

Is Civil Disobedience Ever Justified?

We have examined conscience and the moral law. We now must consider whether we are ever morally justified in breaking the civil law. *Civil law consists of those rules and norms that facilitate and order life in the secular realm.* In a democratic society we have been nurtured on the basic belief that citizens are free to disagree with the law, to speak out against the law, and to work to win uncoerced consent of the community to change the law, but as long as the law remains in force, we have an obligation to obey it. The subject of civil disobedience brings up the more basic questions of the nature and limits of a citizen's obligation to obey the law, and the relation between the authority of conscience and the authority of the state.

We distinguish here between *civil law* and *criminal law*. Criminal law relates to the due process and punishment by the state for aggregated offenses against morality. Therefore, criminal law is more directly related to moral law. Principles parallel to the ones discussed in the previous section would have to be applied if one were to break a criminal law because of one's conscience. The case of German Lutheran theologian Dietrich Bonhoeffer, who participated in an unsuccessful plot to assassinate Adolf Hitler, is often cited as a case of a conscience decision to break a criminal law. Bonhoeffer did not ask others to agree with him, but he felt in conscience that in light of the untold evil the Third Reich under Hitler was inflicting on so many innocent people, such action was justified. Bonhoeffer was arrested, sent to a concentration camp, and put to death in 1945, shortly before the Allied liberation. His *Letters and Papers from Prison*[7] has had a great influence on contemporary theology.

If a criminal law were unjust, of course, and one were fully aware of it, a person would not only be in the right in disobeying it, one would be obliged to do so. An example of this can be found in the Nuremberg trials that dealt with Nazi war crimes following World War II. These crimes included the Jewish Holocaust in which six million people lost their lives. At Nuremberg the argument that one was merely "following orders" in herding innocent men, women, and children into the gas chambers as part of the "final solution," was declared by the court as an insufficient excuse. There exists a "higher law" of right and wrong that must be followed. Many would point to the *natural law*, that law or norm written in the hearts of all men and women to do good and avoid evil, as the source of this "higher law." When Archbishop Oscar Romero in El Salvador told the young recruits in the military not to fire on their own people (which eventually cost him his life), he was appealing in a similar way to the higher law that forbids one to follow an unjust order or law.

There are times when civil laws, those meant to ensure good order in a society, may promote, protect, and perpetuate an unjust situation. In most situations the ones who suffer because of these laws are minority groups within a particular society or state. Minority groups, even in societies or states that embrace democracy, are often left without a voice in the centers of power because of civil laws that proscribe the exercise of their civil and human rights. In the United States during the civil rights movement of the 1960s, African Americans inspired by the charismatic leadership of Martin Luther King, Jr. began to make use of the principles of civil disobedience. Again and again King appealed to a "higher law" as a defense for his breaking of what he claimed were unjust laws. He wrote:

> A just law is a man-made code that squares with the moral law or the law of God. An unjust law is a code that is out of harmony with the moral law. To put it in the terms of St. Thomas Aquinas, "An unjust law is a human law that is not rooted in the eternal and natural law."[8]

The public act of civil disobedience that usually is identified with the beginning of the civil rights movement took place in Montgomery, Alabama, when Rosa Parks refused to give up her bus seat to a white person and move to the back of the bus and stand. The civil law stated that if the bus were full and a white person got on, a black person was to get up and give his or her seat to the white person. When the bus driver told Rosa Parks to move to the back of the bus, her response struck a chord within the black community and eventually among many in the white community as well. She was not going to move, she said, because "my feet's tired."

Through a series of demonstrations, boycotts, sit-ins, and marches, often facing hostile crowds, corrupt government officials, and violent law enforcement officers, the black community finally achieved what had been denied them through the orderly process of law (laws that had, in fact, been discriminatory). The civil rights legislation passed by the U.S. Congress could not, as Martin Luther King, Jr. noted, "make the white man love me, but it could keep him from lynching me." (The confusion between civil law and moral law—the government cannot "legislate morals"—will be discussed later.)

Acts of civil disobedience were also employed in the protests against the Viet Nam War. The anti-war movement found fertile ground among students on university campuses. As one university president who marched with the students as they protested noted, "The students are smart enough to see the injustice of their receiving deferments to continue their education while minorities and poor are sent to fight an unjust war in an unwinable situation." At Kent State University a number of students were shot during a demonstration by trigger-nervous National Guardsmen who had not been trained in crowd control.

Those who are stalled rigidly in the "law and order" stage of moral development would identify any type of civil disobedience as a revolutionary threat to the government, as the following letter from a father to his son who was just entering the University of Tulane at the time will testify:

If you challenge the U.S. government, this is your affair. If you get killed doing it, this is your affair. You see there are constitutional ways to change the U.S. government and I agree that it desperately needs changing. However, if you choose to try to change it by revolution, expect to get shot. Mother and I will grieve but we will gladly buy a dinner for the National Guardsman who shot you. You see, son, they pretty-up in definition all these things you might want to do. When brought down to its basics, it is still just revolution…. The National Guard can shove in a couple of clips and clear Tulane. I think they ought to when students disturb the peace and destroy property.[9]

The matter of abortion, one of the principal moral questions that has divided our society (with "good" Christians on both sides of the issue) can serve as an example of the confusion among many concerning the parameters of civil law and moral law. Some hold that abortion is a civil right (the pregnant woman's right to choose, or the right to privacy), while others see abortion as a human right (the fetus's right to life). The debate as to whether the law should allow abortion (even use tax money to pay for abortion for those on welfare or in the military), or forbid abortion (through a constitutional amendment if necessary), comes down to the question of whether civil law should reflect moral law. If it should, whose interpretation of moral law should it reflect? To put it another way, should moral law determine civil law (what is good should be enforced by law; what is bad should be prohibited) or should civil law determine moral law (what the law allows is morally acceptable; what it forbids is unacceptable)? But this confuses the parameters of the civil and the moral law. The civil law pertains to the good order of society, to the common good as affected by external acts. Martin Luther King, Jr.'s statement that the law can keep one from being lynched, refers to the civil law. The moral law, on the other hand, has to do with our whole selves, both personal and social—interior attitudes, motivations, and both internal and external acts. The moral law calls us to love all of God's people as our brothers and sisters.

Civil law must also be enforceable. In a democracy and pluralistic society such as ours that means there must be a consensus among the people concerning the law. A constitutional amendment prohibiting alcoholic beverages proved to be unenforceable. While such an analogy with abortion would be considered completely unjustified by many, a consensus for enforcing a complete prohibition on abortion does not seem to exist at this time in our society. What is one to do?

In 1973, the U.S. Supreme Court decision *Roe v. Wade* struck down state laws prohibiting abortion. Although that decision made abortion lawful in all fifty states, it did not necessarily make abortion *morally* acceptable. What is allowed by the civil law in a pluralistic society does not necessarily reflect the moral law, although ideally it should. Like abortion, capital punishment is considered morally wrong by many serious Christians. But it is allowed by civil law. Those opposing abortion can work to build the necessary consensus through education, by persuasive argument, and, yes, by civil disobedience. While no group has a right to impose its moral views on others through force, coercion, or violence, it does have a right to bring an issue that it believes needs changing to the attention of the broader community in hope that consensus for corrective action may result. Picketing, marches, sit-ins, and the like, even if they go against civil statutes of law, can be justified in conscience as long as they are peaceful and nonviolent.

Having considered a number of situations in which civil disobedience can be justified, we are now ready to develop a definition of civil disobedience:

Civil disobedience is a nonviolent, public violation
> [*nonviolent*—an essential element of civil disobedience is nonviolence although some distinguish between violence toward persons (always outside the realm of civil disobedience) and violence toward property (sometimes justified when the property is the object of a symbolic action, e.g., disfiguring a missile or pouring blood on it).

public violation—the purpose is to draw the attention of the people to the matter by openly breaching the law.]

of a specific law or set of laws, or a policy of government having the effect of law,
[the action is not to promote lawlessness or a general disregard for government, but is directed toward some specific laws or policies.]

that expresses a sense of justice in civil society
[there is a hope that through the raising of consciousness of the public at large, not only will the matter at hand be changed, but the people as well will have a change of heart.]

and is generally undertaken in the name of a presumed higher authority than the law in question
[here the "higher law" or the universal "law of God" is referred to.]

as a last resort
[the usual procedures or the situation have been attempted with no success.]

for the purpose of changing the laws or situations
[again civil disobedience is directed toward a specific limited goal of changing certain laws or situations that are perceived in conscience to be unjust.]

and with the intention of accepting arrest and the penalty that the prevailing law imposes.
[the acceptance of the arrest and penalty become an essential part of the symbolic action; it is hoped that being punished by the law draws attention to the injustice at hand.]

The matter of civil disobedience and conscience is summarized well in this statement of political philosopher Harrop Freeman:

> If society is going to exist in dependence upon man's moral nature, or his ability to choose the right course from the wrong—on his conscience—then society is also going to have to recognize man's right and duty to follow his conscience even if this leads to civil disobedience.[10]

Having examined the role of conscience in relation to the law, and the situations and circumstances when one in conscience may participate in civil disobedience, we must now consider the broader role of conscience in the social order, not only as individuals but as members of the community of faith interacting with the larger community.

What Is the Role of the Christian and the Christian Community in Social Morality and Social Justice?

From the beginning of our discussion of moral theology we have talked about the person in relationship and how moral responsibility arises out of our various relationships. We also talked about community and how we come to be who we are within relationships that form community. As Christians we are part of the community of faith, the church. Responding within our relationships involves not only our personal responses, but the social responses of our faith communities to the larger society, to the state, and to the world. One aspect of the threefold mission of the church is *to work with others of good will in the socio-political-economic realm to remove those things that stand the way of the coming Kingdom.*

Those things that *stand* in the way of the Kingdom, of the realm of peace and justice, of solidarity and compassion among all of God's people and all of creation, are caused not only by human sin—our turning in on ourselves and refusing to respond within our personal relationships—but also by social sin or structural sin. The mega-relationships among the societal/cultural, the economic/financial/corporate, the political/governmental, and the military/industrial communities have produced a complex of structures that often exploit and destroy people and the environment. Swiss theologian Hans Küng has listed these sobering statistics at the beginning of his book *Global Responsibility.*[11]

- Every *minute, the nations of the world spend 1.8 millions of* dollars on military armaments;

- Every *hour*, 1500 children die of hunger-related causes;

- Every *day*, a species becomes extinct;

- Every *week* during the 1980s, more people were detained, tortured, assassinated, made refugees, or in other ways violated by acts of repressive regimes than at any other time in history;

- Every *year*, an area of tropical forest three-quarters the size of Korea is destroyed and lost;

- Every *decade*, if present global warming trends continue, the temperature of the earth's atmosphere could rise dramatically (between 1.5 and 4.5 degrees Celsius) with a resultant rise in sea levels that would have disastrous consequences, particularly for coastal areas of all earth's land masses.

The cosmic aspect of sin becomes more evident as our global vision expands. But some would argue that the above statistics are of no real concern for the Christian church other than to further prove that the present world is under the sway of the devil and deserves to be destroyed. The church has no role in the "world" other than to condemn it and to gather as many as possible into the community of saints to await the new creation. But the biblical doctrine of the goodness of creation and the Christian understanding of God having come among us in the human being Jesus, remind us that all aspects of the human and of the cosmos have been touched by the divine. The reign of God ultimately embraces all of creation. "Where sin increased, grace abounded all the more," St. Paul reminds us (Romans 5:20), and although "the whole creation has been groaning in labor pains until now" it "will be set free from its bondage to decay and will obtain the freedom of the glory of the children of God" (Romans 8:21–22).

A number of different theologies in recent times have brought the attention of Christians to the moral responsibility they have as a community to join in the effort to transform the structures of society by their prophetic and liberating proclamation, witness, and action. The social gospel movement in the United States in the early twentieth century attempted to apply Christian principles to the social and political order and had a lasting effect on American churches. The political theology coming out of Germany in the late 1960s and 1970s warned of the danger of the privatization of faith and of the gospel. For many, the church has its proper role only in the personal, the private, the individual, and the familial. But whatever affects not only human persons, but also human communities and the environment, is a moral issue and the concern not only of individual Christians but of the Christian community as a whole. While the Christian community does not have a political "plan" for the world, it can and must raise its prophetic voice against those systems and programs that dehumanize people, preventing them from participation in determining their own future. That future is not just the final "day of the Lord" that we patiently await, but the emerging social and political order for which we as a community of faith share the responsibility.

Liberation theology, which had its roots in Latin America in the late 1960s, has had its effects on all of theology. Arising out of the condition of dependence in which the poor in Latin America are held by the international economic, monetary, and trade policies of the industrialized countries and their governments, theology is understood as the *praxis of liberation*. One can *do* theology only by participating in the liberation of the poor and the changing of the unjust social order. Liberation theologians reject the biblicist and doctrinalist approach to theology and accept the correlative approach as long as liberating praxis among the poor in their *situation* precedes or at least accompanies reflection in light of the *message*. Only with a commitment to liberation and a solidarity with the poor and the oppressed, can we understand the true meaning of the gospel message.

Liberation theology puts considerable emphasis on the life and ministry of Jesus. Jesus' preaching of the Kingdom is subversive because it proclaims the end of domination of human beings by human beings. Injustice, privilege, oppression, and narrow nationalism have no place in the universal love preached by Jesus. Liberation theology has been criticized for employing Marxist tools for social analysis, but liberation theology is not Marxist. It has, however, made the whole of theology more sensitive to the way in which the context or situation out of which we theologize has its effect on the theology produced. Other third world theologies—Asian, African—are also contributing to the necessary globalization of theology.

Black theology shares many of the same moral concerns of liberation theology. The God of black theology is a God whose primary passion is freeing the oppressed from the bondage of economic, racial, and social exploitation.

Feminist theology, as has been pointed out earlier, puts much stress on relationships, both personal and social. Moreover, it provides a critique of the male-centered bias of theology and the effects that a patriarchal, authoritarian-dominated church has had on moral teaching both on the personal and societal level. Moral theologian Anne E. Patrick, in *Liberating Conscience: Feminist Exploration in Catholic Moral Theology,*[12] sets out to connect two things that many people regard as unrelated—*conscience and community*—from a feminist perspective. The way Patrick describes the term *feminist* as she intends to use it, gives an indication of the thrust of her work and that of many other women working in the area of moral theology. She says that she uses feminist in a broad sense to indicate a position that involves

(1) a solid conviction of the equality of women and men, and

(2) a commitment to reform society so that the full equality of women is respected, which requires also reforming the thought systems that legitimate the present unjust social order.[13]

It is not males as such that Patrick sees as "the problem," for she presumes that men and women both suffer under the injustices of patriarchy, although in different ways and to different degrees. The goal of feminism that she supports is that which has been stated by theologian Elizabeth Johnson:

> What Christian feminism hopes for is a transformed community. Cooperating with the Spirit of life, feminism hopes so to change unjust structures and distorted symbol systems that a new community in church and society becomes possible, a liberating community of all women and men characterized by mutuality with each other, care for the weakest and least powerful among them, and harmony with the earth.[14]

The community of faith, the church, has a right and an obligation to contribute to the public good of society. In the United States we have a strong, constitutionally based tradition of separation of church and state. This noble experiment has proved to be beneficial both to the church and the state, and has been a model for many others. But the separation clause in the First Amendment never meant to limit religion to the private sphere or to imply the absolute separation of religion or church and society. The way the church makes its contribution, however, needs further clarification. Some limits as well as freedoms exist in this regard. Charles Curran, in *The Church and Morality: An Ecumenical and Catholic Approach*,[15] proposes that the criteria for determining the proper involvement of the church in the political order is that the matter in question (e.g., a proposed law or public policy) must have a truly *political* purpose. (He prefers the term *political* rather than *secular*.) Political here refers to the public realm or the political society. One way to determine what is a truly political purpose is to insist that it is for the defense of the public good or public order. The public order, in turn, involves a further threefold order—an order of justice or social justice, an order of public morality, and an order of peace.

The government can restrict the exercise of religion, for example, by stepping in to prevent human sacrifice, even in the context of religious worship. The government has the right and obligation to protect human rights, especially the right to life. The morality here is public morality, not private morality. When the Supreme Court judged that the practice of polygamy should not be allowed among the Mormons, even though it was one of the tenets of their religion, the reasoning behind the decision was, again, that the practice was against public morality. Likewise, for the sake of public peace, a religion can be prevented from noisy public processions or celebrations in a residential neighborhood in the middle of the night. Curran admits that grey areas will continue to exist, but the criteria of justice and social justice, public morality, and public peace are helpful. They would exclude, for example, public compulsory prayer to God and the erection of religious symbols on public property. These do not have a truly political purpose, that is, a purpose that pertains to the common good of the society as a whole.

The church as the community of the followers of Jesus operates on various levels in its relationship to the broader society. First of all, it should be *a witness, a sign, a model,* to the world of what God wants for everyone (the second of the threefold mission of the church). Its own structures and practices should reflect its commitment to justice and peace, compassion, fairness, the elimination of all discrimination, and a special concern for the poor. It is clear that the divisions in the Christian church and bickering within and among the various denominations have had a negative impact on the broader society. This is a sobering reminder that the church, too, is sinful and always in need of reform. "See how they love one another," should truly be the phrase that identifies the Christian community within the broader society.

If the church is a believable model for life in community, then it also can function as a *teacher* in society, teaching primarily through dialogue, but making its influence felt in upholding and attempting to make more present those values and virtues so necessary for a just society—justice and social justice, ensuring that all people receive what is rightfully theirs in matters of food, shelter, education, health care, job opportunities, and retirement. The church also functions as a *caregiver* in times when the larger society ignores, marginalizes, or neglects particular persons or groups of people. The hospice program, AIDS support groups, or soup kitchens that the church operates are recent examples of direct involvement of the church in society. As was pointed out in the discussion on the church's mission, however, the church as a social service agency functions as a *substitute* until the broader community takes on its rightful responsibility of caring for its citizens. At the same time the church has a role to play in *advocating* changes in structures and socioeconomic situations that are the root causes of the marginalization of individuals and groups.

The church also has a role in *motivating* and *enabling* individuals and groups to realize that society not only has an obligation for all of its members (and in a broader sense the members of the whole human family), but also that a society functions better when all are invited and enabled to participate in determining their own future and the good of the society to which they belong.

While the church, whether local, regional, or universal, has a rightful role in determining the vision, values, and principles that should be present in the political, social, and cultural orders, not only through its individual members, but as a community, it does not have a specific grand plan. Therefore, there are a number of cautions that are in order concerning the church's role in the broader society.

First of all, the church should not be identified with any particular class, culture, party, or ideology. The disastrous results of such identification are recorded on the pages of history when the church became identified, for example, with the Roman empire in the early church; the wealthy Roman families and German princes in the medieval church; the nobility of the Renaissance; the conquistadors and slave traders in the sixteenth and seventeenth centuries; and the trade companies, colonialism, and the aristocracy in the eighteenth, nineteenth, and early twentieth centuries. Regardless of where one places the immediate responsibility for the Holocaust and the indiscriminate destruction resulting from the dropping of the atomic bomb, both are part of the history of the "Christian" West.

During the Viet Nam war, one of the prominent leaders in the church in the United States, after participating in a Sunday morning worship service in the Nixon White house, addressed the press with the phrase, "My country right or wrong, but my country." That is a breakdown of the responsible moral voice of the church in public affairs. The phrase, "My country right or wrong," is idolatry. Especially in a democracy, we must say, "'My country right,' I support it, but 'My country wrong,' I must do everything I can to correct it, including mobilizing the voice of the faith community to right the wrong." The World Council of Churches and the Second Vatican Council, as well as recent pronouncements by church leaders, especially those from the third world, have sharpened the voice of the church in speaking about issues of economic justice, the immorality of nuclear war, the sin of discrimination, and the moral responsibility we have for protecting the global ecosystem.

Within the church certain groups arise that advocate a particular moral stance on certain issues. One such group in the Christian church are those who advocate pacifism. Their call is not for passivity but rather for an active pursuit of peace, at the same time renouncing the use of violence to achieve that peace. Although the Christian church has not accepted (and, it appears to many that at this time it *cannot* accept) pacifism as the stance for the whole church, still the pacifist tradition, with deep roots stretching back to Jesus' own life and teaching, deserves the faith community's support and encouragement. It is one of those "minority reports" within the church that challenges the larger community and the world to ponder the question of whether true peace can ever be achieved by violent means.

Another area where the church should exercise caution is in supporting any particular candidate for political office. Within the political realm, individual church members have the right to exercise their freedom of choice and still not feel alienated from the faith community. When the church publicly endorses a particular candidate, it is putting undue pressure on the candidate who, like all humans, experiences the limitations of finitude and sinfulness. Moreover, in a pluralistic society the democratic process is complex, as are most of the issues affecting public morality. On principles, issues, and policies that affect public morality, the church can and must speak out. But the church should not publicly support or oppose a particular candidate or party, especially if the support or opposition is based on a single issue.

Our Christian faith and conscience call us to respond not only in personal relationships but as members of the community of faith, the church. Whether on the local, regional, national, or international level, the church, after broad dialogue and consultation with its members, can and must speak out, witness, and act to bring its values and vision to bear on the larger society. In its attempt to remove those things that stand in the way of God's Kingdom, the Christian community cooperates and also learns from other individuals and communities. If we believe that God is present in human experience, then somehow God is at work in those of good will who strive with us to make our communities, our world, and the universe a safer, happier, more sustainable, just, and peaceful place for all. We are our brothers' and sisters' keeper. We are responsible together for our world and all of creation.

At the centenary commemoration of the Parliament of World's Religions, held in Chicago in 1993, representatives of fifteen religious traditions of the world, including the four great world religions, issued the following "Four irrevocable directives" as part of its declaration, *A Global Ethic*.[16] They give the call to conscience for a social morality a broad and fitting ecumenical dimension:

1. Commitment to a culture of nonviolence and respect for life.

2. Commitment to a culture of solidarity and a just economic order.

3. Commitment to a culture of tolerance and a life of truthfulness

4. Commitment to a culture of equal rights and partnership between men and women.

Questions for Reflection and Discussion

1. From your own experience, how would you describe *conscience*? Has your perspective on conscience changed any after having read this chapter? If so, how?

2. How would you distinguish between the statement, "Conscience is inviolable," and "Everyone has to do his or her thing"?

3. Can you identify in your own life any perspective that you once looked on as a matter of conscience, but later identified as a part of your superego?

4. How did you react to "A Doctor's Letter to his Son"? At what stage of moral development would you place the father? the son? yourself in making the judgment?

5. What are your thoughts on civil disobedience? Could you picture yourself in a situation in which you would choose to participate in an act of civil disobedience?

6. What insights have you gained from considering the feminist perspective of conscience and community? How do they relate to the moral obligation we have to live "in harmony with the earth"?

Suggestions for Further Reading

Adams, James Luther. "Civil Disobedience: Its Occasions and Limits," in *Nomos XII: Political and Legal Obligation.* ed. J. Roland Pennock and John W. Chapman. New York: Atherton Press, 1970, pp. 293–331.

Callahan, Sidney. *In Good Conscience: Reason and Emotion in Moral Decision Making.* New York: HarperCollins, 1991. See especially chapter 8, "Nurturing Conscience," pp. 199–214.

Curran, Charles E. *The Church and Morality: An Ecumenical and Catholic Approach.* Minneapolis: Fortress Press, 1993. See especially chapter 3, "Catholicity and the Church Moral Involvement in Society," pp. 65–91.

Marinelli, Anthony. *Conscience & Catholic Faith: Love and Fidelity.* New York: Paulist Press, 1991.

McBrien, Richard P. *Caesar's Coin: Religion and Politics in America.* New York: Macmillan, 1987. See esp. chapter 4, "We Hold These Truths," pp. 101–132.

Boff, Leonardo and Virgil Elizondo, eds. *Options for the Poor: Challenge to the Rich Countries,* Concilium 187. Edinburgh: T. & T. Clark, 1986.

Patrick, Anne E. *Liberating Conscience: Feminist Explorations in Catholic Moral Theology.* New York: Crossroad, 1996. See esp. chapter 6, "Toward Liberating Conscience: Spirituality and Moral Responsibility," pp. 170–199, and chapter 7, "Conscience as Process: Choosing Our Common Good," pp. 200–235. See also chapter 1, "Conscience and Community: Catholic Moral Theology Today," pp. 19–39, and chapter 2, "Conscience at the Crossroad: Invitation to Radical Conversion," pp. 40–71.

Ruether, Rosemary Radford. *Gaia & God: An Ecofeminist Theology of Earth Healing.* New York: HarperCollins, 1992. See especially chapter 10, "Creating a Healed World: Spirituality and Politics," pp. 254–274.

Conclusion

Love:
The Final Goal
of the Moral Life

A family loses a child through a sudden illness. The parents and other siblings are devastated. A neighbor, a five-year-old, notices his mother crying when she hears the news. Although close to tears himself seeing his mother so sad, he experiences an inner confusion. Acting on his confusion but also wanting to console his mother, he says, "But Mom, they have a lot of other kids." The reaction of the mother startles him. She turns, walks over to him, sits him down on a chair, and leaning down until their eyes meet says to him through her tears, "Jimmy, you must realize that the love that parents have for their children isn't divided up among the number of children they have. Every child is special. Parents have as much love for the ninth child as there is for the first. There is always an abundance of love. It flows over into eternity. It is what God is."

The mother kisses her little son and presses him to her tear-stained face. Jimmy will never forget.

Where Have We Been?

In Part One of this book we looked at the foundational questions concerning our faith—*"What do we believe, and why?"* This involved looking at *theology* itself (faith seeking understanding) and then at the large questions with which theology deals: *revelation* (God's gracious invitation to us to enter into relationship), *faith* (our Spirit-prompted acceptance and response to the invitation), the *church* (the community of the disciples of risen Jesus called in the Spirit), the *mission of the church* (to preach, witness, and serve the Kingdom), and finally *ecumenism* (the call to unity so that we might carry out the mission effectively). We found the biblical rationale for doing theology in 1 Peter 3:15, "Should anyone ask you the reason for this hope of yours, be ever ready to reply...." We found that the ultimate purpose of theology is prayer—to know the truth that we might love and praise God as we ought.

In the second part of this book we have been considering the moral questions concerning faith—"What as Christians are we to do and be?" We first looked at *moral theology*—our attempt to know and understand how we are to live and what we are do (or not do) and be (or not be) from a faith perspective as disciples of Jesus Christ. We then sought to find out why "good" Christians disagree on basic moral questions. We found the answer in the different ways in which Christians approach moral decision making—the *goal-oriented*, the *rule-oriented*, and the *relational/responsible-oriented* approaches. We noted that moral responsibility always arises from within relationships because humans are by nature relational beings. We come to be who we are through dialogue and sharing within community.

Developing the relational/responsible approach, we then turned to the *human person* and distinguished, for the purpose of discussion and clarification, the *inner* and *outer* levels of the person. We found that at the inner level, freedom is not a freedom of choosing this or that, but *a freedom of defining the person we are going to be.* This inner defining act, which is not a single decision, but the results of our many decisions, is called our *fundamental option.* It is the basic attitude, orientation, and direction in our lives. It is here, at the core of our being, that our fundamental option is directed toward openness, relationships, and mutual and loving responses within those relationships; it is *the life of grace, full humanity—our salvation.* Or, it is directed inward toward selfishness, refusal to enter into and sustain relationships, abandoning responsibility; it is *sin, inhumanity—death.*

Mortal sin and the life of grace must be discussed at this deepest level of our core freedom, our fundamental option. Although our basic direction in life may be toward goodness and wholeness, we know that at times we fall short in responding as we ought within our various relationships. These faults (and some may be serious) compromise and strain our fundamental option, although they do not destroy it. But they do make us aware that we are continually in need of forgiveness and reconciliation within our various relationships.

Freedom must be present if we are to be morally responsible. We examined how *impediments* or blocks to our freedom lessen but do not remove culpability in our moral behavior. Another aspect affecting our freedom are the stages of moral development that we pass through on our way to human and moral maturity. We discussed and critiqued these stages of moral development.

In the development of the moral life we are confronted with certain *values* that are held and cherished by the human community, and certain *norms*, rules, or laws that embody and protect those values. The distinctions between *premoral and moral values* were pointed out as well as the distinctions between *material and formal norms.* We discussed the *virtue of prudence,* so necessary as we attempt to discern between good and bad in particular instances. *Proportionalism,* or the use of *proportionate reason,* as an aid in justifying moral decisions in conflict situations when various responsibilities and values are vying with one another, was explained.

Finally, we turned to the matter of *conscience* and explored the complex meaning, operation, and role it plays in the moral life. We then related conscience to the law, considering situations when *civil disobedience* could be justified, and how conscience calls the Christian and the Christian community to *love of neighbor* in the social and public realm.

Where Are We Now?

In the first letter of John we are told that God is love. We Christians have come to know this God as the mysterious Three-in-One (Trinity)—an unfathomable inner-relationship of love: Creator, Word, and Spirit. Out of unbounded love, God created us as a part of the universe and then invited us into a loving relationship through grace—a sharing in the very life of God. When God chose to reveal the ultimate divine love for us, God spoke and the Word became one of us—Jesus, our brother. This gift of God's love in Jesus is pure gift. It is not something that we earn or deserve. It is sheer grace. This highest form of love, which traditionally has been called *agape*, invites, empowers, and urges us to love God and neighbor in the self-sacrificial manner that God first loved us in Jesus. It is in Jesus that we come to know what God is really like—the unfathomable lover. God is the merciful father in the parable of the prodigal son (or prodigal daughter) whose love for us is beyond our comprehension.

Jesus, as truly one of us, also shows us what we as humans are capable of being. Each of us has within ourselves a yearning, a striving, for some ideal of happiness, a sense of meaning, as we experience love in our various relationships. Traditionally this human love has been identified as *eros*. Some identify it as a drive toward self-fulfillment. Others speak of it as a desire for intimacy. St. Augustine called it the yearning of the human heart for authentic happiness. It is a legitimate and worthy love, enticing us to pursue those premoral values that enhance our lives in relationship, in community—friendship, knowledge, creativity, beauty, joy. We also know, however, that in the drive for self-fulfillment or in the desire for intimacy, this kind of love can turn in on itself. We can become selfish. Then our pursuit of premoral values is not for the purpose of enhancing our love relationships, but for our own self-aggrandizement. The powerful sexual drive within us can become a quest for self-satisfaction alone, for control and domination, rather than being a way of expressing the mutual and unitive aspect of love.

Love need not degenerate this way, however. We are capable of more. And because in Jesus we come to know who God really is and *who we are capable of becoming*, we find in him the model of how authentic human love and God's divine love can come together in the life of discipleship. The reality of the giftedness of love that we experience in our relationships in life, of the life-enhancing joy that we experience in standing up for the cause of justice and right, is mysteriously transformed through grace into an authentic expression of our love of God and neighbor. Our *eros*-love is not left behind, but is preserved yet transcended by our sharing in the *agape*-love that comes to us in and through Jesus Christ. Systematic theologian David Tracy calls this type of love *caritas* (charity). Echoing the words of the prophet Ezekiel (11:19), "I will remove the heart of stone from their flesh and give them a heart of flesh…," Tracy talks about a "displacement-replacement" process of transformation that is made possible by God's grace in Jesus Christ. This transformation

> both restores our weakened and wounded self by real capacity for authentic *eros* and fulfills that constant, powerful force of *eros*-love in all its forms….The continuing transformation of all our *eros*-love by God's *agape* is what *caritas* finally is; *caritas* assumes that the strivings of *eros* are neither irrelevant nor evil in relationship to the gift of *agape*.[1]

The power of love became visible in the ministry and teaching of Jesus. When the "woman of the city" intruded on the meal Simon the Pharisee had prepared for Jesus and his disciples, she embarrassed the host by weeping at Jesus' feet, kissing them, and drying them with her hair. This caused Simon to say to himself, "If he were a prophet, he would know who and what kind of woman this is who is touching him—that she is a sinner." Jesus then spoke to Simon. He reprimanded him for his inhospitality for not having provided the usual water to wash his own and his disciples' feet, and then said, "I tell you, that is why her many sins are forgiven— because of her great love. Little is forgiven the one whose love is small" (Luke 7:47).

In this episode we are brought face to face not only with Jesus' recognition of the power of love in the inner longing of the woman for a transformed life, but also the need at times to awaken those like Simon who are self-satisfied in their religious piety yet insensitive to those who are marginalized—the neighbor. Because our *eros*-love (that love in our ordinary human relationships) also involves our self-interest, we may be tempted to forget who is our neighbor. Jesus not only invited us, but commanded us to love our neighbor as ourselves. It is to be hoped that in our many relationships within community, family, and friendships, in our loyalty to this person, this group, or this cause, our focus need not be on the *commandment* to love, but on the *desire* to do so.

The love that Jesus lived and shared in his life came to a climax when he was unjustly arrested, put on trial, and put to death as an insurrectionist and blasphemer. Through it all he continued his life of love, healing, forgiving, and sharing. The religious and secular rulers who put him to death were threatened by his goodness, truthfulness, and honesty. His love uncovered in them their own corruption, exploitation, and hypocrisy. The fragility and weakness of human love (the need we all have for forgiveness) was tragically displayed when Judas betrayed Jesus and most of the disciples abandoned him. Peter even denied with a curse that he knew him. Jesus died on the cross forgiving his persecutors and promising life in the Kingdom to the thief who recognized this great lover dying beside him. Here we see the great expression of human love, to lay down one's life for one's friends, and the greatest expression of divine love, God was in Jesus reconciling the world to God's self.

Then it happened. The God of love raised up the Beloved into a new creation, and through the power of the Spirit this new creation was made available to the disciples and to us. A new life, a new creation through the risen Christ in the power of the Spirit, became the new power of love in the world. "Do you love me?" the Risen One asked Peter, not once but three times. When the repentant Peter assured Jesus that he did, Peter was told, "Feed my sheep"— share that love. In the first letter of Peter we read, "Above all, maintain constant love for one another, for love covers a multitude of sins. Be hospitable to one another without complaining. Like good stewards of the manifold grace of God, serve one another with whatever gift each of you has received" (4:8–10).

"Why do you persecute me," the risen One asked Saul (Paul) as he made way his to Damascus to arrest the followers of "the Way." When Saul inquired who this was who had blinded him with overwhelming light, the reply was, "I am Jesus whom you are persecuting," and Paul became a lover. Later, he could write to the followers he had gathered into the community at Corinth, "If I have faith to move mountains, but do not have love, I am nothing. If I give away all my possessions, and if I hand over my body so that I may boast, but do not have love, I gain nothing. Love is patient; love is kind; love is not envious or boastful or arrogant or rude. It does not insist on its own way; it is not irritable or resentful; it does not rejoice in wrongdoing, but rejoices in the truth. It bears all things, believes all thing, hopes all things. Love never ends" (1 Corinthians 13:2–8). This is the love that brings us into touch with the moral values, those qualities of life without which we are not fully human, fully saved, or fully Christian.

The goal of the moral life is love. If moral theology is our attempt to know and understand what we are to do and what we are to be, then the answer to what we are to do is *to love*, the answer to what we are to be is *to be lovers*. As Edward Schillebeeckx says, "God is accessible above all in the praxis of justice and love. 'No one has seen God; if we love one another, God abides in us and his love is perfected in us' (1 John 4:12)."[2] Isn't that what the Christian moral life is all about? It is the love of God expressed in our love for others and for all of God's creation. It is a love known and experienced in the beauty of creation, in the family of humankind, and within the faith community. This love is based ultimately on God's love for us that comes through Christ in the power of the Holy Spirit. The life of discipleship is the life of grace, the life of love.

Questions for Reflection and Discussion

1. How would you respond to the statement, "Love is the final goal of the moral life"? Does this make the journey toward full humanity, living the *graced life,* too simple? Can we be truly human without the threat of punishment and damnation?

2. What issues in moral theology do you believe were not sufficiently covered in the second part of the book? Does the *relational/responsible* approach to moral decision making give you a basis for exploring those issues? If not, why not?

Suggestions for Further Reading

LaCugna, Catherine Mowry. *God for Us: The Trinity and Christian Life.* New York: HarperCollins, 1993. See the final chapter, "Living Trinitarian Faith," especially "Trinitarian Life: Living God's Life with One Another," including Ecclesial Life, Sacramental Life, Sexual Life, Christian Ethical Life, and Spiritual Life, pp. 400–410.

McFague, Sallie. *Models of God: Theology for an Ecological, Nuclear Age.* Philadelphia: Fortress Press, 1987. See chapter 5, "God as Lover," 125–155.

Schillebeeckx, Edward. *Church: The Human Story of God.* New York: Crossroad, 1990. See especially "*Ethics as a* religious challenge," pp. 91–98.

Notes

CHAPTER ONE—THEOLOGY: A DEFINITION

1. William James, *The Varieties of Religious Experience* (Cambridge, MA: Harvard University Press, 1985, orig. ed., 1902).

2. Rudolf Otto, *The Idea of the Holy* (New York: Oxford University Press, 1958, orig. ed., 1917).

3. Andrew Greeley, *The Great Mysteries* (New York: HarperCollins, 1985), 3–5.

4. See D. Mackenzie Brown, *Ultimate Concern: Tillich in Dialogue* (New York: Harper & Row, 1965), 145–46.

5. Andrew Greeley, *The Jesus Myth* (Garden City, NY: Doubleday, 1971).

6. Karl Barth, *Evangelical Theology* (Garden City, NY: Anchor Books, 1964), 1–10.

7. Karl Barth, *Church Dogmatics* (Edinburgh: T. & T. Clark, 1936–1969).

8. The popular name given to *Enchiridion Symbolorum* compiled by Heinrich Denzinger in 1854. Most recent English version is *The Sources of Catholic Dogma*, translated by Roy J. Deferrari from the thirtieth edition (New York: Herder, 1963).

9. *The Catechism of the Catholic Church* (Washington, DC: United States Catholic Conference, Libreria Editrice Vaticana, 1994).

10. Paul Tillich. *Systematic Theology*, Vol. I (Chicago: University of Chicago Press, 1951), 59–66.

11. David Tracy, *The Analogical Imagination: Christian Theology and the Cultural of Pluralism* (New York: Crossroad, 1981), 405.

12. *Alfie*, Paramount/Sheldrake film on play by Bill Naughton, 1966. Song: lyrics by David Hall, music by Burt F. Bacharach, 1966.

CHAPTER TWO—REVELATION AND FAITH

1. Woody Allen, "The Scrolls – Two," in *Without Feathers* (New York: Warner Books, 1976), 26–27.

CHAPTER THREE—SCRIPTURE AND TRADITION

1. See *Encyclopedia of American Religions*.Vol. II, ed. J.Gordon Melton (Tarrytown, NY: Triumph Books, 1991), under entries "Church of Jesus Christ of Latter-Day Saints," 188–89, and "Reorganized Church of Jesus Christ of Latter-Day Saints," 203–04.

2. The childhood wonders of Jesus come from the *Infancy Gospel of Thomas,* a mishmash of legend and novelistic folklore that attempts to fill in the gaps between Jesus' birth and his visit to Jerusalem at the age of twelve. The *Gospel of Thomas*, on the other hand, is a serious, if controversial work appreciated by scholars for the light it sheds on the canonical gospels. See John P. Meier, *A Marginal Jew: Rethinking the Historical Jesus* (New York: Doubleday, 1991), chapter 5, pp. 114–115 for a brief commentary on the *Infancy Gospel of Thomas*, and pp. 123–139 for an extended discussion of the *Gospel of Thomas*.

3. Referred to by Jaroslav Pelikan in *The Melody of Theology: A Philosophical Dictionary* (Cambridge, MA: Harvard University Press 1988), under the entry "Tradition," pp. 252–256.

4. Comparison is based on Vatican II's *Dogmatic Constitution on Divine Revelation*, chapter II, with footnotes. The references to Vatican II are from *The Documents of Vatican II*, ed. Walter Abbott (New York: America Press, 1966).

CHAPTER FOUR—CHURCH: ITS MEANING AND MISSION

1. Karl Rahner, *Foundations of Christian Faith* (New York: Seabury Press, 1978), 295–298.

2. *Dogmatic Constitution on the Church*, no. 8.

3. Elizabeth Schüssler Fiorenza, *In Memory of Her: A Feminist Theological Reconstruction of Christian Origins* (New York: Crossroad, 1983).

4. *The Playboy Interview*, ed. G. Barry Golson (New York: Wideview Books, 1981), 456–488. (Original interview by Robert Scheer, Nov. 1976).

CHAPTER FIVE—THE QUEST FOR CHURCH UNITY

1. See for example, Brian Swimme and Thomas Berry, *The Universe Story* (New York: HarperCollins, 1994). See also Anne Lonergan and Caroline Richards, eds., *Thomas Berry and the New Cosmology* (Mystic, CT: Twenty-

Third Publications, 1987). See also Rosemary Radford Ruether, *Gaia and God: An Ecofeminist Theology of Earth Healing* (New York: HarperCollins, 1994).

2.   Karl Rahner, *Foundations*, 178–93. See also "Natural Science and Reasonable Faith," in Rahner, *Theological Investigations*, XXI (New York: Crossroad, 1988), 16–55.

3.   David Toolan, "At Home in the Cosmos: The Poetics of Matter = Energy," *America* 174/6 (February 24, 1996), 8–14. See also Brennan R. Hill, *Exploring Catholic Theology: God, Jesus, Church, and Sacraments* (Mystic, CT: Twenty-Third Publications, 1995), especially chapter 3, "God, Science, and Creation," 70–102, and Diarmuid O'Murchu, *Quantum Theology: Spiritual Implications of the New Physics* (New York: Crossroad, 1997).

4.   *The Church in the Modern World*, no. 92.

5.   "A Look at the Consultation on Church Union: An Interview with COCU General Secretary Daniell Hamby," *Ecumenical Trends* 24/2 (February 1995), 1, 9–15. See also Gerald F. Moede, *The COCU Consensus: In Quest of a Church of Christ Uniting* (Princeton, NJ: Consultation on Church Union, 1985).

6.   "Uniatism, Method of Union of the Past and the Present Search for Full Communion," *Ecumenical Trends* 22/8 (September 1993), 3–7.

7.   *Baptism, Eucharist and Ministry*, Faith and Order Paper No. 111 (Geneva: World Council of Churches, 1982).

8.   "Roman Catholic/Pentecostal Dialogue," *Ecumenical Trends* 25/9 (October 1996), 16.

9. See John Paul II's encyclical *That They Might be One (Ut Unam Sint)* par. 88–96 in *Origins* 25/4 (June 8, 1995), 68–70. See also Archbishop John Quinn, "Considering the Papacy," *Origins* 26/8 (July 18, 1996), 119–128.

10. Heinrich Fries and Karl Rahner, *Unity of the Churches: An Actual Possibility* (Philadelphia: Fortress Press, and New York/Ramsey: Paulist Press, 1985).

11. Raymond Brown, *The Community of the Beloved Disciple* (New York: Paulist Press, 1979), 164.

CHAPTER SIX—MORAL THEOLOGY: A DEFINITION
1. Timothy O'Connell, *Principles for a Catholic Morality.* rev. ed. (New York: HarperCollins, 1990), 241–251.

CHAPTER SEVEN—METHOD IN MORAL THEOLOGY

1. H. Richard Niebuhr, *Responsible Self: An Essay in Christian Moral Philosophy* (New York: Harper & Row, 1963). The three positions are summarized on pages 60 and 61.

2. See Gerard S. Sloyan, *Catholic Morality Revisited: Origins and Contemporary Challenges* (Mystic, CT: Twenty-Third Publications, 1990). See chapter 3, "Is There a Natural Law?" 45–62, for a discussion of natural law from a relational/responsible perspective.

3. For a presentation of the sacrament of marriage from a relational/responsible perspective see Bernard Cooke, *Sacraments and Sacramentality*, rev. ed. (Mystic, CT: Twenty-Third Publications, 1994). See esp. chapter 7, "Human Friendship: Basic Sacrament," 78–92.

4. For a good introduction to a tremendously creative area of theology see *Thomas Berry and the New Cosmology*.

5. Charles Curran, "Official Catholic Social and Sexual Teachings: A Methodological Comparison," in *Readings in Moral Theology No. 8*, ed. Charles E. Curran and Richard A. McCormick (New York: Paulist Press, 1993), 536–558. This chapter first appeared in Curran, *Tension in Moral Theology* (Notre Dame, IN: University of Notre Dame Press, 1988), 87–109.

6. John Paul II, *The Splendor of Truth* (*Veritatis Splendor*), *Origins* 23/18 (October 14, 1993), 297–334.

7. *The Catechism of the Catholic Church.*

8. See discussion by Richard A. McCormick, *The Critical Calling: Reflections on Moral Dilemmas Since Vatican II* (Washington, DC: Georgetown University Press, 1989), 348–350.

9. McCormick, *The Critical Calling*, Chapter 19, "Therapy or Tampering: The Ethics of Reproductive Technology and the Development of Doctrine," 329–350.

10. For an overview of these three approaches see Richard P. McBrien, *Catholicism: New Edition* (New York: HarperCollins, 1994) 996–999.

CHAPTER EIGHT—A SHIFT IN MORAL THEOLOGY

1. The chart is drawn from material in O'Connell, *Principles for a Catholic Morality*, chapter 6, "The Human Person," 65–76.

2. McBrien, *Catholicism*, 955 notes that Pope John Paul II in his 1993 encyclical *The Splendor of Truth*, is insistent on the point that an individual act can change the fundamental option (no. 65). McBrien adds, "Catholic moral theologians agree with him."

CHAPTER NINE—HUMAN FREEDOM AND ITS LIMITATIONS

1. See Lawrence Kohlberg, "Stage and Sequence: The Cognitive Developmental Approach to Socialization," in *Handbook of Socialization Theory and Research*, ed. David Goslin (Chicago: Rand McNally, 1969).

2. See Dee Reid, "Low IQ Is a Capital Crime," in *The Progressive*, 52/4 (April 1988), 24–26.

3. Carol Gilligan, *In a Different Voice: Psychological Theory and Women's Development.* (Cambridge, MA: Harvard University Press, 1982).

4. Gilligan, *In a Different Voice*, 173. For an assessment of Gilligan's contributions, see Cynthia S. W. Crysdale, "Gilligan and the Ethics of Care: An Update," *Religious Studies Review* 20/1 (January 1994), 21–28.

CHAPTER 10—DEVELOPMENT OF THE MORAL LIFE: VALUES AND NORMS

1. McBrien, *Catholicism*, 965.

2. James J. Walter, "Proportionalism," in *Encyclopedia of Catholicism*, ed. Richard P. McBrien (New York: HarperCollins, 1995), 1058.

3. See Richard A. McCormick, "Some Early Reflections on *Veritatis Splendor*," *Theological Studies* 55 (September 1994), 485–86.

4. McCormick, *The Critical Calling*, 134.

5. For a criticism of this position by theologians who insist that even if the procedure were to secure semen for medical examination, and therefore morally speaking it were classified as a medical act, it still seems likely that the church teaching would condemn it, see Ronald Lawler, O.F.M. Cap., Joseph M. Boyle, Jr., and William E. May, "Masturbation," in *Readings in Moral Theology No. 8*, eds. Curran and McCormick, espcially pages 365–66.

6. Anne E. Patrick, *Liberating Conscience: Feminist Explorations in Catholic Moral Theology* (New York: Continuum, 1996), 160.

CHAPTER ELEVEN—CONSCIENCE: THE FINAL ARBITER OF THE MORAL LIFE

1. O'Connell, *Principles for a Catholic Morality*. The following discussion is based on what O'Connell describes as conscience/1, conscience/2, and conscience/3, 110–113.

2. Thomas Aquinas, *IV Sentences*, dist. 38, q.2, a. 4, quoted in McBrien, *Catholicism*, 972.

3. John W. Glaser, "Conscience and Superego: A Key Distinction," in *Conscience: Theological and Psychological Perspectives*, ed., C. Ellis Nelson (New York: Newman Press, 1973), 175–176.

4. *In Defense of Creation: The Nuclear Crisis and A Just Peace* (Nashville: Graded Press, 1986).

5. John Paul II, *The Splendor of Truth*.

6. McBrien, *Catholicism*, 973–74.

7. Dietrich Bonhoeffer, *Letters and Papers from Prison* (New York, Macmillan, 1962).

8. Martin Luther King, Jr., *Why We Can't Wait* (New York: Harper & Row, 1963), 84–85.

9. Paul Williamson, "A Doctor's Letter to His Son," in *The Eloquence of Protest*, ed. Harrison E. Salisbury (Boston: Houghton Mifflin Co., 1972), 28.

10. Harrop Freeman, "Case for Disobedience," in *Hastings Law Journal* 17 (1966), 437, quoted in Robert T. Hall, *The Morality of Civil Disobedience* (New York: Harper Torchbooks, 1971), 3.

11. Hans Küng, *Global Responsibility* (New York: Continuum, 1996), 2. Statistics come from *Justice, Peace and the Integrity of Creation*, a preparatory document for the 1990 World Assembly of the Christian Churches that met in Seoul, Korea, March 5–13, 1990.

12. Patrick, *Liberating Conscience*, 7.

13. Patrick, *Liberating Conscience*, 7.

14. Elizabeth Johnson, "Feminism and Sharing the Faith: A Catholic Dilemma" (Tulsa: University of Tulsa Warren Center for Catholic Studies, 1994), 6, quoted in Patrick, *Liberating Conscience*, 8.

15. Charles Curran, *The Church and Morality: An Ecumenical and Catholic Approach* (Minneapolis, Fortress Press, 1993), 70, 73–74.

16. *A Global Ethic*. eds., Hans Küng and Karl-Josef Kuschel (New York: Continuum, 1993), 24–34.

CHAPTER TWELVE—LOVE: THE FINAL GOAL OF THE MORAL LIFE

1. David Tracy. *On Naming the Present: Reflections on God, Hermeneutics, and Church* (Maryknoll, N.Y: Orbis Books, 1994), 103. See also Evelyn Eaton Whitehead and James D. Whitehead, *A Sense of Sexuality: Christian Love and Intimacy* (New York, Doubleday, 1989), chapter 5, "Caritas— Love Realized and Transformed," 74–88.

2. Edward Schillebeeckx, *Church: The Human Face of God* (New York: Crossroad, 1990), 98.

Index

abortion, 150, 155, 205-206; and civil disobedience, 229-230; and diseased uterus, 206; and ectopic pregnancy, 206; and Roe vs. Wade, 230

Abraham, and sacrifice of Isaac, 49-50; common father of Christians, Jews, and Muslims, 124-125

Abrahamic minority, church as, 94

absolutes in moral theology, 205

Adam and Eve, and sexuality, 156-158

Adams, James Luther, 241

addiction and sin, an analogy, 181-182

agape, 246

aid to Third World, 150

Alfie, 30, n 251

Allen, Woody, 49, n 252

ambush theology, 222

Anabaptist and Free churches: Amananites, Amish, Hutterites, Mennonites, Quakers, 117

Anglican/Episcopal Church 3, 112, 114, 127

anonymous Christianity, 96

Anselm, of Canterbury, 2; and definition of theology, 19-20

anthropology. 149; (also see theological anthropology)

apocalyptic writing, characteristics of, 37-41

apocryphal writings, defined, 76; *Gospel of Thomas*, 71, n 252; Infancy Gospel of Thomas, 252; *Shepherd of Hermas*, 70; *Teaching of the Twelve Apostles (Didache)*, 70;

Aquinas, Thomas, 2, and beginning of human life, 168-169; and conscience, 219-220; and human acts, 153; and *Summa Theologicae*, 25, 31; and unjust law, 227; n 255; Leo XIII and renewed study of, 26

Aristotle, and Aquinas, 25; and human acts, 153; and natural law, 148; and theory of knowledge, 21

asceticism, 101

Assumption of Mary, 44, 46

Athanasius, Bishop, 72

Athenagoras, Patriarch, 133

Augustine, of Hippo, 24, 30; and salvation, 94, 96

B.C.E.; C.E., 61

Baltimore Catechism, 96, 110

baptism, adult, 87; infant, 86; and confirmation 86, and dedication, 87

Baptist Church, 3, 117-118; and the Southern Baptist Convention, 118

Barth, Karl, 22-23, 25, 30, 94, 178, n 251

Berry, Thomas, n 252, n 254

big bang theory, and our relation to the cosmos, 164-165

black theology, 93, 235

Blenkinsopp, Joseph, 80

Boff, Leonardo, 121; and Virgil Elizondo, 242

Bonhoeffer, Dietrich, and disobedience to criminal law, 226, n 256

Boyle, Jr., Joseph M., n 255

Boyle, John P., 172

Branch Davidians, 50, 101

Brown, Raymond E., 54, 80, 121, 137-138, n 253

Brown, D. McKenzie, n.251

Cahill, Lisa Sowle, 151, 215

Callahan, Sidney, 241

Calvin, John, 22, 56; and double predestination, 94

canon law, and juridical vision of church, 24

canon of scripture, defined, 72; Greek canon, 74; Hebrew canon, 74-75; of the New Testament, 72-73; of the Old Testament (Catholic/Protestant divergence), 73-76

caritas (charity), 247

Carr, Anne E., 121, 185

Carter, President Jimmy, and anti-discrimination in the Church, 103; and the Baptist Church, 117-118; and *The Playboy Interview*, n 252

catechism, defined, 30, 43

Catechism of the Catholic Church, 26, 166, n 251, n 254

Catherine of Sienna, 13

Catholic social teaching, and the relational/responsible method in moral theology, 165-166, n 254

celibacy and ordained ministry, 105

Christian ethics, as distinctive, 148-150

church polity, defined, 111; episcopal

Of Related Interest. . .

Exploring Catholic Theology
God, Christ, Church, and Sacraments
Brennan Hill
Using Scripture, history and the thoughts of major theologians past
and present, the author presents the basic theological teachings that
underlie Catholic beliefs.

ISBN: 0-89622-661-1, 400 pp, $19.95 (order M-44)

The Creed
Berard L. Marthaler
This book is unique among the many commentaries on the classic
formulas of Christian faith. It does not simply relate the Nicene-
Constantinopolitan Creed and the Apostle's Creed to the apostolic
faith of the New Testament, but illumines these ancient formulas by
presenting them in light of contemporary theological issues. It links
the present to the past by drawing on recent biblical scholarship,
liturgical studies, theological explanations and historical research.
This revised edition features an updated and expanded text, the addition of a glossary, and enhanced bibliographic resources at the end of
each chapter.   ISBN: 0-89622-537-2, 456 pp, $19.95 (order B-75)

Faith, Religion, & Theology
A Contemporary Introduction
Brennan Hill, Paul F. Knitter
and William Madges
Newly updated, this popular text is a favorite to introduce college
students to the critical differences between faith, religion and theology. A solid foundation for their future studies and search for
meaning. The authors blend the theoretical with the practical to
offer a contemporary view of faith and what it means.

ISBN: 0-89622-725-1, 472 pp, $19.95 (order C-18)

Available at religious bookstores or from:

 **TWENTY-THIRD PUBLICATIONS**
XXIII P.O. Box 180 • Mystic, CT 06355

1-800-321-0411
E-Mail:ttpubs@aol.com